'Sam'

'Sam'

Marshal of the Royal Air Force the Lord Elworthy KG, GCB, CBE, DSO, LVO, DFC, AFC, MA

A Biography

Richard Mead

Foreword by Marshal of the Royal Air Force
the Lord Craig of Radley GCB, OBE

Pen & Sword
AVIATION

First published in Great Britain in 2018
by Pen & Sword Aviation
An imprint of Pen & Sword Books Limited
47 Church Street
Barnsley
South Yorkshire
S70 2AS

ISBN 978 1 52672 717 6

A CIP catalogue record for this book is
available from the British Library.

Typeset in Ehrhardt
by Mac Style

Printed and bound in the UK
by TJ International Ltd, Padstow, Cornwall

Pen & Sword Books Limited incorporates the imprints of Atlas,
Archaeology, Aviation, Discovery, Family History, Fiction, History,
Maritime, Military, Military Classics, Politics, Select, Transport,
True Crime, Air World, Frontline Publishing, Leo Cooper,
Remember When, Seaforth Publishing, The Praetorian Press,
Wharncliffe Local History, Wharncliffe Transport,
Wharncliffe True Crime and White Owl.

For a complete list of Pen & Sword titles please contact
PEN & SWORD BOOKS LIMITED
47 Church Street, Barnsley, South Yorkshire, S70 2AS, England
E-mail: enquiries@pen-and-sword.co.uk
Website: www.pen-and-sword.co.uk

Contents

Foreword

by Marshal of the Royal Air Force
the Lord Craig of Radley GCB, OBE

It is a privilege to have been invited to introduce this remarkable life story of one of the Royal Air Force's finest and most respected leaders, Marshal of the Royal Air Force the Lord Elworthy, always known as Sam.

After University and having been called to the Bar, Sam spent a couple of years flying part-time with the Royal Auxiliary Air Force before being granted in 1936, at the age of almost twenty-six, the permanent commission which he had long craved. Like many before and after him, Sam joined the newly fledged Royal Air Force for the love of flight, of escape into the third dimension. No one could have foretold then that this was to be the start of a most amazing and meteorically successful service career, taking him on to leading his own service as Chief of the Air Staff, and then to becoming Chief of the Defence Staff in 1967. He crammed into the intervening 30 years of regular service exceptional talent as an aviator, deeds of great courage and gallantry on operations in Bomber Command and the most stressful and demanding challenges of command and operational staff duties throughout the Second World War. By May 1945 when the war in Europe was won he had reached the rank of Air Commodore aged thirty-three. Thereafter his career never really faltered. A natural and revered leader, he went from strength to strength, always standing out head and shoulders above his contemporaries. His impressive list of awards, not least his peerage, and of decorations in both war and peace, bear testimony to the very high opinion in which he was held.

This extensively researched book covers not only all the stages in Sam's RAF career but his whole life. Born in New Zealand in 1911, he moved to the United Kingdom in 1924 to attend boarding school at Marlborough and then in 1930 to study Law at Cambridge. After handing over as Chief of the Defence Staff in 1971 and a further seven years of numerous and demanding responsibilities in the UK, he and his beloved wife Audrey decided to settle back in New Zealand, where he died in 1993. The author successfully deals with every period in the long life and times of Sam.

Like many others in the RAF and beyond, I greatly admired Sam. It was my good fortune to be on his personal staff when he became Chief of the Defence Staff. No individual I have known before or after was so charismatic, so greatly admired and yet so disarmingly modest about his own fine personal attributes and achievements.

Introduction

In the summer of 1945 the strength and reputation of the Royal Air Force stood very high. There could be no doubt in anyone's mind about the contribution it had made to the defeat of the Axis powers. The performance of Fighter Command in the Battle of Britain was widely and correctly perceived as having prevented the invasion of the United Kingdom, which would have assured German domination of Europe. The contribution of the RAF to the campaigns in North Africa, Italy, North-West Europe and Burma was immense, whilst Coastal Command, in conjunction with the Royal Navy, had by mid-1943 effectively won the Battle of the Atlantic. The longest campaign of all, lasting from the very beginning to the very end of the war in Europe, had been carried out by Bomber Command, which incurred more casualties, proportionate to its size, than any other British armed formation.

What followed was, unsurprisingly, an anti-climax. An era of peace, albeit interspersed from time to time with military actions on a relatively small scale, has lasted to this day. It was accompanied by different priorities for the British Government, including health, education, trade, industry, social security and the environment, whilst defence assumed a lower level of importance. There was nothing new about this; indeed, arguably it has always been thus in a democracy in peacetime.

For the RAF during the war the primary focus was always on today and tomorrow: activity was dominated by Operations, to which everything else was subordinated. In order to keep ahead of the enemy, development was very rapid, not only in new aircraft but also in the armament and equipment which made them ever more effective fighting machines. Only four years after the last bi-plane fighters had been in action, the first jet fighters entered service. In peacetime, however, the priorities changed. Instead of concentrating on today and tomorrow, the focus was on years, if not decades, ahead. There was less demand for heroes such as Guy Gibson and Douglas Bader and more for men of both vision and application who could look into the future whilst at the same time managing the present.

Happily, there was a deep well of talent on which to draw. The Chiefs of the Air Staff during the late 1940s and the 1950s were men who had held relatively high command during the war, whilst those of the 1960s and 1970s had all served in action but also had long experience of the very different peacetime service. All were distinguished in their way, but none more so than Air Chief Marshal Sir Charles Elworthy, subsequently Marshal of the Royal Air Force the Lord Elworthy, who became not only Chief of the Air Staff, but also Chief of the Defence Staff, at the very top of the British armed services.

Sam Elworthy, as he was known by all and will be called in this book, has always intrigued me for a number of reasons, not least because he was actually a New Zealander. In carrying out my research I discovered that, relative to the size of its population, the contribution of New Zealand to the leadership of the Royal Air Force in the Second World War and the three decades which followed was immense. During the war itself, eminent New Zealanders included Air Chief Marshal Sir Keith Park, the Air Officer Commanding 11 Group of Fighter Command during the Battle of Britain and later the Allied Air Commander-in-Chief in South-East Asia Command, and Air Marshal Sir Arthur 'Maori' Coningham, the AOC of the Desert Air Force in North Africa and the Second Tactical Air Force in North-West Europe. During the 1960s New Zealanders at one time or another led Transport Command, Fighter Command and the Near East and Far East Air Forces, and sat on the Air Council.

All these men had joined the RAF because of the limited opportunities in New Zealand. With no Air Force of their own during the Great War, hundreds of adventurous young New Zealanders joined the Royal Flying Corps and many, including Park and Coningham, received permanent commissions in the peacetime RAF. The New Zealand Permanent Air Force was established in 1923, but it remained a small and poorly resourced part of their armed services until 1937, when, by that time renamed the Royal New Zealand Air Force, it was established as an independent service with equivalent status to its Army and Navy counterparts. For young men wishing to make a career in military aviation before then, there was only one option: travel to the other side of the world and join the RAF. Sam Elworthy differed from most of the others in that he had less far to travel, as both his secondary and further education were undertaken in England. However, his enthusiasm for military flying could never have been satisfied in his home country and he, too, had no alternative but to join the RAF.

Sam has long attracted my professional interest as an important link between the RAF at the height of its fame and power during the Second World War and the RAF of today, much reduced in size but still one of the most capable air forces in the world. He began his service in the mid-1930s on bi-planes with a maximum speed of 184 mph. In the last stages of his career, in the late 1960s and early 1970s, he was intimately involved in the decisions to purchase the Lockheed Hercules and the Panavia Tornado, both of which are still in service today. Such was the variety of activity in the RAF that Sam's career cannot be regarded as either typical or atypical; but it still illustrates very clearly the momentous changes which took place during that period.

Whilst I was familiar with the general outline of Sam's service career, I had little knowledge of the detail of his life. The more I looked into it, the more I thought that a second generation New Zealander, who rose to become the professional head of the United Kingdom's armed services, a peer of the realm and a Knight of the Garter, would make an admirable biographical subject. I decided to approach his eldest son, also a former RAF officer, Air Commodore Sir Timothy Elworthy, and his only daughter, Clare Cary. An inherently modest man, Sam had declined to write an autobiography and had rejected all approaches from would-be biographers. As I have found before in similar circumstances, there was some understandable reluctance by his family to adopt a different stance, but over twenty years had passed since their father's death, and they and their two brothers, Anthony and Christopher, both of whom live in New Zealand, agreed that it was time to put a remarkable life on record.

I found to my delight that Sam rarely threw anything away. Apart from a very brief period in the early 1920s he did not write a diary of record, but he did keep a pocket appointment diary from 1952 onwards which provided a very useful framework to his activities. He also kept his flying log books, which are of vital interest in the pre-war and wartime years and provide some guide to his activities well into the 1950s. He gave three interviews on his RAF career, one to the Imperial War Museum describing the early years of his service up to the end of the first year of the war, the other two to the Air Historical Branch which cover the whole period up to his appointment as Chief of the Defence Staff and fill in a great deal of detail about his work.

Even more significantly, less than two years before he died, he was persuaded by his sister, Di, and one of his nephews, John Jeffares, to be interviewed on video about his life as a whole. The result was nearly eight hours of recollections, from his early childhood to the years of retirement in New Zealand. Whilst it is of outstanding value to a biographer for its content, it also, in a way which is next to impossible to derive from the printed word, reveals a most attractive personality with a highly developed sense of humour.

There was a great deal of other material, including letters and photograph albums, made available to me by Sam's family, who also pointed me in the direction of people who had known him well and were happy to be interviewed. Among the most important collections were the accounts by Audrey, Sam's wife, of a number of journeys made by them both in the 1960s and early 1970s. It became very quickly apparent to me that this had been a partnership of equals. Audrey was a highly intelligent, observant and articulate chronicler, and her social skills were of great value to Sam in his career. Very sadly, she developed Alzheimer's disease, the more so since hers had been, in its way, a brilliant mind.

There was one other reason for me to write about Sam Elworthy. He is the only one of my biographical subjects whom I actually met, and the occasion has stuck in my mind ever since, notwithstanding that our encounter was very brief. The date was 4 June 1964, and Sam's appointment diary is succinct, reading simply 'Marlborough CCF'. My own diary entry is not much longer: 'Inspection Day. Spoken to by Chief of Air Staff.' The occasion was the annual inspection of my school's detachment of the Combined Cadet Force by a very senior officer of the armed forces. Not being a natural soldier, sailor or airman, I was in the band, in which I played the trombone and held the exalted rank of corporal. The CCF duly paraded, and Sam arrived, to be greeted by the Commanding Officer and escorted around the assembled ranks, stopping now and then to talk to a cadet. When he arrived at the band, to my horror he headed directly for me! He was a tall man, perhaps because of which he had a slight stoop. He also had a very penetrating look. The exchange went like this:

Sam: How long have you been playing the trombone, Corporal?
Me: About two years, sir.
Sam: What would you like to do when you leave school?
Me: I'm hoping to go to university, sir.
Sam: Have you ever thought about joining one of the armed services?
Me: (Very firmly) No, sir!
Sam: (With, I recall clearly, a twinkle in his eye) I see. Well, thirty-five years ago I was a corporal trombonist in this band and look where it got me!

At which he turned and strode away. He probably did not even hear my loud 'SIR!', the only possible answer in the circumstances!

Chapter 1

The Elworthys of Pareora

There is a strong link between the Elworthy family of New Zealand and the County of Somerset in South-West England, but its origins and history are unknown before the middle of the eighteenth century. It is tempting to seek some ancient connection between the family and the village of Elworthy, which lies on the eastern flank of the Brendon Hills and is old enough to have been mentioned in the Domesday Book, but none has ever been proved. Instead, the first of the Elworthys of whom there is a record is Thomas, born in about 1757, who married Hannah, the widow of Henry Cole or Coles at the Church of St John the Baptist in Wellington, Somerset on 21 January 1782.

At that time Wellington was a centre for the wool industry, and Thomas had been working as a wool comber in the factory owned by the Were family and later by Thomas Fox, the grandson of Thomas Were. Whilst apparently remaining Fox's employee, Thomas established a small venture of his own in a cottage in the town, but sometime after 1800 he acquired land on which he built a worsted mill. This was in due course expanded into a successful serge manufacturing business into which, as soon as they were old enough, Thomas brought his two sons, William and Thomas the Younger. A fire destroyed the original mill in 1822, but a new and improved facility was built on the site and immediately prospered. The grounds also incorporated a substantial house, which stands there to this day.

Thomas the Elder died in 1834, leaving the business to his sons, who, by the time that they retired in 1858, were both wealthy men. Thomas the Younger had married Jane Chorley, a local girl and the daughter of a gentleman farmer, on 16 November 1826. As was the custom of the time, they produced a large family of four boys and four girls. The youngest boy, Edward Elworthy, born in 1836, was the grandfather of Sam Elworthy, the subject of this book. Coming from a family of staunch Baptists, Edward was educated at the West of England Dissenters' Proprietary School in Taunton.[1]

Edward's father, Thomas Elworthy the Younger, died in 1860, at which time Edward was still living at home with his mother. As a younger son, his prospects in England were limited, and he had no interest in going into the Army or the Church. Instead, two years later, he sailed for Australia to make his fortune, although he was by no means short of funds as the result of an inheritance from his father. The reason for his going is obscure, but it may have been because of the relationship between his eldest brother Fred and Robert Tooth, an entrepreneur who had business interests in Australia and New Zealand. This relationship ended in disaster for Fred, but was cordial at the time of Edward's departure. Edward landed in Sydney, but almost immediately set out for Queensland, where he obtained a job working on a sheep station, his experience of his family's interests in wool giving him an advantage which quickly led to a management position. The record of his stay there is unreliable, but it is said that he bought significant blocks of land around Toowoomba and Dalby which he was later to sell at a profit. In 1864, however, he moved on to the South Island of New Zealand, establishing himself in South Canterbury, and in October of that year he acquired for £18,500 a half-interest in some 60,000 acres of mostly leasehold land on the Pareora River south of Timaru, together with 25,000 merino sheep. Six months later, he acquired the balance of the leasehold for £15,000.

In March 1866 Edward left his new property in the hands of a capable manager, Henry Ford, and sailed for England, with the specific intention of getting married. The object of his affections was Sarah Shorrock, whom he had met before sailing for Australia, although where or when is not known. Her family were also mill-owners, in their case producing cotton in Over Darwen, Lancashire, some 250 miles from Wellington. Sarah, also called Sally, was born in 1844, the eighth of the ten children of James Shorrock, a prosperous member of the local community and a justice of the peace. By the time of her introduction to Edward Elworthy she was living with her family in a substantial house in Darwen, Astley Bank.[2] Like the Elworthys, the Shorrock family were Nonconformists, in their case Congregationalists, and the couple were married on 16 January 1867 at the Independent Meeting

House in Darwen. After a brief honeymoon they sailed for New Zealand, arriving at Edward's property on the Pareora in May 1867.

On his return, Edward began a process which would continue for many years, converting a number of his leaseholds into freeholds by purchasing them from the Government of New Zealand and the Canterbury Provincial Council. There was a very strong tactical element to this which involved initially acquiring freeholds at the entrances of valleys and gorges or along roads and waterways, making the land which was cut off markedly less attractive to others and thus cheaper to buy in due course. This process continued when he and Sarah returned to England from March 1872 until February 1874, as he left comprehensive instructions to Henry Ford on how to act in his absence and followed these up with frequent letters. Although there were a number of temporary setbacks, particularly when land that he wished to buy could only be acquired at a high cost from others who had had the same idea, and some problems over mortgages, he persisted, until by the early 1890s he owned nearly 40,000 acres freehold. In 1895 he drew up a will leaving 26,000 acres of the best land, now called Holme Station, to his three surviving sons and authorizing his executors to sell the remainder, which would provide for the rest of his family and pay off any residual mortgages.

Edward was no farmer – after the resignation of Henry Ford in 1876 he continued to employ other managers – but he was a shrewd businessman and a prominent member of the local community. He served on the local council and became a justice of the peace, a member of the Timaru Harbour Board and the boards of various charitable institutions and the chairman of the Timaru Agricultural and Pastoral Association. Some of his business ventures, notably those associated with freezing and exporting meat, were less successful, but he still managed to accumulate considerable wealth.

When Sarah first arrived at Holme Station the accommodation was scarcely more than a shack with a tin roof, but before very long a more substantial building was erected which was extensively rebuilt after the couple's return in 1874 from their two-year stay in England. This would prove necessary for what was to become a large family. Edward and Sarah produced eleven children, six sons and five daughters, of whom three sons and one daughter died in childhood. Of the other four girls the eldest, Maude, born in 1868, married twice but had no children, and Edith, eighteen months younger, never married but acted as a companion to her mother after her father's death. Ethel, born in 1876, would marry William Bond, have three daughters of her own and live not far from Holme Station before moving to Southland. The youngest of all the children, Muriel, born in 1883, was to marry Sydney Williamson, who had New Zealand roots but was wealthy enough to set himself up as an English country gentleman. He and Muriel, with five children, rented a series of large houses, the most significant of which was Heligan in Cornwall, of which they were tenants from 1929 until the middle of the Second World War. There they acted as frequent hosts to Elworthy relatives visiting from New Zealand.

One of the defining characteristics of many middle-class New Zealand families such as the Elworthys in the nineteenth and early twentieth centuries was that they still considered themselves to be British, very often referring to the United Kingdom as 'Home'. Notwithstanding the long voyage, they visited the mother country frequently, often staying for periods not of months but of years, during which they rented property. Many of them liked to have their children educated there, if not at school, then at least at university. This was certainly true of Edward and Sarah Elworthy, and, even after Edward's sudden death in 1899 from a heart attack at the age of only sixty-two, Sarah travelled frequently to Europe with Edith and, on occasion, with some of her other children. Back in New Zealand, she moved out of Holme Station and into a large house in Christchurch, living for a further thirty-five years.

The three surviving boys, Arthur, Herbert and Percy, born respectively in 1874, 1878 and 1881, inherited Holme Station when Edward died. In accordance with their father's will, that part of the estate which had been retained was divided into three properties of roughly equal size. Arthur and Herbert had already come of age, and the former farmed not only his own part, which retained the name of Holme Station, but also the land which had been left to Percy, until such time as the latter had completed his education. Herbert took over the third part, Craigmore, on which he built another large house.

Arthur and Herbert were educated largely in New Zealand, partly by tutors and partly at Baker's School near Akaroa, but also at prep schools in England during the family's stays there. Herbert also attended Christ's

College in Christchurch, the oldest public school in New Zealand. Both men married relatively early, Arthur to Ella Julius in 1900 and Herbert to Gladys Cleveland in 1905, both produced large families and both were conscientious stewards of their properties.

Percy Elworthy, Sam's father, was born in Timaru in a house on Le Crens Crescent, where Sarah had gone for her confinement. She and Edward had only returned two weeks previously from two years in England and, in Percy's words, 'Even if I was not born at Home I was conceived there – a thought which I find very satisfactory.'[3] Following a two-year stay in England in 1888–9 he was educated initially in New Zealand, first at the Cathedral School, the prep school for Christ's College, and then at the College itself. He was not a good student. 'I did as little work as possible,' he wrote later 'broke every school rule and was beaten without ceasing in consequence.'[4] He did, however, enjoy sport, becoming a member of the rugby fifteen for two successive years and winning the swimming championship. It was as early as this that he made up his mind to have his own sons, should he have any, educated in England.

After Edward's untimely death Sarah embarked on a Grand Tour with Edith, Herbert, Percy and Muriel, sailing first to San Francisco, from where they went down to Los Angeles and on to the Grand Canyon, before travelling on to England, where Sarah had one objective in mind, to get Percy into Cambridge. To achieve this she relied on Edward's first cousin once removed, Arnold Wallis,[5] a fellow and bursar of Corpus Christi College. He recommended Trinity Hall and, having somehow satisfied the entrance requirements, Percy matriculated there in the autumn of 1900.

Perhaps unsurprisingly, Percy did not have a distinguished academic career at Cambridge, but once again he excelled at sport. In his first year he represented Cambridge against Oxford in the Cottenham Steeplechase, but his horse fell at the last fence and he was badly concussed, losing his memory for some considerable time and being sent to Capri to recuperate. He also took up rowing, becoming a member of the crew both of the Trinity Hall First Boat, which won the Thames Cup at the Henley Royal Regatta in 1902, and of the Clinker Fours Boat, which won the Intercollegiate Cup. He was urged to stay on at Cambridge for a third year, in the hope of being chosen for the Cambridge Blue Boat against Oxford, but his brother Arthur insisted that he return to New Zealand to take over the property left to him by his father. He thus failed to take his degree.

Initially, Percy farmed in partnership with Arthur from his return in 1902 until 1910, when the two properties were separated. For the first two years, however, he lived in Pareora Cottage with Herbert, until the latter decided to build a family house on Craigmore. Percy himself erected a bungalow on his own property, Gordons Valley, named after a boundary rider who had worked for the first owners of what was later to become Holme Station. He also planted a large number of trees, including species from England, which enhanced the property considerably.

By 1905 Percy was keen to follow his brothers into marriage. His choice of partner fell on Bertha Julius, a younger sister of his brother Arthur's wife, Ella, whom he had known since his schooldays in Christchurch, where she lived with her parents. Their father was the Bishop of Christchurch, Churchill Julius, a significant figure in New Zealand ecclesiastical history. Julius was born in Surrey in 1847 and educated at King's College, London and Worcester College, Oxford, before being ordained deacon in 1871 and priest in 1872. His subsequent appointments included two in Somerset, as curate in South Brent[6] and vicar in Shapwick. A member of the evangelical movement of the Church of England, in 1878 he was appointed vicar of one of its strongholds, Holy Trinity, Islington.

In 1883 Julius invited the Bishop of Ballarat, who was visiting from Australia, to preach at Holy Trinity, and not long afterwards he was surprised to be invited to become the vicar and archdeacon of the pro-cathedral parish of Ballarat, one of the country dioceses of the State of Victoria. He accepted immediately and sailed to Australia with his wife and family the following year. He was a great success in Ballarat, becoming closely involved with the pastoral and educational work of the parish. His reputation spread, and in 1889 he was nominated to succeed to a forthcoming vacancy in the diocese of Christchurch and was duly consecrated bishop the next year.

Percy had come to Bishop Julius's notice before his brother Arthur's marriage to the Bishop's older daughter. Whilst at Christ's College he used to break out of school at night to visit Ella. In due course he was caught, brought before the headmaster and expelled. He immediately went to see Julius to assure him that his daughter's reputation was intact. The Bishop, who was a member of the governing body of the school as its Warden, was so charmed by the boy that he had the expulsion overturned, even before Percy's parents knew of it. Notwithstanding this, he was clearly aware that Percy had a wild streak in him and, when approached for his younger daughter's hand in marriage in 1907, insisted that Percy should see rather more of the world before settling into matrimony.

Percy took the Bishop at his word and set off for Southern Africa, accompanied by his friend, Carlisle Studholme. The two young men trekked up to the Limpopo River and thence into Portuguese East Africa, shooting big game as they went, many of whose heads were sent back to decorate the walls of his new house in Gordons Valley. Percy had a bad attack of malaria, which required two periods of hospitalization, but eventually was well enough to travel on to England, where he knew that Bertha Julius was visiting. At the end of the year he followed her back to New Zealand, proposed and was accepted.

Percy Elworthy and Bertha Julius were married in Christchurch Cathedral on 1 October 1908. The ceremony was performed by Archdeacon Harper, Bishop Julius gave away the bride and Studholme was the best man. The reception, for some 800 guests, was held in Bishopscourt, the residence of the Bishop. The newly married couple honeymooned in the North Island. Percy was something of a pioneer motorist in New Zealand and they went everywhere by car, notwithstanding that few roads were made up. After a number of misadventures, and not a little damage to the car, they eventually arrived in Auckland, whence they returned to Gordons Valley, where Percy had the bungalow converted into a large house by the addition of a second storey.

Unlike his two older brothers, Percy never made any attempt to become a farmer, instead employing a succession of managers to run the property, the first of whom was Bob Oliphant. Whilst in New Zealand he would indulge his passion for motoring, pioneering a number of routes, including the road over the Crown Range between Queenstown and Wanaka.[7] He kept up the practice of frequent visits to England, and it was there in 1909 that his first child, Janet, was born. The couple returned to New Zealand in the following year and it was at the house at Gordons Valley, in the '40-acre bedroom', so called because of its enormous size, that Samuel Charles Elworthy was born on 23 March 1911.

Chapter 2

Childhood and Schooldays

The doctor drove over from Timaru in a gig to assist at the birth, which was just as well as the baby weighed in at over 10lbs. Percy and Bertha wanted him to be called Sam rather than Samuel, but the Registrar made out the birth certificate in the names of Samuel Charles, which is what he remained for official purposes, although nobody called him anything but Sam until nearly 50 years later, when his second name asserted itself in circumstances not of his own choosing. To compound the confusion, he was baptized, on 15 May 1911 at St Mary's, Timaru, in the names of Julius Sam!

Two further children followed in quick succession, Anthony Churchill, Tony to most but 'Tort' to family and close friends, in June 1912 and Mary Antoinette, always known as Anne, almost exactly a year later. Childcare was substantially in the hands of the nanny, who from about the time of Sam's birth was Nurse Jensen, a Dane who was always called Nin. She would remain with the family for fourteen years. Her presence allowed considerable freedom to Percy and Bertha, who were able to travel widely within New Zealand in one of the many cars which they owned over the years and, in early 1914, to visit New Guinea and the Dutch East Indies.

Whilst Percy took an interest in the development of his estate, he took none in the day-to-day business of farming, leaving it entirely to the manager, although from time to time he would ride round on his horse to see what was happening and ensure that everyone was working hard. Other than travel, much of his life was devoted to sports, particularly those in which horses were involved. He rode to hounds, steeplechased and played polo at the Pareora Polo Club, which had been founded by him and his two brothers in 1904. As far as field sports were concerned, he was an enthusiastic shot, pursuing duck in Gordons Valley and pheasants, partridges and grouse in England, and he used to go on an annual stalking expedition in New

Zealand. He was less keen on fishing, but was persuaded to participate on a number of occasions.

Percy was highly patriotic and, when Great Britain declared war on Germany in August 1914, he immediately sought to enlist in the New Zealand Armed Forces. According to his own private memoirs, he had been suffering from sinusitis and the relevant medical authority would not pass him fit for active service. Moreover, the New Zealand Government made it clear that, for the time being, they would not be taking married men with large families. However, it is apparent from notices in the local press that he, Studhome and others offered their services as a garrison for Samoa, which had been seized from the Germans. This offer having been accepted, Percy reconsidered what must have looked like a very uninteresting prospect and managed to get out of it by claiming that he needed to go to England to undergo an operation, presumably for his sinusitis. The house was shut up, his brother Arthur agreed to oversee the affairs of the farm, with Bob Oliphant in day-to-day control, and on 11 February 1915 Percy, Bertha, the children and Nin boarded the SS *Remuera* for the journey round Cape Horn to England.

The voyage was uneventful until after the ship left Rio de Janeiro, when she was warned that the German armed merchantman SS *Prinz Eitel Friedrich*[1] was in the area. The passengers were lined up on deck, ready to take to the lifeboats, whilst the captain sent an uncoded signal to HMS *Caernarvon*, which was believed to be nearby. The German ship intercepted the message and made off, although it turned out later that *Caernarvon* was too far away to have been of any assistance.

On arriving in England, Percy rented a large house on the edge of Richmond Park and then, his sinusitis having been cured, possibly by the sea air, went to sign up at the War Office. He had an introduction to a cavalry general who turned out to be away, so he rather foolishly told the recruiting officer that he would take anything else and found himself posted to a battalion of the Prince of Wales's Leinster Regiment, which was in barracks in Plymouth. On reflection this was not at all to his liking. Whilst at Cambridge he had not only joined the Cambridge University Mounted Infantry but had been visited by the Colonel of the 6th Dragoon Guards with an invitation to join the regiment, in which Charles Elworthy, a cousin from whom Sam derived his second name, had served and been killed in the Boer War. He had declined at the time, but he retained a strong preference for the cavalry. He contacted a friend in the 1st Life Guards, the Marquess of Tweeddale, who persuaded his commanding officer, Sir George Holford, to apply for Percy to be transferred to the regiment.

1st Life Guards was divided into two separate units, the fighting regiment in France and the reserve regiment in London, the latter with responsibility for recruiting and training. As Percy was initially based at Knightsbridge Barracks with the reserve regiment, the family took a house closer to the centre of London, Grove Lodge[2] in Hampstead. Percy was sent off on a machine gun course at the Small Arms School at Hythe, becoming on his return the reserve regiment's Machine Gun Officer. He subsequently went on a course in 'Bombing', which taught the use of the Mills Bomb, the standard British hand grenade of both world wars. An expert horseman, he was then asked to instruct new recruits in riding, which he did in a camp on the Epsom Downs, where a sports meeting was subsequently held.

Three months after joining, Percy crossed to France on his posting to D Squadron of the fighting regiment, commanded by John Jacob Astor V, later Lord Astor of Hever. The regiment was stationed at Verschocq in the Pas-de-Calais. It had seen action in the First Battle of Ypres in late 1914 and had then served as infantry. When Percy arrived it was back in its mounted role and was to form part of the cavalry force massed to exploit a breakthrough on the Somme in July 1916. In the event, this never happened, and the regiment reverted to an infantry role. In the winter of 1916/17 Percy was lent temporarily to the 4th Battalion of the Seaforth Highlanders, which was holding the line opposite the Hohenzollern Redoubt near Loos. Not long before he arrived, a German sporting a large moustache and wearing a sheepskin coat had infiltrated the British trenches, killed a British officer and escaped, and a reward was offered for his capture should he do the same again. By coincidence, Percy was also sporting a large moustache and wearing a sheepskin coat and was up close to the front line and nearly within hand grenade range of the German trenches, when he was apprehended by an NCO of the Middlesex Regiment, the Seaforths' neighbours. He was immediately marched back through the trenches, to cries for revenge from the soldiers he passed. Luckily, he was allowed to lead his captors to a trench where he knew his Adjutant was stationed and was released, albeit reluctantly.

Later in 1917, Percy was invalided back to England, suffering from a duodenal problem and subsequently from appendicitis, for which he was operated on in the military hospital in Belgrave Square. By this time the family had relocated to 47 Cadogan Place, which was conveniently close to both the hospital and Knightsbridge Barracks. Following his recovery, Percy was charged once again with training recruits and occasionally took part in the mounted escort to the King and Queen.

This was at the time of the Zeppelin raids on London, which Sam and the other children loved, not only because they found them exciting, but because they were woken up, assembled on the stairs away from the windows and given cups of Bovril. Whilst they were still in Hampstead they had actually seen one of the airships being shot down. Sam's other abiding memory of this time was the sight of convalescent soldiers walking around in their blue uniforms and red ties. By then he was attending his first school, the pre-preparatory Gibbs School in Sloane Street. The first evidence of scholarship came in a letter to his father written on 18 October 1916. It read: 'DARLING DAD WE MISS YOU VERY MUCH KILL A LOT OF GERMANS LOVE FROM SAM'!

Percy, now a captain, managed to return to France once he was fully fit, but not to his regiment. Instead, he was appointed aide-de-camp to Major General John Vaughan, who had commanded 3 Cavalry Division and was now based at GHQ British Expeditionary Force in Montreuil-sur-Mer as Inspector of Quartermaster General Services. Percy's new job involved a great deal of travelling around the many corps of the BEF. At the beginning of the second week of November 1918 he was sent up to Valenciennes to obtain information about the horses of some Canadian gunners, failed to return to GHQ and instead joined the advance to Mons, near where he found himself on Armistice Day. Back in London, Bertha bought flags for herself and the children and they went out on the streets to celebrate. After Percy's return from France he rode in the procession for President Woodrow Wilson, who visited London in December 1918.

Percy was discharged from the Army in January 1919 after a short but not undistinguished career, in which he had been fortunate to survive and had made many friends, something which would stand him in good stead for the time he and Bertha would spend in England in future years. Just after his return from France, however, there was a major family tragedy. Sam, who shared a room with his older sister Janet, awoke one night to find her missing from her bed. He got up to look for her and was told that she had fallen ill during the night. She had appendicitis, but was not taken to hospital. Instead, a doctor operated on her on a table in the house. The appendix was removed, but she contracted peritonitis and died two days later. She had been a most attractive child, gentle, unselfish and happy, and her death left a significant hole in the family.

The Elworthys returned to New Zealand shortly afterwards on the SS *Rotorua*, travelling for the first time through the Panama Canal, which had opened in 1914. When they had left New Zealand, Sam had been three, Tony two and Anne only one, so they had had little opportunity to make the most of what Gordons Valley had to offer. Now they could, to some extent, spread their wings. They were joined, moreover, in November 1919 by a fourth sibling, Alice Diana ('Di'), who in due course cheerfully accepted that she was a replacement for Janet.

One of the requirements of a country childhood was the ability to ride, and Sam, whilst by no means a gifted horseman, was judged to be Best Boy Rider at the Timaru Show, largely as a result of being mounted on an excellent pony: Percy, however, never allowed his children to play polo. They all learnt to swim and to shoot, whilst Sam and Tony were taught to climb in the mountains around Mount Cook. The family kept a shack at Lake Tekapo, where they used to go for weekends and for longer holidays to swim, boat and fish, and there were other attractive sites not far away such as Mount Nimrod, already a nature reserve by the beginning of the twentieth century. Expeditions were often affairs involving the wider family, with frequent visits to and from Holme Station and Craigmore. Arthur Elworthy's older son, Edward, went off to Oxford in 1920, but his two daughters, Rachel and Betty, were still living at home, and his younger son, John, was to become a very close friend of both Sam and Tony. Herbert's eldest children, Harold and Margaret, were too senior, but the other four, Rona, Cecil, Elizabeth and Josephine, were much the same age as Sam, Tony and Anne, and there were plenty of picnics and, later on, tennis parties.

Whilst the children were still young, contact with their parents was strictly rationed. The four of them lived in the nursery wing of the house under the care of Nin, taking all their main meals there. At teatime, however, they would go to the drawing room and knock on the door to be admitted. They would then spend an hour with their parents, letting them know how they had been occupying their time and being given what Sam was later to call 'useful things to do'. Exactly an hour later, Nin would appear and take them back to the nursery. On occasion they would participate in joint activities. Bertha was very keen on amateur dramatics, producing and directing a number of plays and pantomimes and even painting all the scenery. The children were roped in as required, as were other members of the wider family.

Although Percy was determined that the children should undergo their secondary education in England, his own experience of prep school in Christchurch had probably decided him against sending them there, so instead he engaged a tutor, Frank Ivey, who was to be with the family for five years. Ivey provided a good grounding in the prep school curriculum, and the children doubtless benefited from receiving personal attention. As they would have been at school, however, they were subjected to corporal punishment if they failed in their work. Sam did not escape this, but he got off relatively lightly compared to Tony, who was all too frequently chastised. Although it was usually Ivey who administered the punishments, Bertha was particularly intolerant of underperformance. She was disparaging of Tony, but reserved much of her criticism for Anne, whose behaviour never seemed to measure up to the standard set by Janet. Anne's life was made increasingly miserable, and this resulted in almost complete estrangement from her parents later in life.

After five years had passed, Sam was fast approaching the age when he would have to go to public school, and so the entire family, together with Nin and Ivey, packed up and set off again for England, once more leaving Gordons Valley in the hands of a manager, who by this time was Bob Johnston. They sailed in the *Rotorua* on the reverse journey through the Panama Canal, departing from Wellington on 9 February 1924 and arriving at Southampton on 16 March.

Percy had originally hoped that Sam would go to Winchester, but it was clear that he would only be accepted if he won a scholarship and this required a good knowledge of Greek, which Sam had never learnt. There was no alternative in contemplation as the family set out for England, but on the ship they met Alwyn Warren, a New Zealander who had recently graduated from Magdalen College, Oxford and was returning to theological college in England with a view to being ordained.[3] He was an old boy of Marlborough College and suggested approaching his former housemaster, C. A. Emery, to see if he could help. Percy leapt at the idea, and Warren duly went to see Emery to tell him about Sam.

By that time Common Entrance, the exam on which admissions were decided, had already taken place for the next term, which would start in May. Emery, however, said that if Sam came to see him at Marlborough, he would give him the papers, invigilate them himself and, should Sam perform well enough, ensure that he had a place. Sam went down to Marlborough for three days to take the exams, staying with Emery in his house, Summerfield; about a week later, he was hugely relieved when Percy received a telegram from the housemaster to say that he had passed with credit.

Marlborough came as something of a shock to Sam, who, unlike the overwhelming majority of the other boys, had not been through the preparatory school system. Hitherto he had always lived in great comfort, but now he found himself subjected to a harsh regime. With a number of other boys, he lived in a dormitory in which there was only minimal heating in winter. The food he was later to describe as 'deplorable'. There were only two baths for the twenty-six boys in the house, one of which was reserved for the 'bloods', as the most senior boys were called, whilst the remainder shared the other. The result was that, even after scraping off excess mud before getting in after a rugby game, a thick layer of sludge would build up at the bottom of the junior bath which was hardly conducive to good hygiene.[4] If the baths were bad, the lavatories were much worse, in a yard outside and with no roof and no doors!

Junior boys did not act as personal fags for the seniors at Marlborough, but there was communal fagging, mostly cleaning and tidying the classrooms and other common areas. After the first two weeks a new boys' examination was held in the house, consisting largely of questions on traditions, privileges and school slang. Failure to answer a question correctly resulted in the boy in question being beaten with a slipper. More serious transgressions were punished by the cane, wielded by the housemaster or the head of house in front of the whole house at 9.15 in the evening.

Sam's performance in the Common Entrance exam had resulted in his being placed two forms off the bottom of the school, but this still did not reflect his real academic ability. He won the form prize in his first term, was moved up a form and then promoted yet again in his third term, after which he stayed in the same stream, moving up a form once a year. By his last year he had reached the Upper Fifth, which suggests that his academic performance, whilst not brilliant, was above average. Progress was monitored by weekly form orders. If performance was good, all was well. If not, the boy in question was disciplined, which often meant the cane. The curriculum was a broad one in the Lower School in preparation for taking the School Certificate exam, but it became more specialized in the Upper School, in which the boys were prepared for the Higher School Certificate, passing which was a requirement for university entrance. Sam was in the 'Modern' form, which majored in History, Geography and English rather than Classics, Languages, Maths or Science.

Summerfield at that time was an unusual house for two reasons. Firstly, it took boys of all ages, whereas the rest of the school was divided into junior and senior houses, the boys spending a year or so in the former before moving on to the latter. Secondly, it was about half the size of the senior houses. This meant that it laboured under a considerable disadvantage when it came to competitive sports, but, for this purpose at least, it was combined with another house, C3.[5] On the other hand, the house was small enough for the boys to get to know each other very well and Sam made some good friends, of whom the most enduring was Kit Bowring.

Sam did not distinguish himself on the sports field. He shone in none of the major games – cricket, rugby and hockey – and he was in no other school team. He did take up one particular extramural activity, however, playing the trombone, which he enjoyed, becoming good enough to play in a trombone quartet in the Music Competition. He joined the Officers Training Corps, which in theory was voluntary, although at that time everyone was expected to volunteer. As soon as he was able to do so after basic training, he joined the band, rising in due course to the rank of corporal.

In the summer of 1926 Sam was joined in Summerfield by Tony, who had been at prep school at Heatherdown, near Ascot. Whereas Sam more than held his own academically, Tony failed to do so, coming bottom of every form he was in and being beaten frequently, both for poor work and for various other misdemeanours, which on one occasion involved him bringing a cow into Chapel! Sam later remembered his younger brother bringing one of his weekly orders back to the housemaster with a note on the bottom: 'A. C. Elworthy. 25/25. Privileged lunatic.'

Sam enjoyed his final year at school, when he rose to occupy a position of authority. He became a house captain and, indeed, head of house, but not a school prefect because of Summerfield's small size. He left at the end of the summer term of 1929 and, Percy having accepted the inevitable, Tony left with him.

For the whole of the time that Sam was at school his parents lived in England, Percy setting himself up as a country gentleman. They rented two houses, the first at Membury, actually in Devon but no great distance from the ancestral Elworthy homeland in Somerset; the second, occupied for much longer, was Forbury House, near Kintbury in Berkshire and not far from Marlborough. At the latter they maintained a substantial establishment of butler, cook, parlourmaid, kitchen maid, housemaid, three gardeners and a chauffeur. The butler, Leslie Cox, who was the son of the head gardener, proved indispensable and would return with them to New Zealand in due course.

Percy and Bertha led a most active social life, staying with and entertaining friends and, in Percy's case, enjoying both hunting and shooting. He had a gun in two local syndicates, had more invitations than he could accept to shoot elsewhere and even rented a small moor in Argyllshire for the grouse season. Family holidays were taken in the United Kingdom, either in Scotland or at some seaside location, for which purpose Percy bought a capacious caravan, which he later took back to New Zealand. With the children growing up fast, the formality of the earlier years was replaced by a more free and easy relationship, although Anne was always something of an outsider. Percy was by now called 'Willie' by his children, after the Lewis Carroll poem 'You are old, Father William'.[6]

Percy adored cars, although Sam recalled that he always had difficulty double-declutching on hills, so used to grind to a halt and start again in first gear. In the late 1920s he had no fewer than five at the same time and over the years owned models of many marques, from relatively modest Fords and Austins to more exotic American imports such as Stutzes and Chryslers, as well as top of the range Jaguars and Rolls-Royces; it was in one of the last of these that Sam first visited Cambridge.

Chapter 3

Boats and Planes

Sam was later to regret that he had not left Marlborough a year or more earlier, by which time he had already achieved sufficient credits in the Higher School Certificate to satisfy the admission requirements for Cambridge. On reflection, he would have preferred to have spent the time travelling on the Continent, learning to speak French and German, in which languages he was not at all proficient. As it was, he stayed on, secure in the knowledge that he had a place. He and his father had both visited Cambridge to arrange this when he was still only sixteen, as part of a round trip in the Rolls-Royce which also involved picking up a dog for Di in Macclesfield.

Not unnaturally, Percy's original idea was that Sam should go to his own old college, Trinity Hall, and they accordingly began their visit there. However, Percy had a friend, Doctor Winstanley, who was senior tutor of Trinity College, and they went to call on him as well. Percy then announced that if Winstanley was prepared to be Sam's tutor he would send him there instead, always provided that he satisfied the entry requirements. Winstanley agreed, and Sam was duly admitted to Trinity as a Pensioner on 1 October 1929.

It had been decided some years earlier that Sam would read Law. One of his godfathers, Lord Tomlin, a Lord of Appeal, was asked by Percy for advice on his eldest son's career. Tomlin enquired about the boy's character and was told that he was always arguing with his father, at which he gave his opinion that Sam might well succeed at the Bar, and this duly determined the choice of degree course.

In the event, Sam did not shine academically, achieving third class honours in the qualifying exam and Parts I and II of the Tripos in 1930, 1931 and 1932 respectively. He graduated as a Bachelor of Arts in 1932, but did not find the time to take his Master of Arts degree, for which he became automatically eligible in 1935, until 1960. The reason for his lacklustre performance was that he had found another activity, one which he enjoyed enormously and to which he devoted almost all of his available time, doing the bare minimum of academic work required to keep his supervisors content.

The activity was rowing, not an option which had been available at Marlborough. In this sport Sam rose to the highest level within both college and university and he retained an abiding love for it thereafter. Trinity was a very strong rowing college and uniquely had two clubs at that time: First Trinity Boat Club was open to all members of the college, whilst Third Trinity was limited to old boys of Eton and Westminster.[1] Sam naturally joined the former, which had an illustrious history, having been founded in 1825 and achieved much success subsequently. In the relatively recent past it had produced the coxless fours which won gold in the 1924 and 1928 Olympics, and its record at both Cambridge and outside events, notably the Henley Royal Regatta, was second to none amongst Oxbridge colleges.

With no experience from school, Sam began as a novice in the First Trinity Fifth Boat in the Bumps races which took place over four days at the end of the Lent term of 1930. In a Bumps race the boats take position by division in line astern, with a length and a half of clear water between them: on the first of four days they assume the order of their finishing positions in the preceding year. They start simultaneously, and the objective is to touch ('bump') the boat in front before the finishing line is reached, in which event both boats pull into the side of the river to let those behind row past. On the next day the boats start in the revised order determined by the results of the day before. Furthermore, the top boat in each division exchanges places with the bottom boat of the division above.

The First Trinity Fifth Boat was actually the most successful in which Sam ever raced in the Bumps, bumping the boats in front on four successive days, which entitled each of the rowers to receive an oar, on which were painted their names and the college arms, whilst the cox received a rudder.[2] For the May Bumps of 1930, held at the end of the Summer Term, Sam was promoted to the First Trinity Second Boat, which both started and finished ninth in the top division, having 'rowed over' – neither bumping nor being bumped – on each day.

On the strength of his performance Sam was promoted into the First Trinity First Boat for the Ladies' Challenge Plate at the Henley Royal

Regatta of 1930, a remarkable achievement given that he had only taken up the sport some six months earlier. The boat did not get beyond the second day, however. In the Michaelmas Term of 1930 Sam rowed in the First Trinity Second Light Four, which was beaten in the first round of its competition, but later that term he was in the crew of the First Trinity First Boat which won the Head of the River Race on the Cam, better known as the Fairbairn Cup.

The cox of the First Trinity First Boat in 1930 and 1931 was His Royal Highness Prince Chula of Siam. On one occasion the boat sunk due to exceptionally high winds and the crew had to swim for the bank. Chula, however, had never learnt to swim and immediately began to submerge. He was saved by Sam and, in his gratitude, announced that he would put his rescuer's name forward for the award of the Order of the White Elephant. In the event, it was never bestowed, possibly as a result of the confusion caused by the Siamese Revolution of 1932 which resulted in the absolute monarchy in Thailand becoming a constitutional one.

Sam was to remain in the First Trinity First Boat for the remainder of his university career, going on to become Secretary and then President of the club, but he never emulated the success of his first term of rowing, although by the end of his last term the First Boat stood fourth on the river in the May Bumps. He also continued to row for the college at Henley in both eights and fours, usually progressing far in the heats but never winning a trophy. However, the college four in which he rowed won the Home Park Challenge Cup at the Kingston Regatta in 1931. Later in his college career, Sam also coached a number of the more junior boats.

Sam's quality as a rower was such that, in spite of his brief record, he was invited in the autumn of 1930 to participate in the selection races for the two university Trial Eights, from which the crew to row in the Oxford and Cambridge Boat Race was formed. In the event he was not chosen that year, but in the following year he received his Trial Cap, although he did not row for the university against Oxford. It was possibly in the hope of doing so that, having already graduated, he elected to stay up at Trinity for an extra year, doubtless theoretically to pursue postgraduate studies, but in practice to do what he enjoyed most. He was selected for the Trial Eights again, but yet again missed being picked for the Boat Race. One consolation, however, was that the possession of a Trial Cap made him eligible for membership of the Leander Club, which is limited to the most distinguished oarsmen and which he duly joined.

Not surprisingly, many of Sam's best friends at Cambridge were members of the Boat Club. These included the closest of all, Peter Kenrick; as freshmen in the First Trinity First Boat for the Henley Regatta of 1930, they roomed together, inevitably in the least attractive digs, and formed an immediate and lifelong bond. Kenrick, unlike Sam, was no novice, having been Captain of Boats at Shrewsbury. Patrick Beesly, another Trinity rower, was to be Sam's Best Man some years later. However, although Sam rowed every day of the week, spending up to four hours on the river, he also developed a wide social circle outside the sport, making other longstanding friends, not all of whom were at the university. These included Peter Garran, a young Australian who had come to the UK in the hope of joining the Diplomatic Service, Garran's future wife, Elizabeth Stawell, and Betty Bellair, who was to marry Peter Kenrick, all of whom were introduced to Sam by his cousin John. In their company Sam found plenty of time to enjoy the many balls which were held by the colleges, especially during May Week, and other less formal events. He was also a member of the most famous club in Cambridge, the University Pitt Club, and on its committee for 1932/3.

Percy and Bertha had decided to return to New Zealand in 1930, taking Anne and Di with them and giving up the tenancy of Forbury House. This left Sam and Tony, who had also opted to stay in England, in his case to learn to fly, with no base in the country. The gap was filled by a couple who had formed a close relationship with Percy and Bertha, Ernest and Daisy Hudson, who offered a home from home to the Elworthy brothers. They lived near Ham, a few miles from Forbury, in a large house called Prosperous, standing on the site of an earlier building which had been the home of Jethro Tull, the agricultural pioneer of the early eighteenth century. They had no children but instead lavished affection on two very pampered Pekinese dogs, who were always served first at mealtimes. Sam and Tony were frequent guests, for the first time on their own over the Christmas of 1930, and the Hudsons seem to have acted almost as surrogate parents. Whilst kind, however, they were also very formal. On one occasion Sam had brought his dinner jacket down for the weekend but left the trousers behind.

As there were only the three of them for dinner that evening, he hoped that he might be allowed to dress more casually, but Ernest pointed out that there was just time for him to drive back to London to get them!

Otherwise, Sam's university vacations were largely spent in the UK, often staying with friends. Scotland was a favourite destination, but he also visited France, whither Anne had been sent back by her parents to learn French, boarding with a family in Paris. The Long Vacation in the summer of 1932, however, was spent in New Zealand, the first time he had been back to the country since 1924. He was accompanied by Tony and invited Peter Kenrick to join them. They sailed for New Zealand towards the end of June and remained there until September, as Sam needed to be back in Cambridge for the start of the new term. Whilst there they based themselves at Gordons Valley, but travelled around the country, including to Mount Cook for the skiing. As it turned out, this would be Sam's last visit for nearly fourteen years, partly because Percy and Bertha themselves returned to England in 1934, this time buying Rainscombe, a substantial house near Oare in Wiltshire.

After coming down from Cambridge in the summer of 1933 Sam lived in digs in London and was primarily concerned with studying for his Bar exams and attending the required number of dinners at Lincoln's Inn. However, he felt that he needed another interest in life. After leaving school, Tony, who was obsessed by flying, had taken lessons and duly obtained his private pilot's licence in 1931, although to his great disappointment he failed to get into the RAF because of a thyroid condition. Sam was keen to follow him into the air and would have joined the Cambridge University Air Squadron if the time required had not clashed with rowing. He had actually flown on several occasions, the first of which had been during his stay in England as a small child when he and Percy had been taken up in a Bristol Boxkite at Hendon. Whilst he was at Marlborough he had flown in an Avro 504 at the enormous cost to his pocket money of 5 shillings and he had subsequently flown to Paris more than once in an Imperial Airways Handley Page HP 42. He now discovered that there was an organization called the Reserve of Air Force Officers which, if he was accepted, would not only arrange for him to be taught to fly but would pay him the princely sum of £1 per day for the privilege.

The RAFO had been formed in 1923 as part of a scheme, together with the Royal Auxiliary Air Force and the University Air Squadrons, to provide pilots and airmen to bolster the regular RAF. Initially directed at former RAF personnel, in the late 1920s it was also opened to direct recruitment of those with no flying experience. Flying training in the RAF itself was carried out within the service, but it was decided that training for the RAFO would be contracted out to civilian organizations. In the event, four aircraft manufacturers were selected,[3] carrying out the training at their own airfields close to their factories.

Immediately after coming down from Cambridge, Sam duly applied to join the RAFO, armed with a favourable reference from the Chief Instructor of the Cambridge University Air Squadron. He was accepted, gazetted as a pilot officer on probation on 14 August 1933 and ordered to report to Brough Airfield in Yorkshire for flying training. This was clearly an inconvenient location for someone living in London. However, Sam had a university friend who had also been accepted into the RAFO and who was living and working in Yorkshire but had been ordered to attend the flying school run by De Havilland at Hatfield. Hoping not only to carry out their training closer to home, but also to save the Government money, they applied to exchange postings. They were told in no uncertain terms to do as they had been ordered, which gave Sam an early indication of the sort of bureaucracy which occasionally bedevilled the RAF.

Following his arrival at Brough as one of about fifteen would-be pilots who came from all walks of life, Sam spent the first days exclusively on ground studies, which included lectures on navigation, airmanship, engines and the rigging and fitting of planes. These continued throughout the course, and Sam was graded 'Exceptional'. On 28 August he took his first flying lesson. Initially, the civilian schools had used a wide range of largely superannuated aircraft, but by this time they had standardized on two bi-planes, the De Havilland Tiger Moth and the Blackburn B2; since Sam was on Blackburn's airfield, it was in one of that company's aircraft that he learnt. It differed from the Tiger Moth in that the seating arrangement was side-by-side rather than in tandem.

Sam was lucky in his instructor, Flight Lieutenant Woodhead, who he thought was excellent. Woodhead was particularly keen on aerobatics, indeed one of the aircraft had been specially modified for him to be able to perform them, and he introduced them into his lessons at the earliest possible opportunity, much to Sam's delight. However, the focus in the first instance was on take-offs and landings and, after only just over 10 hours of instruction, Sam went on his first solo flight on 9 September. It turned out that, like Tony, he had a natural aptitude for flying. He continued to undergo intensive training as often as he could get away from London for the remainder of 1933 and into January 1934, by which time he had completed over 25 hours on dual control and almost the same number solo. He achieved his private pilot's licence on 26 February 1934, although it was not until 10 November that he was awarded his RAF flying badge after two further refresher courses at Brough. He was able in the meantime to borrow aircraft from the Hatfield school and, not long after qualifying, flew a Tiger Moth from there to Prosperous and back, taking Tony as a passenger. He occasionally took up other friends and, in the summer of 1935, flew the newly married Peter and Betty Kenrick in a Puss Moth to Le Bourget for their honeymoon as a wedding present.

On 28 January 1935 Sam was called to the Bar at Lincoln's Inn, having been proposed by his godfather, Lord Tomlin. His original intention had been to practise at the Chancery Bar, but it became rapidly apparent that he was unlikely to be able to make ends meet there for many years. 'That way,' as he was to say later, 'lay starvation!' Instead, he became one of the Blue Button Boys at the Stock Exchange. These were unauthorized clerks whose job was to run round the stock jobbers and find out the prices at which they were buying or selling specific stocks; they were expressly forbidden to carry out any dealing themselves. Whilst it was useful training for anyone hoping to make a career in stockbroking, it was also very unexciting.

One of Sam's close friends at Cambridge, Jimmy Wells,[4] had become a member of 600 (City of London) Squadron, Royal Auxiliary Air Force on coming down from university. Encouraged by Wells, Sam now applied to join the squadron and was accepted, exchanging his commission in the RAFO for one in the RAuxAF on 15 January 1935. 600 Squadron had been formed in October 1925, one of four squadrons – the others being 601 (County of London), 602 (City of Glasgow) and 603 (City of Edinburgh) – which made up the RAuxAF at the time. Designated as a light bomber squadron, it initially flew the DH9a and then the Westland Wapiti, but by the time Sam arrived, the latter had been replaced by the Hawker Hart.

The Hart was a highly versatile general purpose bi-plane which was, when it entered service in 1930, faster than any existing RAF fighter, with a maximum speed of 184 mph. It had two small cockpits, the rear one usually occupied by an NCO or other rank, whose day-to-day role would have been on the ground as a mechanic, but who would readily volunteer to act as the Lewis gunner and would prove exceptionally useful in the event of a forced landing, a not uncommon occurrence; if no one was available, then ballast had to be loaded to ensure the correct weight distribution. The Hart was allocated to a large number of squadrons, both in the United Kingdom and overseas, and in due course spawned a number of variants for army co-operation and for use by the Royal Navy, whilst, in the absence of anything better, the Hawker Demon was produced as a fighter.

600 Squadron had a Town Headquarters at Finsbury Barracks, where its members could meet on two nights a week and where classroom instruction was given, but the flying took place at RAF Hendon, where the pilots were expected to spend most of their weekends. Sam was more than happy to do so, as he was in his element. With the exception of the Adjutant, Assistant Adjutant and a few senior warrant officers, all the members of the squadron, whether pilots or ground crew, were volunteers, which in Sam's opinion meant that they tried particularly hard to achieve and maintain the highest standards, whether of flying or of maintenance. Many of the ground crew were there simply because they enjoyed tinkering with engines, one of them driving out to Hendon to do so every weekend in his Rolls-Royce!

The CO was Squadron Leader Peter Stewart, an underwriter at Lloyds, and the officers were largely drawn from banking, stockbroking, insurance, accountancy and the law; Sam found them very congenial. His flight commander was Flight Lieutenant Viscount Carlow, who would in due course take over command from Stewart, only to be killed in a flying accident during the war.

The highlight of each year for the RAuxAF squadrons was their two weeks in camp, where the pilots could practise cross-country flying, bombing and gunnery during the day and let their hair down in the evening. In July 1935 this took place for 600 Squadron at RAF Sutton Bridge in south-east Lincolnshire and also included air defence exercises in the role of fighters. This demonstrated amply that the Hart could still outpace some of the dedicated fighters still in RAF service as well as the bombers, which included models fast approaching obsolescence such as the Fairey Gordon and the Handley Page Heyford. Sam, however, was distinctly unimpressed by the tactics prescribed for fighter attacks, which he considered to be stereotyped actions by numbers: all interceptions were achieved by eyesight alone, with effective ground control still far in the future. Although Carlow was an advocate of radio and carried a set in this aircraft, this was purely a private venture. Communication between two aircraft was carried out by 'zogging', which consisted of the pilot letting his arm hang over the side of the cockpit facing the other aircraft and then moving it up and down from the elbow to represent Morse code, a short movement representing a dot and a long one a dash. It required a great deal of practice.

On 6 July, a week before leaving for Sutton Bridge, the squadron participated in the RAF Review to celebrate King George V's Silver Jubilee. This consisted of a static review of 370 aircraft from thirty-eight squadrons at RAF Mildenhall and a formation flypast at RAF Duxford. Sam had taken his aircraft up to Mildenhall a week earlier, travelling back there for the review. Although the squadron did not participate in the flypast, it nevertheless returned to Hendon in close formation.

A month later, Sam went on holiday to Southern Germany and Austria with John Elworthy. Sam and John were first cousins twice over, by virtue of their fathers being brothers and their mothers sisters. John had spent a lot of time in England, attending the Royal Naval College at Osborne on the Isle of Wight and then the Royal Naval College at Dartmouth, prior to being commissioned into the Royal Navy. His home in England during this period had been with Percy and Bertha, whilst Sam and Tony had become more like brothers to him than cousins.

Sam and John decided to go canoeing on the Danube and two of its tributaries, the Inn and the Salzach, visiting Passau, Salzburg and Innsbruck amongst other cities and towns and enjoying themselves hugely, notwithstanding the very evident rise of National Socialism in Germany and some sympathy for the movement in Austria. Such political developments, however, probably seemed relatively trivial to Sam next to those, one personal and one professional, which were about to decide the direction of his own life in the decades ahead.

Chapter 4

Take-off

It was John Elworthy who was the catalyst for the first of the momentous changes in Sam's life, which had its origins in the early summer of 1935, before the expedition to Germany and Austria. John had just returned by sea from New Zealand and was staying in Sam's flat in Swiss Cottage. By way of entertainment he suggested that they should arrange a game of bridge. Sam agreed and invited a girl he knew, whilst John brought along Audrey Hutchinson, whom he had met and played bridge with on the ship. There was an immediate and mutual attraction between Sam and Audrey; indeed, Sam was later to say that she was the first and only woman he ever considered as a partner.

Audrey was born on 8 November 1910 in Orange, New South Wales, the only child of Arthur and Olive Hutchinson, who had met in Australia after emigrating from England. When she was three years old the family moved to Auckland, where Arthur had been appointed managing director of the Burroughs Adding Machine Company and subsequently became an eminent member of the business community, known for his charitable work as chairman of the Blind Institute, for which he was awarded the OBE. Audrey was educated at the Diocesan High School for Girls in Auckland, where she boarded for two years, and then at Auckland University, where she gained a first class honours degree in English and History. She had visited England once before, but had come this time to take up an appointment as private secretary to the New Zealand High Commissioner and was thus intending to stay for a protracted period. It turned out to be longer than she had anticipated!

Audrey had a bubbly and vivacious personality, but she was also both intelligent and erudite and could hold her own in any company. She had, in particular, a great love of poetry, and her phenomenal memory enabled her to quote at will from the poems she loved best. Most of all, however, she enjoyed meeting people of all sorts and conditions. Quick to praise and slow to criticise, she somehow brought out the best in all those she encountered, and Sam himself was quickly bowled over.

Sam and Audrey spent as much time as possible together, and it was not long before he persuaded her to take to the air, flying her from Hatfield down to Prosperous and back again in a Gipsy Moth. Subsequently, he was delighted to find that she was keen to experience aerobatics and immediately subjected her to loops and a long inverted descent, for the duration of which she was hanging from her straps with every indication that she was enjoying the experience hugely. They went up again for more of the same two days later and, three days after that, on 28 September 1935, they announced their engagement.

The second of the great changes in Sam's life took place shortly afterwards. The overwhelming majority of RAF officers in the General Duties Branch[1] received their commissions, whether permanent or short-service, on graduating from the RAF College at Cranwell. However, it was decided to award a very small number of permanent commissions to university graduates, and Sam, who had enjoyed his time at 600 Squadron enormously and had come to the inevitable conclusion that neither the Law nor the City were meant for him, decided to apply for one of these. He was informed that whilst his application was being considered he would remain in the RAuxAF but be attached to a regular squadron. After an unspecified period, which would certainly be some months, he would be reported on by the commanding officer as to his suitability for a permanent commission. If the report was adverse, he would either be sent to Cranwell or discharged.

Accordingly, on 28 October 1935 Sam was posted on attachment to XV (Bomber) Squadron,[2] which was based at RAF Abingdon. The squadron had been originally formed in 1915 as a training unit but had been sent to France later that year, where it served for the remainder of the war as a reconnaissance and artillery spotting squadron, flying first B.E.2s and then R.E.8s and distinguishing itself at the Battles of Arras and Cambrai. It was disbanded in 1919 but reformed in 1924 as a test flying and experimental unit and was re-designated as a bomber squadron in 1934.

Sam was determined to avoid an adverse report but he entertained serious concerns that, as a weekend flyer, he would not be good enough. These were quickly dispelled, for two reasons. Firstly, the squadron operated Hawker Harts, on which he already had over 120 hours of flying time. Secondly, the standards of efficiency which had been achieved by 600 Squadron were in no way emulated by XV Squadron. The quality of flying was much lower, the enthusiasm less and the leadership distinctly poorer than he had been used to. This was partly due to the squadron commander, of whom he had no great opinion, whilst the flight commanders were elderly flight lieutenants with some 20 years of service. However, two months later, the CO was replaced, first by a short-lived appointee and then by Squadron Leader C. D. ('Bill') Adams, who was a very considerable improvement, whilst the flight commanders were succeeded by younger men, of lesser experience but with greater leadership qualities. Over the next two years of Sam's service with the squadron the standards improved dramatically.

Having received a favourable report,[3] on 3 March 1936 Sam relinquished his commission in the RAuxAF in exchange for a permanent commission in the RAF as a pilot officer, with his seniority backdated to 3 December 1934. At the age of nearly twenty-five he believed himself to be the oldest General Duties pilot officer in the service, and one of his friends, later Air Marshal Sir Anthony Selway,[4] allegedly told him that he hadn't a cat in hell's chance of ever getting beyond the rank of flight lieutenant. However, his immediate future secure, he could now think about getting married. Until then he and Audrey had been living separate lives and had only been able to see one another when he could get away from Abingdon, which had included his leave over Christmas 1935, spent by them both at Heligan with his aunt, Muriel Williamson.

Sam had to apply to his Station Commander, Wing Commander Tommy Elmhirst, for permission to marry, which was duly granted, and the wedding took place in London on 5 June 1936 at St Saviour's, Walton Street. Audrey's parents were unable to come from New Zealand, but her cousin, Phyllis Wilson, helped with much of the planning, and Phyllis's husband gave Audrey away. On Sam's side Percy and Bertha were there, as was Aunt Muriel. The best man was Patrick Beesly, and the chief bridesmaid was Sam's cousin, Elizabeth Elworthy,[5] whilst one of the toasts was proposed by Ernest Hudson. Elmhirst had only allowed Sam three days leave, but one of his RAF friends, Freddie White, who owned his own aeroplane, suggested that Sam should hire a plane and fly to France. After the reception at the Basil Street Hotel, Sam and Audrey picked up a Puss Moth at Heston and flew to Le Touquet, where they dined with Freddie and Lois White, flying to Le Bourget the next day for a night in Paris.[6]

The proper honeymoon had to be deferred until August, when Sam and Audrey crossed the Channel to Dunkirk and then drove down to Dinkelsbühl on the Romantic Road in Southern Germany, before going on to Landeck in the Tyrol and Interlaken in Switzerland. Back in Abingdon, they moved into a furnished house at 44 East St Helen Street, which they rented at £2 a week, whilst a Mrs Wiblin came in every day to cook all their meals and wash up for 17/6 a week. As his gross pay at the time was 12/6 per day, this would not have left much over but for the fact that Sam had a modest allowance from his father. Moreover, he was still expected to dine in the mess on four nights out of seven.

Sam's focus now was on his new career. A routine soon established itself in XV Squadron. Flying took place on most days, with a focus on formation and cross-country flying. Elmhurst, who had commanded the squadron prior to Sam's arrival, had never been keen on the former, believing it to be dangerous. He had been in airships during the Great War, and even Sam, who otherwise admired him, felt that he lacked experience on fixed-wing aeroplanes. The arrival of Adams, whom Sam described as 'a great aviator'[7] and the delegation of formation flying training to one of the flight commanders, Flight Lieutenant MacCallum, solved the problem.

Bombing practice was carried out either on a dedicated range at Otmoor or on a circle marked out on the airfield at Abingdon, although, as the station was also occupied by 40 Squadron and the Oxford University Air Squadron, great caution had to be exercised in case one of their planes was taking off or landing at the time. In March 1936 Sam, accompanied in the rear cockpit by Sergeant Abrook, was sent up to the armament training camp at RAF Leuchars in Scotland to carry out air firing exercises against drogues pulled by other aircraft. Whilst there, he was detailed by Elmhirst to undertake another mission. Elmhirst's wife had inherited Kilconquhar House in Fife and she wanted a good aerial photograph of the property. The photo had to be taken with a hand-held camera, steadied by a wire, so needed considerable accuracy, and a previous attempt by another pilot had produced a very unsatisfactory result, with the images either blurred or showing large expanses of open country. It was evident that the exercise had been carried out at too great an altitude, so Sam solved the problem by making his approach very low over the house, although the application of a considerable amount of throttle was then required to clear the enormous beech trees on the other side. When developed, one of the photos turned out to be exactly what was required, to the extent of even showing the furniture in the dining room. Elmhirst was delighted and kept a copy in his pocket book to show to friends.

Sam was not so lucky, at least at first, in another encounter with the Station Commander. Elmhirst, whom Sam described as 'very GS' (General Staff, inclined to act by the book) had directed that all junior officers should attend court martials as 'officers under instruction' and then write an essay on the proceedings and submit it to him. One court martial attended by Sam involved a case of alleged desertion against a corporal. The findings of the court, that the allegations had been proved, were then sent to the Judge Advocate General for confirmation and sentencing. The prosecuting officer's case, however, depended on evidence given by the accused's mother-in-law, which Sam believed to be inadmissible under the hearsay rules. He said as much in his essay, predicting that the case would be thrown out. He was immediately hauled before Elmhirst, who called him an 'insufferable little so-and-so'[8] who should not presume to criticise his elders and betters. A month later, Elmhirst summoned him back to tell him that the case had indeed been dismissed, on precisely the grounds which Sam had predicted. When asked how he had known, Sam confessed that he had been called to the Bar. Elmhirst got his own back by appointing Sam to prosecute or defend in every subsequent court martial!

On 1 June 1936 Sam was made Adjutant of XV Squadron, an appointment he held for a year and which gave him his first taste of staff work, albeit at the lowest possible level, with responsibility for the roster of duties, for discipline, which was generally good, and for certain aspects of administration. This did not mean that he did any less flying, in contrast to the procedure adopted in the Great War, when squadron adjutants were confined to ground duties, the appointment often being held by reserve officers who were over the age for active operations or by those from branches other than General

Duties. It did mean that he was closely involved with the replacement of the squadron's Harts by Hawker Hinds in the summer of 1936. The Hind was one of the many derivatives of the Hart, the main difference being a new engine, the Rolls-Royce Kestrel V, which provided additional power, increasing both the maximum speed and the service ceiling. The other changes were the modification of the rear cockpit and the replacement of the tail skid by a wheel. The Hind was always seen as an interim stop–gap, pending the introduction of the new monoplane light bombers, the Fairey Battle and the Bristol Blenheim, although it was to remain in frontline service outside the UK until 1941.

Sam had been promoted to Flying Officer on 3 September 1936 and, in the summer of the following year, after handing over as Adjutant, he was appointed Flight Commander of A Flight, comprising his own and three or four other aircraft. Adams's assessment of his ability in his log book for the year commencing 1 June 1936 was 'Exceptional' for each of the four categories – Pilot, Pilot-Navigator, Bombing and Air Gunnery. Just prior to his new appointment, the focus had been on preparations for Empire Air Day, on which the public was admitted to the station to see the squadrons at work, inspect the aircraft on the ground and be treated to a display in the air. Now the emphasis turned to dive-bombing.

Dive-bombing exercises involved planes acting individually, each one climbing to between 5,000 and 6,000ft and then going into a sharp dive to release one bomb at a time out of the eight which were carried, at altitudes of between 1,000 and 3,000ft. The accuracy at 3,000ft was never very good, but at lower levels pilots were expected to drop their bombs within 50yds of the target. Not only the height of the release, but the angle at which it was executed had an effect on the result, with the calculations being done in the pilot's head, although some used home-made instruments to establish the correct angle. The key to accurate bombing was the precise determination of Point X, the position at which the dive commenced.

Most of the dive-bombing was done at Abingdon or Otmoor, although planes were also sent up to RAF Catfoss in Yorkshire, from where they could bomb small ships at sea. The Royal Navy provided a far more substantial target in the shape of HMS *Centurion*, a pre-Great War battleship which had been refitted as a radio-controlled target ship. At the end of August 1937 the squadron relocated for a week to RAF Tangmere, from where it carried out dive-bombing attacks on the ship in the Solent. On his first sortie Sam achieved two hits with two bombs, but was disconcerted to be told that they had been disqualified because he had released them from an altitude of 1,900ft rather than 2,000ft and that this meant that he would have been shot down by anti-aircraft fire. Other pilots had the same experience, with hits being disqualified whilst misses were assessed as good dives.

The problem was that, for largely political reasons, the Royal Navy was determined to show that its ships were not vulnerable to dive-bombing, a stance which echoed that of the US Navy when Brigadier General Billy Mitchell had carried out similar tests over fifteen years earlier. Accordingly, not only were most of the hits disqualified, but the planes were only allowed to bomb one at a time and not in large numbers from multiple directions, as would have been the case in a realistic attack. Once again, the reason given was that they would all have been shot down. The controversy rumbled on, and it was only during the Norwegian campaign and the evacuation of the BEF from Dunkirk that the warnings on the vulnerability of ships to dive-bombing proved emphatically to have been correct.

On 28 October 1937 XV Squadron was visited on an inspection by Air Chief Marshal Sir Edgar Ludlow-Hewitt, who had recently been appointed AOC-in-C of Bomber Command. He had asked for a demonstration of dive-bombing, and Sam was ordered to carry it out on the dive-bombing area at Abingdon, where the large marked-out circle had a stick in its centre. With a combination of skill and luck Sam not only managed to land his bomb in the middle of the circle but actually to knock over the stick, something he had never achieved before. Ludlow-Hewitt, who was not a man to express any emotion publicly, was nevertheless impressed. He had asked Elmhirst to put forward the names of young officers to act as his personal assistant and Sam's was on the list. He was duly interviewed and chosen on the spot.

Sam's immediate reaction was disappointment, as he believed that his new job would require much less flying, the one thing above all others that he enjoyed as an RAF officer. However, he quickly recognized that it would give him a unique opportunity to see a great deal more of the RAF and, in particular, of Bomber Command, which was itself only fifteen months old and in the course of a massive transformation. Until July 1936 all UK-based squadrons, whether bomber or fighter, had been incorporated into an organization called Air Defence of Great Britain, which also included anti-aircraft and searchlight batteries and the Observer Corps. ADGB was divided into a number of geographical zones, with substantially all the bomber squadrons in the Wessex Bombing Area in South-Central England, later divided into a Western and a Central Area. These now became Bomber Command, with its HQ at Hillingdon House, Uxbridge. With the realization that the bombers would have to be as close as possible to the Continent, there was now a major shift to airfields in the East of England, from North Yorkshire down to East Anglia.

In 1935, in the light of German re-armament, it had been decided to expand the number of bomber squadrons from the forty-three agreed upon only a year earlier to seventy, this scheme being modified a year later by a change of emphasis from light to medium bombers. Other expansion schemes were to follow,[9] the results of which were twofold. Firstly, the general expansion and the geographical relocation created a substantial requirement for new airfields, which were built to a very high standard in terms of permanent hangars and buildings but largely retained grass runways. Secondly, a new generation of aircraft was emerging. The light bombers, including the Hart, were being replaced by the Fairey Battle and the Bristol Blenheim, whilst the heavy bombers such as the Handley Page Harrow were superseded by a new generation of aircraft, the Armstrong Whitworth Whitley, the Handley Page Hampden and the Vickers Wellington, all of which entered squadron service during 1937 or 1938. Moreover, orders had already been placed for what would become the four-engined heavy bombers of the Second World War.

Although Ludlow-Hewitt had no responsibility for the construction of airfields and the manufacture of aircraft, he was intimately concerned with the commissioning of the former and the introduction into service of the latter, which included training significant numbers of both aircrew to fly in them and ground crews to look after them. His workload was thus huge, and Sam was there to alleviate the burden as much as possible. This was not easy, as Ludlow-Hewitt was not only a severe taskmaster, who demanded the highest standards of all his subordinates, but an austere man who did not encourage close relationships. A Christian Scientist who neither smoked nor drank, he had an outstanding brain, but little sense of humour. Initially, he made Sam's life extremely difficult, blaming him for everything which went wrong. After about six months, however, Sam had the temerity to answer back on one occasion and, to his astonishment, Ludlow-Hewitt smiled and said that he was quite right. From that moment their relationship improved dramatically, and Sam came to admire his chief greatly and to enjoy working for him.

Sam's main duties involved arranging the AOC-in-C's programme, writing the minutes of his meetings and accompanying him on the many inspections which he undertook within his increasingly far-flung command. It was normal practice to fly to these, and Sam found that he was able to pursue his favourite activity far more often that he had anticipated. On some occasions he and Ludlow-Hewitt travelled together in a Hart, with either acting as pilot, but on others they would fly alongside each other, communicating by way of zogging, at which Ludlow-Hewitt was an expert but Sam was far from completely proficient. He discovered that Ludlow-Hewitt was a complete master of his trade, with an astonishingly detailed knowledge of aircraft. On one occasion they were on an inspection at Grantham and Ludlow-Hewitt asked the CO which engine was installed in the Hart at which they were looking. The CO replied that it was a Kestrel V. The AOC-in-C immediately summoned a Flight Sergeant, who told him that it was actually a Kestrel IIB. 'Put it in your book, Elworthy,' barked Ludlow-Hewitt, 'Squadron commander grossly inefficient'!

If Ludlow-Hewitt had a weakness, it related to casualties, about which he became quite emotional. He insisted on being told about accidents immediately, even if it was in the middle of the night and even after Sam told him that there was no advantage in doing so. He insisted that Sam should phone the station commander immediately to find out the cause and express the AOC-in-C's sympathy. Sam believed that casualties were a crushing burden to him and was not surprised when he was replaced at Bomber Command early in the War, as he was insufficiently ruthless to press on regardless of them. Instead, he was to become an outstanding Inspector-General of the RAF for the duration of the war. Sam, however, believed that he had done more than anyone to improve the training and efficiency of Bomber Command in the run-up to hostilities.

There were some lighter moments for Sam, at least in retrospect. One occurred when Ludlow-Hewitt was summoned to attend a levee at St James's Palace, accompanied by Sam, both of them in full dress uniform. When they emerged, the car which they were expecting to be waiting for them was not there. Sam offered to go off and find it, but Ludlow-Hewitt insisted on coming too. They were accosted by a press photographer, who was taking pictures of all those leaving the palace. Asked for their details, Ludlow-Hewitt was reluctant to divulge anything, but the man persisted and, to make him go away, Sam gave him their names, ranks and occupations. Some days later, the phone rang on Sam's desk outside the AOC-in-C's office and he picked it up to hear the voice of the PA to the Chief of the Air Staff, Air Chief Marshal Sir Cyril Newall. Sam asked him to hold on whilst he put the call through, only to be told that the CAS actually wanted to speak to him. The conversation was brief and one-sided.

'Elworthy?'

'Yes, sir.'

'How's your brother officer?' asked the CAS, then immediately slammed down the phone.

In considerable puzzlement Sam rang the PA and was referred to the newly published edition of *Tatler*. There, prominently displayed, was a photo of the two men with the caption: PILOT OFFICER ALWORTHY AND A BROTHER OFFICER!

Abingdon was clearly too far away for the Elworthys to live there, so Sam and Audrey rented a house called The Mull in Denham, close to Uxbridge. On 27 January 1938, not long after the move, their first child, Timothy Charles Elworthy, was born. Ludlow-Hewitt unbent as far as to have a drink to celebrate the birth. He also gave Audrey a neat whisky, believing it to be sherry, which she knocked back without comment! Sam and Audrey were in Denham for little more than a year, as at the end of 1938 Sam asked to be relieved from his position as PA to Ludlow-Hewitt and, on 11 January 1939, was posted to 108 Squadron at Bassingbourn, south-west of Cambridge.

Chapter 5

Blenheim

Having passed his promotion exam with a distinction, Sam had been promoted to flight lieutenant on 3 September 1938. He was appointed to command A Flight of 108 Squadron, but before he could do so he had to take a conversion course on the Bristol Blenheim Mark I with 114 Squadron at RAF Wyton.

Like its much more successful replacement as a light bomber, the De Havilland Mosquito, the Blenheim started life as a private venture. The initiative in the Blenheim's case came from Lord Rothermere, proprietor of the *Daily Mail*, who in 1934 challenged the aircraft industry to produce a high-speed, twin-engined, 6-passenger aircraft for use by himself and other businessmen. The Bristol Aircraft Company had been working on just such a plane and persuaded Rothermere to fund the development of what became the Type 142, which flew for the first time in April 1935. It proved to be faster than any fighter then in service with the RAF, which accordingly decided to carry out an evaluation of its potential as a light bomber, aided by Rothermere's decision to present the aircraft to the nation for that purpose.

The evaluation proved successful, a large order was placed and the Blenheim I entered service in March 1937. The relocation of the prototype's wing from a low to a mid-position enabled an enclosed bomb bay to be incorporated into the fuselage, carrying up to 1,000lbs of bombs (usually 4 x 250lbs). A dorsal gun turret was also added, with one Vickers machine gun, whilst an additional forward-firing .303 machine gun was built into the port wing. The plane was powered by two Bristol Mercury radial engines which produced a top speed of 278 mph at 15,000ft, and it had a crew of three, a pilot, a navigator/bomb-aimer and an air gunner/wireless operator.

Sam went solo in a Blenheim for the first time on 16 January 1939, returning to Bassingbourn two days later. He had visited the station on four occasions with Ludlow-Hewitt and was thus familiar with its two squadrons, 104 and

108. The latter had been formed in November 1917 and, equipped with DH 9 bombers, had served in France for the last five months of the Great War, only to be disbanded in July 1919. It was re-formed in January 1937 at Upper Heyford as part of the Expansion Scheme, moving subsequently to Bassingbourn under the command of Squadron Leader J. H. Powle.

The eight months which Sam spent at Bassingbourn were largely uneventful. He was the only substantive flight lieutenant in the squadron and thus the most senior officer after Powle. There was a significant intake of officers from the Royal Air Force Volunteer Reserve who proved to be good material, but they were very inexperienced at first. A great deal of flying and navigation training took place, the latter all still carried out by dead reckoning, but there was relatively little bombing training, partly because no directions had been received on what sort of targets the aircraft were likely to be ordered to attack. There was also very little night flying as the Blenheim had been specifically introduced as a day bomber. At the time, its speed and strict formation flying were together thought to be all that was necessary to protect it from attacks by enemy fighters, an assumption which was later to prove all too tragically false.

The only relief in a relatively tedious programme came when a party of Romanian Air Force officers arrived in August for a conversion course following an order to Bristol for thirteen aircraft, which were to be delivered in November. As Sam was later to say, at least they didn't kill any of them!

Sam and Audrey were renting a house in nearby Royston. Although the storm clouds of war were gathering, the normal peacetime routine included a number of opportunities for leave, and they managed to get away for the Henley Royal Regatta and to stay on more than one occasion with Percy and Bertha at Rainscombe.

In the third week of September, following the declaration of war on Germany, both 104 and 108 Squadrons were ordered to relocate to RAF Bicester, where they became Group Pool squadrons as part of 6 (Training) Group, which had recently been formed in Abingdon under the command of Air Commodore W. F. McN. Foster. Their purpose was to conduct six-week operational training courses for aircrew who had already qualified as pilots at elementary and service flying training schools or as navigators/ bomb-aimers and wireless operators/air gunners at the equivalent schools.

In addition to the Blenheims, the squadron also had the use of a number of Avro Ansons.

Sam's arrival at Bicester was dramatic. A young pilot officer in 108 Squadron had reported that his aircraft was unserviceable because of a failed airspeed indicator. Keen to get all the planes to Bicester, Sam said that he would take it himself. It turned out not only that the airspeed indicator was out of action but also that there was a hydraulic leak, rendering the undercarriage useless and compelling him to make a belly landing at his new airfield.

Powle was now appointed Chief Ground Instructor at Bicester, and command of the squadron was assumed by Wing Commander P. J. A. Hume-Wright. Sam remained in command of 'A' Flight, but in practice he became one of the senior flying instructors, taking up trainee pilots and sometimes complete crews on most days and often several times a day. There were a significant number of crashes during training, many of which were caused by engine failure shortly after take-off. Sam believed that the principal reason for the crashes, which were often fatal, was adherence to the established procedure of gaining height as quickly as possible so that, in the event of a failure, the aircraft might be at a sufficient altitude to allow a safe landing. This usually worked with bi-planes such as the Tiger Moths used at elementary flying schools, which had good gliding characteristics, but seldom with heavy twin-engined monoplanes. Sam realized that the safer course of action was to gain not height but speed, as the achievement of sufficient velocity would usually allow the plane to be flown on one engine for long enough to be able to make a safe landing.

He was even more concerned about the policy on training for night flying, which was now on the curriculum notwithstanding the Blenheim's designation as a day bomber. The Central Flying School was the main authority on training, but the huge proliferation in types of aircraft meant that it had not always kept up with their particular characteristics. It had also lost sight of the fact that night flying in peacetime was aided by lights from streets, buildings and cars, providing bearings for the pilots. The imposition of a strict blackout meant that such aids were no longer available and, in particular, that the pilots had no natural horizon. The dictum from the CFS, that all night flying should be carried out solo and should consist of pilots flying 'circuits and bumps' later and later in the day, eventually progressing through dusk to complete darkness, led to a large number of disastrous crashes, with inevitable fatalities.

Sam quickly realized that the trainee pilots were becoming disorientated. Notwithstanding the rule that such flying should be carried out solo, he decided that he should accompany the trainees, not handling the cockpit controls himself, as there was only one set for the pilot, but sitting beside them and telling them what to do, instilling in them the necessary confidence to do it themselves. The results were extraordinary, with the number of accidents falling dramatically. Initially, Sam told nobody in authority what he was doing, but as soon as he had proved that the method worked he put a paper up to Foster, who arranged a meeting with representatives of the CFS. The latter, possibly motivated by professional jealousy, pointed out that Sam was not a qualified flying instructor and insisted that he should follow official policy. Sam countered that teaching pupils to fly in the first instance was quite different to converting them subsequently on to a much more complex aeroplane. In spite of the CFS's opposition, the results of Sam's methods were undoubted, and the AOC, and in due course the Directorate of Flying Training, came down in his favour.

Arrangements were immediately made at 104 and 108 Squadrons to designate their most experienced officers as night flying instructors, following the procedures pioneered by Sam. On 1 January 1941, many months after he had left Bicester, Sam was awarded the Air Force Cross, specifically for his work on night flying training. In his letter of congratulation Foster wrote, 'I put you top of my list, and I always greatly admired your gallant and constructive attitude with regard to dual on Blenheims at night.'[1]

There were other hazards to night flying, including one alarming episode at RAF Weston-on-the-Green, a relief landing ground which was in regular use for training flights but had little in the way of buildings or slit trenches. Whilst Sam's Blenheim was on the ground at dusk, a German intruder arrived over the airfield and, spotting it, turned to come in for an attack. Sam and his crew dived into the nearest ditch when the first bomb fell some 300yds away. It was followed by three others in quick succession, the last of which exploded very close to where they were sheltering but did them no harm. This was the first time that Sam had come under enemy fire.

One other significant event had taken place at Bicester in the autumn of 1939. In 1937 a contract had been placed by the Air Ministry with Handley Page for the construction of two prototypes of its proposed HP 57 four-engined bomber. When the first of these was nearing completion, it was realized that the company's own airfield at Radlett was too small and it was decided to use Bicester instead. The final assembly took place in one of the hangars there, and the aircraft was rolled out for its maiden flight on 25 October. The company's chief test pilot, Major Jim Cordes, was accompanied by its flight test observer, E. A. Wright, but Cordes asked for a volunteer to accompany them as his crew, and Sam put up his hand. He was thus in at the beginning of what turned out to be a successful career for the subsequently named Handley Page Halifax. Although it was outshone as a bomber by the Avro Lancaster, because of the Lancaster's flying characteristics and its astonishing ability to carry ever heavier bomb loads, it proved to be more adaptable in many other ways, operating not only as a bomber but also as a maritime reconnaissance aircraft in Coastal Command and as a freighter and troop carrier, whilst a number were employed on clandestine operations. At the end of the war it was still equipping over twenty squadrons in Bomber Command, including all those in 4 Group.

For the duration of Sam's posting to Bicester he and Audrey rented 6 Hazelmere Gardens in North Oxford, where she signed on as an air raid warden. She was already pregnant when they moved, and their second son, Anthony Arthur Elworthy, subsequently known in the family as Ant or Anto, was born in the John Radcliffe Hospital on 10 March 1940.

A month later, 104 and 108 Squadrons were disbanded to re-form as 13 Operational Training Unit, with Sam, who had been an acting squadron leader since moving to Bicester, as Chief Flying Instructor. The expansion of Bomber Command now demanded a restructuring in its training activities and 7 (Training) Group was formed in July, with its headquarters at Bicester and 13 OTU as one of its units. This brought Sam into contact for the first time with an officer with whom he would in due course form a close relationship, the newly appointed AOC, Air Commodore the Hon. Ralph Cochrane. That would have to wait, however, as on 26 August Sam was posted at short notice to an operational squadron.

82 Squadron had originally been formed as an army co-operation squadron in 1917 before going to France, where it flew Armstrong Whitworth FK8s for reconnaissance and artillery spotting. Disbanded after the Great War, it was re-formed in 1937 and equipped first with the Hawker Hind and then the Blenheim I. In 1938 it re-equipped with the Blenheim IV, which had an elongated nose, more powerful engines and more machine guns, two instead of one in the mid-upper turret and two in a remote controlled rear-firing mounting beneath the nose, together with provision for carrying small bombs under the wings. In August 1939 the squadron moved to RAF Watton, an expansion station in Norfolk, as part of 2 Group.

The early months of the war were spent largely on sweeps over the North Sea, the squadron scoring what was at the time considered a major success by sinking a U-Boat in March 1940. On 1 May command was assumed by Wing Commander the Earl of Bandon, an Irish peer. Paddy Bandon was a one-off, a practical joker par excellence, referred to by many as 'The Abandoned Earl', but he was also an inspiring leader who managed to enjoy popularity and respect in equal measure. Under his command, 82 Squadron was as good as any when the Germans struck through Belgium and Luxembourg on 10 May. However, it saw no action until four days later when six of its planes attacked a crossroads between Breda and Tilburg without loss. On the following day Bandon led twelve planes to Monthermé to bomb a troop concentration, once again returning unscathed. The squadron's luck, however, was about to run out.

On 17 May twelve Blenheims, led this time by Squadron Leader Paddy Delap, were sent to attack German troops moving through the Belgian town of Gembloux. For the first time in the squadron's experience, the appalling vulnerability of the Blenheims was exposed. Not only was the light anti-aircraft fire effective, but the Messerschmitt Bf 109s were waiting. One by one the British planes were shot down. Twenty-two out of thirty-six crew were killed, three were taken prisoner and eight, including Delap, managed to crash land or bale out successfully and escape to the Allied lines. A single plane, badly shot up, staggered back to Watton, where its pilot was met by Bandon with the words 'Where's everybody else, Morrison?'

The initial reaction of Bomber Command was to share the remaining ten aircraft around the rest of 2 Group and disband the squadron. This

Bandon refused to consider. Initially, he pooled his remaining resources with those of 21 Squadron, the other occupant of Watton, whilst over the course of the next few weeks 82 Squadron was rebuilt. On 1 July, however, Bandon himself was promoted, to be replaced by a quite different character, Wing Commander Edward Lart. Unlike his predecessor, Lart was cold and humourless, but he shared one characteristic with Bandon in that he was apparently fearless, flying himself on every possible occasion and invariably pressing on against the odds. The Battle of Britain was now in full swing and most operations were directed against German airfields on the Continent or invasion barges, incurring losses, but not excessive ones.

On 13 August, however, disaster struck again. The squadron was ordered to attack a German airfield at Ålborg in northern Denmark, at the extreme end of the Blenheim's range. The formation was spotted and the defences alerted. Those aircraft which were not shot down by flak were finished off by Messerschmitt 109s. Of the men in the eleven planes which attacked, twenty were killed, including Lart, and thirteen taken prisoner. One plane returned early due to an apparent fuel problem. The pilot, Sergeant Baron, was charged with cowardice and court-martialled: he was in due course acquitted and went on to be awarded the DFM in 1941 and, shortly afterwards, to be killed in action.

Once again, 82 Squadron was re-constituted. New planes arrived and a new CO was appointed, Wing Commander J. C. Macdonald, better known as 'Mad Mac' or 'Black Mac'. Squadron Leader McMichael was appointed to command A Flight, with Sam taking on B Flight. He brought with him from Bicester two men whom he rated very highly and who would act as his crew throughout his time at 82 Squadron, Pilot Officer (shortly afterwards Flying Officer) Bill Collins as his navigator/bomb aimer and Sergeant Leslie Gayfer as his wireless operator/air gunner, the three of them flying in the same aircraft, T2165 or 'M for Mother', until the last weeks of Sam's appointment.

After much debate Sam and Audrey had decided that it would be safer for the children to spend the rest of the war in New Zealand, whither Sam's parents had already returned, having disposed of Rainscombe because the New Zealand Government had threatened to sell Gordons Valley compulsorily unless its owners lived there permanently. Percy and Bertha agreed to look after Tim and Anthony, who were duly despatched with a reliable nurse by sea from Tilbury. The ship attempted to pass down the English Channel, but the threat from German aircraft was too great, so it turned round, unloaded all its passengers at Tilbury again and then sailed up the East Coast and round Scotland to Greenock, where they were picked up for the voyage. As wives were not permitted at Watton, Audrey moved out of the house in Oxford and rented rooms behind the King's Arms in Bicester, at the same time joining the Mechanised Transport Corps, which was not part of the armed services but an entirely female civilian organization providing drivers for government departments and foreign dignitaries.

In the meantime, Sam was in the thick of the action. He thought that his first operation, carried out on 29 August, three days after his arrival, would also be his last. On that day the squadron despatched six aircraft to bomb various targets, Sam's being an aqueduct on the Dortmund–Ems Canal. He was only too aware that Wing Commander Roderick Learoyd had won the VC by doing the same thing in a Handley Page Hampden just over a fortnight earlier, operating at night but still encountering formidable defences. In Sam's opinion, if he could repeat this feat in daylight, there would be no decoration fit for him! As it happened, there was no cloud cover, which was called for in daylight bombing, so he aborted, dropping his bombs instead around some minesweepers at Den Helder and scoring some near misses.

Thereafter, the tempo built up. The Battle of Britain was still in full swing and invasion was believed to be imminent, so the focus was initially on bombing the invasion barges in the Channel ports and the German long-range gun positions on the Straits of Dover. Initially, all the operations were carried out in daylight, but the pilots were given orders to seek an alternative target if there was inadequate cloud cover. This provided an excuse for the more timid pilots to do exactly that. After some time the all too frequent lack of cloud cover in the beautiful summer weather of 1940 resulted in operations being switched to night-time, but in contrast to the practice adopted later, bombers leaving one after another in a stream, the pilots could select their own times of departure and thus made their attacks alone. Sam himself was always one of the first to take off and on some occasions had landed again before the last plane set out. On arrival near the target, the aircraft would drop a flare and then circle round it, hoping to pick up a landmark which would lead the pilot to the target. If he failed to find it, he would select an alternative target and drop his bombs there instead. Unsurprisingly, Sam was deeply unhappy, believing the whole system to be hopelessly inefficient.

In the first week of September there was a major invasion alert. All personnel were recalled from leave, aircraft were bombed up ready to fly and arrangements were made to put into effect Operation *Banquet*, whereby every available non-operational plane, most of which were being used for training or army co-operation, would be deployed to airfields such as Watton which were closer to possible invasion locations, in this case the coast of East Anglia. When the threat lifted in early October, the emphasis changed again, with night-time raids being conducted further afield on airfields, marshalling yards, oil refineries and other industrial targets. For the first time the aircraft were penetrating Germany itself, flying to Duisburg, Hamburg, Bremen and Gelsenkirchen. The raids were almost entirely ineffective, but night fighters were non-existent at the time, so casualties were low and were caused more often by pilot error, bad weather or mechanical problems than by enemy action.

On 14 December Sam succeeded Macdonald as CO of 82 Squadron, with promotion to acting Wing Commander, his immediate superior now being Group Captain T. M. ('Bill') Williams, the Station Commander at Watton. From the beginning of October the squadron had operated from Watton's satellite airfield at Bodney, 4½ miles away. Unlike Watton, Bodney comprised little more than Nissen huts and basic hangars, and the squadron office remained at Watton. On the other hand, both officers and NCOs were accommodated in Clermont Hall, a substantial mansion nearby, although they messed separately. The grounds of the house were full of game and many of the officers spent their spare time shooting. One highly popular member of the squadron was its Intelligence Officer, Flight Lieutenant Douglas, known to all as 'Uncle Duggie', who sported a Military Cross alongside the row of Great War medals on his chest. Something of a father figure to the young officers around him, he was keen to fly as often as circumstances permitted, so that he could debrief the crews more effectively, and Sam took him along on a couple of raids.

The New Year began much as the old one had ended, with attacks on targets in Germany and Occupied Holland, Belgium and France. Attacking an oil refinery in Rotterdam on 11 January at 1,000ft, Sam could feel the explosions of his bombs shaking his aircraft. On 7 March, with twenty-six operations behind him, he was awarded the Distinguished Flying Cross. Five days later, he led eight aircraft on a raid on Bremen and the airfield at De Kooy which proved to be one of the most satisfactory thus far, prompting a signal of congratulation from the AOC of 2 Group, Air Vice-Marshal Stevenson.

Since the disaster at Ålborg seven months earlier, 82 Squadron had been extremely active, but had not had a particularly difficult time. Now its fortunes were to change. In the wider war, Winston Churchill's most pressing concern was the Battle of the Atlantic, in which the balance of power had swung significantly to Germany, with losses from U-Boats rising alarmingly due to the adoption of 'wolf pack' tactics and a breakout into the Atlantic by the battle-cruisers *Scharnhorst* and *Gneisenau*, which had between them sunk or captured twenty-two ships. On 6 March Churchill issued a directive which switched the emphasis to the war at sea, as a result of which 2 Group was given the main responsibility for sinking all enemy ships on coastal routes, initially from the German coast to the Brittany peninsula, but later extended to include Norway. In order to do so effectively, it switched back from night to daytime operations.

The first such operation by 82 Squadron was mounted on 15 March against shipping off the French coast at Dunkirk, and almost immediately losses began to mount, both from flak ships and from German fighters covering the convoys. The most successful raid was carried out by six aircraft led by Sam on shipping off Le Havre on 31 March. Coming in at below 200ft, Sam and one of his fellow pilots, Sergeant Robert Smith, each attacked a tanker of about 3–4,000 tons, guarded by two flak ships which put up a hail of fire. Smith made two direct hits on his target ship, setting it on fire, whilst Sam missed on his first run but came back for a second run with three hits. Both ships were later confirmed destroyed.

Two days later, however, Sam suffered a near disaster. The targets this time were Hamstede and Flushing airfields, which commanded the sea lane from Rotterdam to Antwerp. Sam later described the operation:

I was out on my own near Flushing and was about to bomb an ammunition dump when I was set upon by a couple of 109s. We did our bombing and then began a ten-minute fight. It seemed more to me. Gayfer, my gunner, was doing his stuff well and I don't think the Jerries liked it very much but they were persistent and we were being repeatedly hit. Then Gayfer got a bullet through his leg and immediately after had his turret blown off. Still we kept flying until a cannon shot put both of his guns out of action. Then another cannon shot got us amidships and burst just behind me, but the armour plate[2] saved me. The aircraft was filling with smoke and fumes and for some time we could not see. Then I saw Bill Collins calmly folding his maps and neatly packing his charts and Navigator's instruments into his bag. He is my observer and he told me afterwards that he didn't think that he would need them again. Up to now it had been the usual unequal running fight but when both my rear guns had gone I turned and tried to get a smack at the Jerry with my fixed front gun. After manoeuvring I got my sights on him and pressed the firing button. Nothing happened. The high pressure air container which operated the gun had been hit and all we could do then was take all the avoiding action we could. We were repeatedly hit but the old Blenheim held together. One engine packing up. One rudder control shot away. The Trimmers blown off, the turrets smashed and no guns left. At last the Jerries turned away, presumably out of ammunition. We staggered home safely. My poor old bus T2165M which had carried me on every trip is now so much scrap, a complete write-off.[3] We had 80 0.5" machine gun hits and five cannon shell hits. We came home blissfully ignorant of the damage that had been done. Why the old bus did not break up I don't know. Gayfer is O.K. though still in hospital and has been awarded the D.F.M.[4]

Sam had managed to get away by a mixture of brilliant flying, aggressive attacking and sheer luck. What he did not mention in his letter was another casualty of the action. Audrey had given him a little Lalique glass elephant as a mascot, which he always placed on the ledge above his control panel. After landing back at Bodney he found that it was on the floor, with its head broken off. Next to it was the bullet which had probably done the damage. He kept both for the rest of his life.

Sam carried out one further operation and it proved to be almost as eventful. On 10 April he led nine aircraft in a raid on Borkum and shipping off the Friesian Islands. The attack was made at almost sea level and caused considerable damage, but then four Messerschmitt 110s appeared. One of the Blenheims went down into the sea, whilst another lost an engine. Sam ordered the rest of the formation to head for home, whilst he escorted the damaged aircraft back himself. Bill Collins took photos of the raid with Sam's Leica camera and, some time later, Sam received a call from the AOC-in-C Bomber Command, Air Marshal Sir Richard Peirse, asking for a print from one of the negatives, which was presented to Churchill.

Sam had received both his AFC and his DFC from the King, the first at Mildenhall in January and the second, accompanied by Audrey, at Buckingham Place in mid-April. On 17 April the award to him of the Distinguished Service Order was announced. After referring to the raids on Le Havre and Flushing the citation ended with the words: 'By his magnificent leadership and complete disregard of danger, Wing Commander Elworthy had brought his squadron to the highest peak of war efficiency.' To his great pleasure, the only other awards announced that day were also to members of 82 Squadron, a DFC to Flight Lieutenant S. J. Monroe and two DFMs, one of which went to Gayfer and the other to Sergeant Smith for his exploits at Le Havre.

By this time Sam had completed thirty-five operations and was ordered by the AOC not to undertake any more, pending a posting elsewhere. As it happened, the squadron had by that time been relocated temporarily to RAF Lossiemouth, on the north-east coast of Scotland, from where it was to carry out sweeps along the coast of Norway. Sam accompanied his men to control the operations rather than fly with them. Very little was achieved, whilst some aircraft and their crews were lost. The squadron returned to Bodney on 3 May and, three days later, Sam was posted to HQ 2 Group.

Chapter 6

Bomber Staff

No. 2 Group had been formed in March 1936. After two years at Abingdon the HQ relocated to Wyton and then, in October 1939, to Castlewood House, Huntingdon. As a squadron commander, Sam had had frequent contact with the leading figures. The AOC, Air Vice-Marshal Donald Stevenson, was to become a controversial figure in Bomber Command, but at the time of Sam's arrival he had been in post for barely three months. The Senior Air Staff Officer (SASO) was Sam's former Station Commander at Watton, Bill Williams, with whom he had formed a good relationship. Sam himself was one of ten wing commanders, who dealt with administration, intelligence, engineering and training, as well as Sam's own function, operations.

At the time of Sam's arrival, 2 Group controlled all the RAF's UK-based Blenheims, other than those in the OTUs and two squadrons detached to Coastal Command. Its stations were all in Norfolk and Suffolk and, from north to south, were West Raynham, with a satellite at Great Massingham, Swanton Morley, Horsham St Faith, Watton, with a satellite at Bodney, and Wattisham. Polebrook, in Northamptonshire, was added to the Group in July 1941, specifically to take the newly formed 90 Squadron's Flying Fortresses: these aircraft, however, were to prove unsatisfactory for the group's purposes and were phased out in early 1942. Sam had been concerned that he would be required to do little or no flying himself, but the dispersed geography of the group meant that he actually spent a great deal of time piloting himself and others, including the AOC and occasionally Peirse, the AOC-in-C, on visits to the stations. The HQ flight, which was based at nearby Wyton, consisted of single-engined De Havilland Hornet Moths, Miles Magisters and Percival Proctors.

Sam's main role was to receive the outline plan each day from Bomber Command HQ, which identified targets and specified the weight of attack on each, and to convert it into detailed orders for all the squadrons, allocating the targets, finalizing the numbers of aircraft and setting the outward and return routes. Since many of the targets were shipping, there was a Royal Navy lieutenant commander on the staff to provide intelligence and liaison when necessary. Sam was also required to report back to Bomber Command on the results of the operations of the previous day or night, communicated to him by the squadrons.

When Sam arrived, the focus on shipping, with which he had been so intimately involved in 82 Squadron, remained at a high level of intensity. Peirse, much to his annoyance, had been forced to divert his larger bombers from industrial targets in Germany to ports and other coastal installations, but it was 2 Group which bore the brunt of the new strategy through its daylight raids. Stevenson executed his orders, to deny all shipping lanes to the Germans, with a ruthlessness which was to prove extremely costly to his crews. Many operations were carried out against specific targets, not only convoys which had been identified by intelligence, but also airfields and harbour installations; more general sweeps were also mounted in areas of sea which were divided into 'beats'. Each beat was given a letter or a number and allocated to squadrons on a daily basis. Sweeps were usually conducted by small groups of aircraft, which made their approach at very low levels, sometimes less than 50ft. They would fly directly towards the enemy coast, turning three miles out at a right angle to fly along it and then at another right angle to return to base. Any vessels spotted would be attacked, but they were usually accompanied by flak ships and the defensive fire was always considerable, whilst the Germans also flew fighter patrols over convoys.

At the end of April 1941, shortly before Sam arrived at 2 Group HQ, a new operation was initiated, called *Channel Stop*. The intention of this was to close the Straits of Dover to all German shipping, using Blenheims by day and Royal Navy MTBs by night. This involved deploying one squadron at a time from 2 Group to RAF Manston, a fighter airfield in Kent, to carry out operations at short range. Although the aircraft had protection from escorting Spitfires, which to some extent fended off the German fighters, they could do nothing about the flak, which was heavily concentrated in the area. Losses mounted rapidly and squadrons were only able to stay at

Manston for a fortnight before being relieved. Churchill continued to take a close interest, visiting 2 Group on 6 June.

The most important naval base on the French Atlantic coast was Brest, where *Scharnhorst* and *Gneisenau* had taken shelter following their successful cruise. Numerous operations were mounted by night and by day; for the latter, squadrons from 2 Group were despatched to RAF Portreath and RAF St Eval in Cornwall for specific operations. Towards the end of June, Sam took Peirse on a tour of inspection of both airfields, borrowing for this purpose a Blenheim from 82 Squadron, with Collins and Gayfer as his crew.

Operations with a different objective had begun somewhat tentatively in January 1941. These carried the codename of *Circus* and were sequentially numbered, amounting to over 100 during the course of 1941. Like *Channel Stop*, they were mounted in conjunction with the fighters of 11 Group, which provided an escort of Spitfires. Most of the targets were in North-West France and consisted initially of ports in the Pas-de-Calais and Normandy, but subsequently of airfields, army camps, ammunition dumps and industrial installations further afield. The intention was to bring the Luftwaffe to battle, diverting it from daylight raids on the United Kingdom, in which cause they were only modestly successful.

Circus and the attacks on the two German battleships came together on 24 July in Operation *Sunrise*, with 2 Group Blenheims and a fighter escort mounting a successful raid on Cherbourg as a diversion, whilst first 90 Squadron's Flying Fortresses and then Wellingtons and Hampdens from other groups bombed Brest, claiming a number of hits on the *Gneisenau* and the cruiser *Prinz Eugen*, whilst newly introduced Halifaxes bombed La Pallice, whither *Scharnhorst* had sailed, damaging the ship sufficiently to force her back to Brest for repairs.

Circus 81 was mounted initially with a different objective. One of Fighter Command's most charismatic commanders, Douglas Bader, had been shot down over France and, whilst struggling to get out of his cockpit to parachute to safety, had parted company with his artificial right leg. Bader was much admired by the Germans, and a message was sent to the RAF by Adolf Galland of the Luftwaffe offering safe conduct to a plane to drop a replacement. Sam arranged for the new prosthesis to be delivered to his office, whence he despatched it to the squadron chosen for Operation

Leg. Instead of the single aircraft which the Germans were expecting, five Blenheims and a large fighter escort arrived over the designated drop zone at St Omer, dropped the package and went on to attempt to bomb Gosnay power station, although they were foiled by the weather!

On 12 August there was one significant diversion from *Circus* and *Channel Stop*. Operation *77* was mounted as part of an attempt to persuade the Germans to withdraw fighters from their Eastern Front, on which Great Britain's newest ally, the Soviet Union, was in headlong retreat. It consisted of a large-scale daylight attack on two of the most important power stations in Germany, Knapsack and Quadrath, both near Cologne. Fifty-four Benheims were dispatched, thirty-six to Knapsack and eighteen, including nine from 82 Squadron, to Quadrath. Fighter cover was provided to a limited extent by Westland Whirlwinds on the outbound leg and by Spitfires from the Dutch coast on the return journey. Both power stations were hit and for public consumption the raid was claimed as a great success, but the results were far short of the destruction which was sought and did little to encourage the Germans to withdraw fighters from Russia. Ten Blenheims were shot down, 18.5 per cent of the attacking force.

The losses incurred on daylight raids in the summer of 1941 were indeed terrible. On one day in particular, Sam had to send out orders to three squadrons, one after another, to carry out attacks on a convoy which was believed to be carrying strategically important cargoes, and all of them were decimated. He was one of a number of officers, including Bandon, now commanding RAF West Raynham, who tried to persuade Stevenson of the futility of such sorties. The AOC was deaf to their opinions, continuing to mount operations in which the odds on significant losses were high and not in any way commensurate with their value. In one incident, Stevenson became so angry with those protesting against his tactics that he hurled an inkwell against the wall, shouting, 'Churchill wants it!' However, even Churchill was having second thoughts, writing to the Chief of the Air Staff, Sir Charles Portal, on 29 August:

> The loss of seven Blenheims out of seventeen in the daylight attack on merchant shipping and docks at Rotterdam is most severe. Such losses might be accepted in attacking *Scharnhorst*, *Gneisenau* or *Tirpitz* or a

south-bound Tripoli convoy, because, apart from the damage done, a first-class strategic object is served. But they seem disproportionate to an attack on merchant shipping not engaged in vital supply work. The losses in our bombers have been very heavy this month and Bomber Command is not expanding as was hoped. While I greatly admire the bravery of the pilots, I do not want them pressed too hard. Easier targets giving a high damage return compared with casualties may more often be selected.[1]

If Portal communicated this to Stevenson, there is not much evidence that the latter was listening. He continued to mount daylight raids, and his squadrons, who nicknamed him 'Butcher', continued to take severe casualties. It would be the end of the year, however, before he was replaced by a more considerate commander.

Largely because of the heavy losses, this was not a happy time for Sam in terms of his professional duties, as may be seen from a portrait of him by the war artist Eric Kennington, who was commissioned by the Air Ministry to draw members of the RAF, his other subjects including Learoyd and Bader. In it Sam looks drawn, and it seems that he was preoccupied with an operation in progress at the time, breaking off all through the sitting to use the telephone and receiving news of the results before it had finished.

There were, however, occasionally more pleasant distractions, one of which was the visit of the King and Queen to 2 Group in August. Sam, with Peirse, Stevenson and Williams, escorted the royal couple around Watton.

Best of all, Audrey was now living with him again, the two of them taking the top floor of the Old Prison Governor's House in Huntingdon. She was, however, absent for much of the time as she had taken on an important assignment. The 'Bundles for Britain' movement had been established in the United States shortly after the outbreak of war on the initiative of Janet Murrow, the wife of Edward R. Murrow of CBS News, whose broadcasts from London during the Battle of Britain and the Blitz made such an impression on America. It was supported by American women of all social classes who put together bundles of clothes, many of which they had made themselves, and other necessities for distribution to hospitals in Britain. In the United Kingdom Clementine Churchill was the Honorary Sponsor, and John Winant, the US ambassador, was the Chairman of the London Committee.

Audrey had been recruited by a very close friend, Beatrice 'Babs' Rathbone, who was American by birth and also a close friend of Janet Murrow, who had been one of her bridesmaids. Babs had married John Rathbone, MP for Bodmin, whom she had met when they were both undergraduates at Oxford in the early 1930s. Rathbone was at the time a member of the University Air Squadron and subsequently joined the Royal Air Force Volunteer Reserve and trained on Blenheims. With both of their husbands away on active service, Babs shared Audrey's rooms in Bicester, but the two couples managed to spend part of the men's leave in December 1940 together at Par, in Rathbone's constituency. Soon afterwards, Rathbone joined 82 Squadron and was killed on his first operation. On that very day Babs arrived at Watton with Parliamentary papers for her husband to sign, and Sam had to tell her that he was missing, driving her back to Bicester himself. She later succeeded Rathbone as MP for Bodmin, whilst Audrey took up the role at 'Bundles for Britain' which was to visit and then write reports on the hospitals to the branches which had adopted them.

Many of the hospitals had been badly damaged by German air raids and all were desperately short of blankets, bed linen, clothes and medical supplies. One of Audrey's great skills was her written English, which was not only grammatically excellent, but also highly descriptive and often very moving. This took up a great deal of her time: by early September 1941 she had visited and reported on over forty hospitals, including Queen Victoria Hospital, East Grinstead, where she established a particularly close relationship with Archibald McIndoe, the pioneer of plastic surgery and a fellow New Zealander. Her work produced an enormous response. As the Executive Director of Branches for the movement wrote, 'It is largely due to your straightforward and utterly dramatic reports that America's imagination has been fired to aid the voluntary hospitals.'[2]

As a result of this, the Murrows became lasting friends of Sam and Audrey. Babs Rathbone married again, this time to an old friend serving as an officer in the King's Royal Rifle Corps, Paul Wright,[3] and they and the Elworthys remained close for the rest of their lives.

Because of the atmosphere at 2 Group HQ it was doubtless with a sense of relief that Sam was posted to the staff of Bomber Command on 20 October. He had come to the attention of Peirse, the AOC-in-C, on a number of occasions, and it was probably no coincidence that Bill Williams had preceded him there and was now Deputy SASO. Sam was appointed Wing Commander Ops 1(b), one of five Wing Commanders Ops at that time, with responsibility for Plans as well as Operations.

Bomber Command HQ was situated in a wooded area near the village of Walters Ash, a few miles north of High Wycombe. For security reasons it was given the codename Southdown and its postal address was simply GPO High Wycombe. It was divided into three parts, the hub of which was officially named Site 1 but was popularly known as 'the Hole'. On it were two houses used as offices, but the majority of the complex lay underground beneath two grassy mounds and consisted of a network of passages and a huge Operations Room, with constant artificial lighting and air conditioning. One wall was covered by a large blackboard, setting out the groups and squadrons at the command's disposition. On another was an equally large map of Europe, on which officers of the Women's Auxiliary Air Force marked up with tapes the targets and routes for the day or night. In the middle of the room was a desk for the AOC-in-C. Site 2 consisted of a large, modern country house, which contained the officers' mess and living quarters, although most of the married officers, including Sam, were in accommodation elsewhere. Site 3 contained the barracks for the other ranks, together with garages and workshops.

Security on the site was inevitably very tight, giving rise to one incident which, years later, had an amusing and beneficial consequence. Summoned late one night to an urgent meeting in the 'Hole', Sam, who had been in the mess, decided to borrow a bike to get there more quickly. In the complete blackout he rode straight into a barbed-wire barrier across the road, on which he cut himself quite badly, being removed to the first-aid post to be patched up. Years later, he received a letter from Personnel to say that he was entitled to some tax relief in respect of a war wound, which turned out to relate to this event!

In terms of the command structure, Operations and Plans, as well as Intelligence, Army and Navy Liaison and Public Relations, came directly under the SASO, Air Vice-Marshal Robert Saundby, known to his friends as Sandy, who was next in importance only to the AOC-in-C. All other staff branches came under the Air Officer Administration ('AOA'), AVM Ronald Graham, except for Training, the responsibility of AVM John Capel.

Sam's first few months at High Wycombe were difficult ones for Bomber Command. Although the Stirling and the Halifax had begun operations in the first quarter of 1941, they were still heavily outnumbered by the twin-engined medium bombers, the Hampdens, Whitleys and Wellingtons, together with the disappointing Avro Manchesters. Not only did these lack range and bomb load, but they had no navigational aids. The result, as illustrated in a report produced by Mr D. M. Butt of the War Cabinet Secretariat on the initiative of Lord Cherwell, the Prime Minister's Scientific Adviser, and based on the analysis of aircraft photographs, was that only one in four night bombers managed to drop its load within five miles of its target. In the context of this, losses of 3.5 per cent by night, not to mention 7.1 per cent by day, were unacceptable. Whilst a new strategy was being considered, operations were sharply reduced over the winter of 1941/2.

The immediate casualty of Bomber Command's failure was Peirse, who was removed on 8 January 1942 and sent out to become AOC-in-C in India, just as a Japanese invasion was threatening. His replacement was AVM J. E. A. Baldwin, to whom it was made clear that he was only a caretaker. It was perhaps unfortunate that during the 'interregnum' an event took place which did nothing to improve Bomber Command's reputation.

Sam's responsibilities involved preparing plans not only for day-to-day operations but also for certain contingencies, one of which was a potential break-out by the *Scharnhorst* and *Gneisenau*. Very late on the evening of 11 February, the two battle-cruisers, in company with the *Prinz Eugen* and several destroyers, sailed out of Brest and up the English Channel, covered by protecting fighters and aided by poor weather, including very low cloud. There was a complete intelligence breakdown on the British side and the ships were only spotted by a Spitfire of Fighter Command over twelve hours later, when they had reached a point opposite Le Touquet. By this time, most of Bomber Command's squadrons had been stood down for the day and there was thus a tremendous scramble to get airborne, the first aircraft not taking off until 13.30. Although 242 sorties were flown, most of the aircraft failed to find the ships and those that did scored no hits. In Sam's opinion, their ability to carry out accurate visual bombing with success from a few thousand feet was negligible. About halfway through the operation, Saundby, who had arrived back from a meeting in London, suggested that it might be more profitable to sow mines in the path of the ships and the remaining aircraft were switched to this. As it happened, the two larger ships did hit mines but still managed to reach port safely.

The so-called 'Channel Dash' did little for the reputation of either the RAF or the Royal Navy, notwithstanding the heroism of the six Fleet Air Arm Swordfishes lost in a suicidal torpedo attack. Although dropping mines had much more impact than was realized at the time,[4] the failure of the bombers more generally helped to strengthen the belief in high places that Bomber Command was not fit for purpose. A new leader was sought and the Chief of the Air Staff, Air Chief Marshal Sir Charles Portal, had just one such in mind, Air Marshal Arthur Harris. With the support of the Secretary of State for Air, Sir Archibald Sinclair, his name was put up to Churchill, who readily agreed to his appointment, which took place on 22 February 1942.

Harris, always known as Bert to his friends and colleagues, was, along with Portal, Lord Dowding and Lord Tedder, one of a very small number of towering figures in the RAF during the Second World War. He was also, by a long way, the most controversial. A fighter pilot in the Great War, Harris had experimented with the use of one of the RAF's transport planes, the Vickers Vernon, as a bomber whilst in command of 45 Squadron in the Middle East in the 1920s, and then with the Vickers Valentia in an official bomber role in the UK. Service in the Air Ministry as Deputy Director of Operations and Intelligence and then Deputy Director of Plans had given him a wider appreciation of the RAF's role in the event of war, and it was followed by command of 4 Group, equipped with the new Whitley, in 1937. For the first year of the war he was AOC 5 Group, flying Hampdens, whose minelaying role he valued more highly than their bombing, before becoming successively Deputy Chief of the Air Staff and then Head of the British Air Staff in the USA, where he built valuable contacts with the USAAF.

Harris is always associated with the policy of area bombing, which he executed so vigorously throughout his tenure as AOC-in-C Bomber

Command. However, he was not its architect. Although Great Britain had bent over backwards to avoid civilian casualties during the first year of the war, in practice area bombing had been taking place since the winter of 1940/1, at least in part in retaliation for the Blitz and in particular the devastating raid on Coventry on 14 November 1940. The formal acknowledgement of the change in policy preceded Harris's appointment, albeit by only a week, with the promulgation of General Directive No. 5, which set out all those targets within reach of the brand new navigational aid, *Gee*, and stated specifically that the objective was to 'focus attacks on the morale of the enemy civil population and in particular the industrial workers'. This directive was also a result of the belated realization, following the Butt report, that, even with *Gee*, night-time precision bombing was next to impossible. Yet a bombing campaign had to be pursued, as it was the only way of directly attacking Germany at the time.

Sam became a huge admirer of Harris, describing him subsequently as 'a man of great courage, drive and force'.[5] However, up to the time of the new AOC-in-C's appointment Sam had had only had one brief previous encounter with him, whilst attending a conference with Ludlow-Hewitt before the war, during which he had been chastised by Harris for failing to produce a staff car at the right time and in the right place. It is likely that Harris had forgotten the incident, but Sam was initially wary of him. Not very long afterwards his fears were to be more than justified, but before that happened there was an unusual departure from the HQ routine.

By early 1942 the Germans were beginning to use night fighters with much greater confidence, due in great part to the development of a new radar system, codenamed *Würzburg*. A number of radar stations were established on the routes taken by Bomber Command aircraft, one of which was identified by photo reconnaissance as being at a location near Bruneval, north of Le Havre. A Commando raid to seize the installation and transport it back to the UK for scientific examination was devised by Lord Louis Mountbatten's Combined Operations HQ and Major General 'Boy' Browning, commanding 1 Airborne Division. Bomber Command had a stake in the venture, due to the effect that *Würzburg* was having on its raids, and Sam participated in the planning, as one of 4 Group's squadrons, No. 51, was providing the twelve Whitleys needed to carry in the paratroopers.

Moreover, the command supplied an experienced radar mechanic, Flight Sergeant C. W. H. Cox, to photograph the radar set and to dismantle and bring back as much of it as possible. The operation was mounted on the night of 27/28 February from a non-Bomber Command airfield, RAF Thruxton, and Sam and Lieutenant Colonel Charles Carrington, the Army liaison officer at High Wycombe, went to see it off and then travelled on to Portsmouth to meet the returning raiders and their trophies.

The raid, under Major John Frost[6] of the Airborne Division, was outstandingly successful. The parachute landing was on target, the installation was captured with modest casualties and Cox managed to disassemble the equipment, the key parts of which were then carried to the beach nearby and brought off by the raiders on to landing craft, from which they were transferred to motor launches. Sam had gone out in a destroyer to meet the returning vessels and he welcomed back Cox, who was later to receive a Military Medal for his actions.

'Do you believe in horoscopes, sir?' asked Cox.

'No', replied Sam.

'Neither do I', said Cox, 'but it's my birthday today, and I looked at my horoscope in the paper and what did it say? – "A quiet and uneventful day"!'[7]

Sam's days were rarely so interesting. More often he was part of a strict routine, which began with 'morning prayers'. SASO, the Group Captain Ops, the Wing Commander Ops 1(b), the Group Captain Intelligence and the senior Meteorological Offer met first for a preliminary look at the weather, an assessment of the previous night's operations and a general review of priority targets. The intention of this gathering was to try to anticipate as far as possible what the AOC-in-C would decide, so as to have the answers ready. At 09.00 sharp Harris would appear, by which time other operations staff, Carrington and Captain de Mowbray, the Royal Navy liaison officer, would have joined the group. There would be a more formal presentation of the weather and any other key factors, based on which a list of potential targets were handed to Harris. He would then make his decision without further discussion, after which the meeting was at an end, although Harris might stay on for a discussion with Saundby on the previous night's events. In the meantime the G/C Ops and W/C Ops 1(b) would ring each of the groups, providing them with the target and the make-up of the bomb load.

There would then be a further discussion between them and Saundby on the defences, based on which the routes would be established and communicated to the groups.

Sam considered that Saundby, a consummate staff officer, was in many ways the perfect counterpart to Harris. However, he also believed that the SASO was himself incapable of making major decisions. The staff on a number of occasions pointed out to him difficulties arising from Harris's choice of target or route, but Saundby was adamant that once the AOC-in-C had spoken he was not to be challenged. On at least one of these occasions, Sam was so concerned that he went to see Harris himself and found him perfectly agreeable to a change. The relationship between Harris and Saundby went back to 45 Squadron in the Middle East, when the latter had been one of the former's flight commanders: they had remained good friends, Harris even inviting Saundby to share his residence, but the relationship was perhaps both too close and, on Saundby's side, too subservient. Although considered by Sam to be a thoroughly good man in most respects, Saundby somehow lacked the moral courage to express a contrary opinion to his chief.

As he was responsible for Plans, Sam had a number ready for consideration by the time that Harris became AOC-in-C. One of these concerned the relative merits of incendiaries and high explosives. Solly Zuckerman, the RAF's Scientific Adviser, had done a lot of work on this issue, as a result of which Sam suggested that more damage would be done with an 80:20 ratio of incendiary to high explosive, rather than the other way round, which at the time was the accepted combination. He was supported in this by the Director and Deputy Director of Bombing at the Air Ministry, Air Commodore John Baker and Group Captain Sydney Bufton, and the three of them concluded that the best target to demonstrate this would be Lübeck.

When the proposal was put to Harris, he was not impressed. In Sam's words:

He wanted to know what the houses were built of and I told him that they were all brick houses. Before I could continue with the briefing he said, 'Bricks, you bloody fool, when did bricks burn?' I attempted to explain the use of wooden joists in the roof and walls and that we were certain it was the kind of place that would burn well. But he didn't like the plan and got impatient with me. He wasn't at that time convinced that the fire-incendiary business was the right idea, and from that moment I got more and more stick until suddenly he said, 'Look. I don't think you are any use to me. You are fired, so get out!' So out I went.[8]

Sam consulted Saundby, who was sympathetic but told him to disappear and check in due course where his new posting would be. Totally mortified, he had no alternative but to return to the house nearby in Walters Ash where he and Audrey were living as paying guests of their friends, Bill and Pete Lord. Audrey had by this time left 'Bundles for Britain', first working for Operational Research at the HQ and then taking a job in a factory in High Wycombe which manufactured armatures used in electric motors. She was, moreover, on a night shift at the time, away from 6.00 pm to 8.00 am, and she wanted to sleep during the day. After five days doing very little other than worrying about his future, Sam was called by Saundby with the news that the AOC-in-C wanted to see him. Harris told Sam that he had been unfair to him, as what had happened was not his fault, and if Sam was prepared to stay, he would welcome it. However, if he chose to go, he would understand. Sam replied that if Harris was prepared to have him, he would like to stay.

From that day on, Sam never looked back. Lübeck was bombed on the night of 28/29 March. The raid, as confirmed by photographs and intelligence, was one of the most successful of the war, destroying over 30 per cent of the built-up area and damaging many other buildings.[9] As a mark of Harris's confidence in him, on 5 May Sam was promoted to acting group captain and appointed Group Captain Ops, the senior operations officer at Bomber Command HQ.

His appointment came at a time of great change. The new four-engined heavy bombers were beginning to supplant their twin-engined predecessors, although it would be the autumn of 1943 before the Wellington carried out its last Bomber Command sortie. *Gee*, which enabled navigators to establish their precise position by radio signals from a 'Master' and two 'Slave' stations, was being fitted to the leading aircraft, and in spite of the fact that the Germans worked out how to jam it, it was proving to be invaluable in getting the bomber streams over the North Sea both outbound and inbound.

Heavier and more effective medium capacity (MC) bombs were replacing the general purpose (GP) bombs which had been the staple of the RAF since the Great War, and incendiaries were being more intelligently deployed. Perhaps most importantly of all, political support was strong.

On the night of 30/31 May 1942 Harris launched the first 'Thousand Bomber' raid on Cologne. In fact, 1,047 aircraft were deployed, which required a great deal of complex planning from Sam and his colleagues. From the point of view of the destruction caused this was a great success, due in large part to the weather conditions, which were ideal. The propaganda value was huge, the most dramatic statement of intent by Harris on how he proposed to carry out his bombing campaign. The information that 369 aircraft came from Operational Training Units and Flying Training Command rather than from front line squadrons, and that losses amounted to nearly 4 per cent, was not disclosed.

In fact, 'Thousand Bomber' raids were to be very much the exception, not the rule, for the rest of the war. Losses from the OTUs, in particular, were extremely high and, without drawing extensively on them, Bomber Command rarely had enough aircraft or trained crews to be able to mount such operations. It proved to be far more effective to send out smaller groups of aircraft, albeit often several hundred strong, more frequently.

One major development now began to take shape. The Butt report had led to a great deal of thinking in the Air Ministry on ways to improve bombing accuracy. The driving force behind this was Bufton, who put forward a strong case for creating a specialized marking force, which would precede the main bomber formation and put down coloured flares to identify clearly to bomb aimers where they should drop their loads. Bufton rapidly converted his own immediate superiors, Baker and Norman Bottomley, the DCAS, and a number of others were consulted, both in the groups and at Bomber Command HQ, one of whom was Sam.

Harris was strongly opposed to the proposal, disliking intensely the concept of an élite force and believing that groups should do their own marking. In this he was largely supported by his group commanders. He was partly motivated by what he saw as a move away from area bombing towards precision bombing of selected industrial or military installations, which he dismissed as 'panacea' targets. The arguments for and against were aired over the next few months, with Harris becoming more and more irritated by the men he privately referred to as 'the three Bs'. However, the results of the bombing campaign did not go in his favour. Two further 'Thousand Bomber' raids – in fact, the numbers were just short of 1,000 in the first case – on Essen and Bremen failed to emulate the success of the first, and overall the accuracy of the bombers remained poor. In August Portal, supported by his Vice-Chief, Wilfred Freeman, came down in favour of what was to be named the Pathfinder Force, and Harris was forced to agree to its formation.

To be fair to Harris, on this and several other key issues, once the decision had been taken at the top, he supported it loyally and vigorously. In this case one important element was in his gift, the choice of the new force's commander. Bufton proposed Basil Embry, then Station Commander at RAF Wittering, a forceful and inspiring leader who had managed to escape back to Britain after being shot down earlier in the war: he would have been an excellent choice,[10] but possibly just because it was Bufton's idea, Harris turned him down. Instead, he chose Wing Commander Donald Bennett, an Australian who had similarly been shot down and escaped. Bennett had served under Harris in 210 Squadron between the wars and had impressed him subsequently. He was only six months older than Sam and, by the end of the year, would become the youngest Air Vice-Marshal in the RAF.

Each of the bomber groups was ordered to provide one squadron to the Pathfinder Force, which was officially formed on 15 August with its HQ first at Wyton and then in Huntingdon. Its first raid was on Flensburg three days later. Over the coming months it developed new marking techniques and was re-designated 8 (PFF) Group in January 1943. In due course it became a volunteer-only group, its crews required to carry out forty-five operations for their first tour, against thirty for the rest of Bomber Command, and they were given promotion and pay of one rank ahead of where they would otherwise be. The PFF began by employing all the aircraft types then in use in Bomber Command – the Lancaster, Stirling, Halifax and Wellington – before standardizing on Lancasters. Moreover, a year after its formation, 8 Group was joined by 109 Squadron, which flew the remarkable De Havilland Mosquito, and this aircraft was to become an integral part of the group's operations, in due course equipping over half its squadrons.

Harris's first year in command effectively set the tone for the rest of the war. In October 1942 6 (RCAF) Group began to form, manned entirely by Canadian squadrons and paid for by the Canadian Government, and in the same month operations were extended to the major industrial cities of Italy – Turin, Milan and La Spezia. Other than for 2 Group, which had now thankfully given up its Blenheims in exchange for much more effective Mosquitos and Douglas Bostons, bombing remained almost exclusively confined to night-time operations. One exception was the low level Augsburg Raid on 17 April which, whilst successful in terms of the damage done to the MAN[11] factory, was disastrous in terms of losses, with seven out of twelve Lancasters shot down. The outbound leg of a raid on the Schneider factory in Le Creusot on 17 October was also flown in daylight; whilst the results were disappointing in terms of the damage caused, all but one of the ninety-four Lancasters returned that night, due largely to the complete absence of flak en route and over the target.

One other major development was the arrival in England of the US Eighth Air Force, which began operations from airfields in East Anglia in August 1942. Whilst in Washington, Harris had established an excellent relationship with the commander of its advanced elements and overall commander from December 1942, Major General Ira Eaker, whom he invited to be his house guest when he first came to England. Their strategies, however, were entirely different – Harris focused on night-time area bombing, Eaker on daylight precision bombing – but the combination would in due course prove to be devastating.

If Harris hated the concept of élite formations in his command, he hated scientists even more, but in the spring of 1943 he found himself compelled to deal with one of them. Barnes Wallis came with an excellent record as an aircraft designer, having conceived the Wellington, unquestionably the best bomber of the early years of the war, whose considerable ability to accept damage was made possible by his geodetic construction technique. However, Wallis had now come up with a proposal to which Harris was only persuaded to give any time at all by the insistence of Portal.

One day in mid-February 1943, Sam was summoned by Harris, who instructed him to go up to the Air Ministry, where he would be briefed by Portal. The meeting was a short one, Portal sending Sam on to Vickers

House to meet Wallis, with orders to put himself at his disposal for as long as Wallis wanted and then to write a report on Wallis's proposition for himself and Harris. Wallis immediately took Sam down to the National Physical Laboratory at Teddington, where he was shown marbles being fired by a catapult from one end of a water tank, skipping over the water and eventually hitting a low wall at the other end. Wallis then explained that he was proposing to build a bomb, weighing about 10,000lbs, which would be spun and then dropped from bombers in a similar manner with a view to destroying some of the key dams supplying power to the Ruhr Valley, the greatest industrial area in Germany. Sam, warned in advance by Harris about long-haired scientists with crazy ideas, was initially deeply sceptical.

On the following day Sam was taken by Wallis down to Dorset. There he boarded a Wellington piloted by Captain 'Mutt' Summers, Vickers' chief test pilot, and took his seat in the rear gun turret. The aircraft flew low over the sea on a course parallel to Chesil Bank and duly dropped its load, a half-scale model of Wallis's proposed bomb. From his seat Sam could see the device bouncing along the surface of the sea below, and for the first time he wondered if the idea was as ridiculous as he had initially thought. On his return he wrote a report to Portal and Harris which concluded that Wallis should be taken seriously. He was sent for immediately by Harris.

'You bloody young fool, what did I tell you about scientists?' was the AOC-in-C's reaction.

Sam persisted in his recommendation that Harris should invite Wallis to see him. This duly happened and, in the meantime, Portal had authorized the conversion of three Lancasters to carry *Upkeep*, as the full-scale bomb was codenamed.

The result was the most famous bombing operation of the war. A new squadron, 617, was formed under the command of Wing Commander Guy Gibson, and some of the best crews in Bomber Command were posted to it. On the night of 16/17 May 1943 nineteen Lancasters took off to attack the dams. Eleven of them reached their targets and breached the Möhne and the Eder Dams, although they failed with the Sorpe, largely due to its different construction. Flooding caused much destruction in the Ruhr, exacerbated by the loss of both water and power supplies. The raid was widely acclaimed by Great Britain and its allies. On the other hand, eight aircraft were lost, a very high proportion of the squadron, but perhaps commensurate with the risks and the results. Gibson was awarded the Victoria Cross.

Sam, who represented Bomber Command HQ at the early meetings on the Dams Raid at the Air Ministry and who was thus one of the few people who knew why there were so many Lancasters flying around at a very low height and with no bomb doors, was present at RAF Scampton to welcome back Gibson and his surviving crews on their return from the raid. Most unusually, Harris was there himself, with Ralph Cochrane, now the AOC of 5 Group, and Barnes Wallis, the last in tears because of the losses. Sam, however, had not come up from High Wycombe. Instead, he travelled the few miles from RAF Waddington, to which he had recently been posted as Station Commander.

Chapter 7

Waddington

RAF Waddington, situated some four to five miles south of Lincoln, next to the eponymous village and between the ancient Roman Ermine Street and the modern A15, was a station of long standing, having been acquired in 1916 and used initially for training. It consisted at that time of a very large area of grass, on which were built ten hangars and some buildings for accommodation. Following the end of the Great War it was effectively mothballed until 1926, when it was placed under the command of 6 (Special Reserve and Auxiliary Air Force) Group, welcoming in September of that year its first occupant, 503 Squadron, whose task was to train reserve pilots.

Waddington was a major beneficiary of the Expansion Schemes of the mid-to-late 1930s. Additional land was acquired, extending the airfield right up to the A15, which for the time being became its eastern boundary. The three hangars on the opposite side of the airfield were pulled down and replaced by five large Type C hangars and a number of substantial brick buildings for use as offices, messes, accommodation, stores and workshops, most of which remain in use by the RAF to this day, together with a Fort-type control tower. The station came under the command first of 6 (Training) Group, then 3 Group and lastly 5 Group, in which it would remain until after the end of the coming war. Two regular squadrons, 50 and 110, took up residence in May 1937, followed by two more, 44 and 88. A number of other squadrons were to serve there between then and 1945, but 44 and 50 were to be amongst the longest-lasting occupants. Both were equipped with Hampdens at the beginning of the war, mounting operations against naval targets on the very first day.

When Sam arrived on 14 April 1943 to assume command from Group Captain K. P. Lewis, the incumbent squadrons were 9 and 44, both of which were by then operating Lancasters. The latter was commanded by Wing

Commander John Nettleton, the South African hero of the Augsburg Raid, for his role in which he had been awarded the VC, and it was with Nettleton that Sam made his first flight in a Lancaster one month later, spending an hour flying over the Lincolnshire countryside.

However, 9 Squadron was there for only a matter of hours before moving to the satellite airfield of Bardney, eight miles east of Lincoln, much to the dismay of its air and ground crews, as the temporary accommodation at this newly constructed airfield was distinctively inferior to the comfortable arrangements at Waddington. Moreover, 44 Squadron was to leave for RAF Dunholme Lodge at the end of the following month. The reason for these moves was the decision to lay concrete runways, to accommodate which additional land had been acquired to the south of the original airfield. Whilst satisfactory for Hampdens, the grass runway at Waddington, as at many similar airfields, had proved to be less suitable for the much heavier Lancasters and was beginning to show signs of serious wear and tear. Construction units moved in and very quickly began work on three runways forming an A shape, the main one of which, 03/21, ran from just east of north to just west of south and was 2,060yds long, whilst the two cross runways, used relatively rarely, came in at 1,450 and 1,510yds respectively. There was also a concrete perimeter track and dispersals for two squadrons, about half of which were on the far side of the A15, where further land had been acquired. A new Villa-type control tower was built, although the old tower remained in use for radar operations. The last of the old 1916 hangars were demolished.

Sam, however, was not at Waddington to oversee construction work. Instead, whilst continuing to be based there with a substantial majority of his staff, he was given operational and administrative command of Bardney and a second satellite airfield, Skellingthorpe, about two miles south-west of Lincoln, both of which had been constructed during the war with concrete runways. Skellingthorpe was occupied by 50 Squadron, another former resident of Waddington. This meant a great deal of inconvenience for Sam, as it was traditional for the station commander to attend crew briefings and often to greet the crews on their return from operations.

From time to time he was also required to visit the HQ of his superior formation, 5 Group. When he arrived it was based at St Vincent's Hall in

Grantham, which was sufficiently far away to justify flying there in his Tiger Moth, but in November 1943 it relocated to Morton Hall, Swinderby, a short drive from Waddington. Sam was delighted to be in 5 Group as he had great respect for its AOC, Air Vice-Marshal the Hon. Ralph Cochrane, a descendant of the famous Royal Navy officer of the Napoleonic Wars and the South American and Greek Wars of Independence, Thomas Cochrane, Earl of Dundonald. Cochrane had served in airships during the Great War but had converted to fixed wing aircraft shortly afterwards on the advice of Lord Trenchard. In 1922 he was appointed a flight commander of 45 Squadron in Iraq, with Harris as his squadron commander and Saundby as his opposite number in the other flight, the three of them forming a tightly-knit team. As a result, he commanded the complete confidence of both the AOC-in-C of Bomber Command and the Deputy AOC-in-C, as Saundby had now become. In the late 1930s Cochrane had produced the blueprint for the establishment of the RNZAF and went on to be its first Chief of Staff.

Sam had first served under his AOC relatively briefly in the summer of 1940, when Cochrane was appointed to command the newly formed 7 (Training) Group, which included 13 OTU. He had realized immediately that Cochrane was a man of enormous ability; indeed, he was to say subsequently that he thought that he had the best brain in the RAF. Sam, however, did not have a particularly easy time of it, as the AOC was a tough taskmaster and not always solely on current operations. A few months after taking up his appointment at Waddington, Sam was summoned by Cochrane to be told to write an appreciation of the raid by the USAAF on the oil installations in Ploesti, Romania. He protested that he was quite untrained for such work, having never attended staff college, but was told to get on with it. He later realized that the paper itself was never intended to be used but was Cochrane's way of testing him for ideas.

When Sam arrived at Waddington, his three squadrons, 9, 44 and 50, were substantially engaged on what later became known as the Battle of the Ruhr. This had begun whilst Sam was still Group Captain Operations at High Wycombe and he had been closely involved in its planning. The targets were the towns and cities of the most heavily industrialized area of Germany, Bochum, Essen, Gelsenkirchen, Krefeld, Dortmund, Duisburg, Düsseldorf and Oberhausen, together with nearby Cologne. All of them were attacked by the squadrons from Waddington, for as long as it was open, Bardney and Skellingthorpe. With the weather improving as spring became summer, the incidence of raids increased. For the most part Bomber Command would call for 'maximum effort', which meant that every squadron was required to put into the air all its available aircraft, and there were, inevitably, a large number of losses.

There were occasional deviations from 'Happy Valley', as the Ruhr was ironically named by the aircrews, with two raids on the Skoda factory in Pilsen, both unsuccessful, and several on targets in Italy. More popular with the aircrews were 'Gardening' operations, although they were not exactly devoid of risk. These were concerned with minelaying in sea areas from the Oslo Fjord in the north to the mouth of the Garonne in the south, all of which were given the codenames of plants. By way of example, on the night of 28/29 April, mines were laid by 44 Squadron on 'Jasmine' off the Baltic Coast and by 50 Squadron on 'Silverthorne' and 'Daffodil' and 9 Squadron on 'Verbena' and 'Nasturtium', all of which were in the Kattegat and the Sound between Denmark and Sweden. The mines were acoustic or magnetic devices, their descent from the aircraft stabilized by parachutes so that they would enter the sea vertically.

Harris did not encourage his senior commanders to go on raids; indeed, where group and base commanders were concerned, he positively forbade it, on the grounds that they were so well informed on highly sensitive technical, tactical and strategic matters that, if captured, they could be of enormous help to the Germans. He was less strict on station commanders, and many of them felt that both their own understanding of what was involved and the morale of their crews would be improved if they went on operations from time to time. Sam was no exception, and on the night of 12/13 July he went on his first raid since early April 1942, in a Lancaster of 9 Squadron piloted by its commander, Wing Commander Pat Burnett, of whom he held a high opinion. The target was Turin and casualties across the squadrons involved were high at 4.4 per cent. One of those who lost his life was John Nettleton, whose aircraft was shot down crossing the Brest Peninsula on its return journey.

A fortnight later, on the night of 27/28 July, Sam flew with Burnett again. Whereas on the previous occasion he had been travelling in a supernumerary capacity, effectively as a passenger, this time he was acting as the flight engineer, the member of the crew responsible for the smooth operation of all the aircraft's systems, mechanical, electrical, hydraulic and fuel. The flight engineer, who sat on a drop-down seat next to the pilot and above the entrance to the bomb-aimer's position, played a particularly important role on take-off, adjusting the throttles as appropriate whilst the pilot concentrated on holding the aircraft steady on the runway until sufficient velocity had been achieved to lift off. He was the first and usually only choice to attempt to fly the aircraft in the event of the pilot being killed or incapacitated, although flight engineers were not trained pilots.[1]

The target was Hamburg, which had recently taken over from the Ruhr as Bomber Command's main objective, and this was the night of the great firestorm. The techniques adopted by the Pathfinders of 8 Group were starting to prove highly effective, helped by the introduction of new navigational devices, the first of which was *Oboe*, which, like *Gee*, depended on radio beams transmitted from ground stations in England. It had the great advantage of being immune to jamming by the Germans, but was necessarily confined in each raid to a few aircraft, which were usually provided by 8 Group's Mosquito squadrons. *Oboe* also had a limited range due to the curvature of the earth. The other introduction was *H2S*, a radar underneath the aircraft which transmitted images of the ground below to a screen in the navigator's compartment. Although effective, particularly when land was juxtaposed with water, it had one immense disadvantage when in early 1944 the Germans discovered a way for its transmissions to be picked up by night fighters.

Three nights before the Hamburg raid, another new device had been employed for the first time. This was *Window*, strips of paper backed with aluminium foil which were dropped in bundles, mimicking aircraft and completely fooling the radar defences. Not only was this employed again on the night of Sam's trip to Hamburg, but the marking by the Pathfinders was reasonably accurate and there was a lack of 'creep-back' by Main Force bomb-aimers wanting to unload and get away as quickly as possible. The temperature on the ground was high and there had been no rain for some weeks, so everything was tinder-dry. There was a high proportion of incendiaries being used, setting off fires which started to come together, merging and sucking in oxygen, causing those caught in shelters to be asphyxiated. Destruction was enormous and about 40,000 people died, whilst much of the rest of the population fled the city. Sam was later to say that he could smell the smoke at 20,000ft.

The full moon and clear skies in mid-August meant that operations over Germany were temporarily abandoned in favour of Italy, but there was one important raid which required such conditions, on the German research establishment at Peenemünde, where the V2 was being developed. This was the first major operation in which a Master Bomber was used by the Pathfinders, providing instructions for the marking and then circling the target throughout the attack to guide in the Main Force. In the case of Peenemünde the technique proved to be very successful in terms of accuracy, and considerable damage was inflicted which caused delay to the rocket programme, although 40 planes were lost out of 596, a very high percentage. Between them, 9 and 50 Squadrons contributed 23 aircraft with no losses.

Shortly afterwards Harris switched the emphasis to Berlin, one of the most difficult targets due to the distance from England (which meant that *Oboe* could not be used), the city's very considerable defences and the difficulty of differentiating between its industrial and residential areas. After only two weeks Harris moved on to other targets, with a view to returning to the German capital during the long nights of winter. By the time this happened, Waddington, construction work complete, had become a going concern as a bomber station again.

On 13 November 467 Squadron Royal Australian Air Force arrived to take up residence. The squadron was no stranger to operations, having been in action since late 1942. It comprised three flights, but one of these was hived off to form A Flight of a new RAAF squadron, No. 463. Five days after arriving, 467 Squadron flew to Berlin, with 463 Squadron joining in for the first time on the night of 3/4 December.

The return to an active role by Waddington coincided with a significant change in the organization of Bomber Command, one which was to affect Sam directly. The increasing number of stations within each Group, amounting by this time to ten or more, provided the AOCs with a problem of control. For each of the Groups other than 8 (PFF) Group and the newly forming 100 (Bomber Support) Group, which would henceforward take over responsibility for electronic counter-measures and night-fighter intruder operations over Germany, their stations were now grouped into threes, one being the Base Station, usually with solid pre-war infrastructure. This would house virtually all the administrative functions, some specialist activities and a central maintenance operation. The other stations, of which there were usually two, were those constructed during the war with temporary facilities. They continued to have engineering activities appropriate to the everyday requirements of their squadrons, although major overhauls were conducted at the Base station. They also had their own operations, intelligence and flying control staffs, but these were no longer responsible to Group but to the senior officers of each branch at the base station.

Each of the bases was given a two-figure number, the first figure denoting the Group and the second the Base. Thus Waddington became the HQ of 53 Base, with Bardney and Skellingthorpe as its two substations, each with its own station commander. Sam reverted to being station commander of Waddington alone. He was not at all happy with this reorganization, saying later:

> I still believe that the system was quite unnecessary. In fact, in my view, in many ways it worsened matters rather than improved them, because there was a tendency to select officers as base commander who were fairly senior, who for the most part, I think – and their subsequent careers justify this view – were not high calibre men. Equally important, they were not men who were obviously destined for higher staff jobs for those officers couldn't be spared ... Indeed, some proved to be operational liabilities by trying to take too great a part in activities when they really didn't know what they were doing.[2]

It would be easy to accuse Sam of pique at being effectively demoted, if not in rank, then in responsibility. However, less than a year later he would find himself coming into frequent contact with a number of base commanders, so his views were born of experience. In any event, he made an exception for the new base commander of 53 Base, Air Commodore Allen Hesketh, with whom, although twelve years his senior, he formed an excellent relationship.

In spite of his misgivings, what this meant for Sam was that he could now get on with the business of running Waddington and its two squadrons, relieved of the responsibilities which lay with the base commander and the inconvenience of having to make frequent visits to Bardney and Skellingthorpe. Waddington was in itself a major enterprise. Sam had responsibility for about 2,200 men and women, of whom the aircrew, numbering some 280 at full strength, represented just the tip of the iceberg. There were a large number of staff branches or units in addition to the squadrons – Operations, Administration, Engineering, Intelligence, Signals, Meteorology, Flying Control, Medical, Airfield Defence and even NAAFI – and 15 per cent of the total personnel were lady officers and WAAFs.

The hub of activity was the station headquarters, which housed Operations and Intelligence, the briefing room and the Intelligence Library, where post-raid debriefings took place. Sam's own office was there, manned by a small staff of which the most important member was the Station Adjutant, Flight Lieutenant Henry Locke, a former and future schoolmaster who was highly efficient at his job. Most of the engineering took place either at the dispersals, where minor repairs could be effected by the riggers and fitters attached to each aircraft, or in one of the large hangars, which were used for major repairs and scheduled overhauls. In some cases an aircraft was sufficiently badly damaged to be towed up the A15 to a facility established by its manufacturer, A. V. Roe & Co Ltd, at Bracebridge Heath, just to the north of the airfield.

Sam's day was an exhausting one. It would effectively begin with the receipt of orders for the night ahead from 5 Group, on which all departments, led by Operations, would put together the plan of action for communication to the squadrons in due course. Based on this, the amount of both fuel and ordnance could be calculated and those aircraft which were available for the raid could be refuelled and then bombed up by the armourers.

The briefing took place in the afternoon. Once the crews were all present and seated, Sam would enter with the squadron commanders. On the wall at the front would be revealed the target for the night ahead, with the routes there and back. There would then be presentations by the Met Officer on weather conditions en route, over the target and on the return journey, the Flying Control Officer on take-off procedure and the Intelligence Officer on likely defences, followed by the Squadron Commanders, after which Sam would wish them luck and wrap up. If possible, he would then see the aircraft off, before trying to catch some sleep. About an hour before the first aircraft was due back, he would return to the Station HQ to establish the progress of the raid from the Operations Room and then join the debriefing staff to greet the crews on their return.

Audrey was at Waddington with Sam. She was invaluable in maintaining morale, entertaining in the station commander's house and taking part when possible in any extramural activities, such as sports days. However, she also had a full-time job of her own. Every morning she would bicycle off to Bracebridge Heath, where she was employed as a welder, repairing damaged Lancasters.

That Sam ran Waddington very tightly was amply demonstrated when on 11 January 1944 the station was visited by the Inspector-General of the RAF, who was none other than his old boss, Edgar Ludlow-Hewitt. Based on past experience, Sam had a very good idea of how the inspection would be carried out and he had prepared accordingly.

His Engineering Officer suggested that one particular aircraft parked at the beginning of the tour should be looked at, but Ludlow-Hewitt turned to Sam and said, 'I don't think you'll expect me to look at that one, will you?'

'No, sir' replied Sam.

'I rather suspect that that one has only just been delivered here.'

'Quite right, sir.'[3]

Instead, the Inspector-General selected an aircraft himself, one which was clearly showing its advanced age. It was spotlessly clean. Ludlow-Hewitt was so impressed by his inspection that he was moved to congratulate the ground crews, not a common occurrence.

Although there was little relaxation for Sam, there was an occasional break in routine, especially when visitors from other bases or stations were involved. One of these was Air Commodore Bobby Sharp, AOC of 54 Base at Coningsby and formerly a fellow Blenheim squadron commander. Sharp was a strong character who managed to get Cochrane to persuade Harris to allow him to go on raids, as result of which he was in due course awarded a DSO shortly after his promotion to Air Vice-Marshal, a very rare feat. He had an unusual aircraft as his personal 'hack'. This was an American

P-47 Thunderbolt fighter, lent to him by the USAAF, in which he arrived at Waddington one day. Sam asked if he could take up the aircraft and, on the strength of a brief look at the instruction manual, spent an exhilarating thirty-five minutes in the air.[4]

Operations continued relentlessly, albeit pausing for nearly two weeks in December 1943 because of the weather, but then accelerating through the early months of 1944 as conditions improved. The Battle of Berlin was at its height, with 463 and 467 Squadrons, led respectively by Wing Commanders Rollo Kingsford-Smith and Josh Balmer, visiting 'the Big City', as it was called, four times in both November and December 1943, and six times in January 1944. In spite of *Window*, German night-fighter capability was increasing significantly, with the Luftwaffe on occasion able to put into the air almost as many aircraft as the RAF, although they were themselves at risk from the Beaufighter and Mosquito night fighters of 100 Group, which operated *Serrate*, a device which homed in on the Germans' radar.

Losses were frequently high and, unsurprisingly, had a serious impact on morale. Sam became particularly concerned at the incidence of sickness among the aircrews, with individuals being signed off operations by the RAF doctors in respect of relatively trivial maladies, the all too frequent result of which was that a whole crew was grounded. Sam called all the aircrews together and told them that if he found anyone malingering he would have him court-martialled for cowardice in the face of the enemy. The rate of sickness dropped significantly, and morale actually rose.

Following the Dams Raid, Sam had continued to take an interest in 617 Squadron, which was being used by Cochrane to deliver precision attacks on specific enemy targets, in so doing developing a marking capability which was already going beyond that now in use by 8 (PFF) Group. He became friendly with its new CO, Wing Commander Leonard Cheshire, and at the end of January 1944 was invited to take part in a practice run over the bombing range at Wainfleet in a Lancaster of 617 Squadron piloted by an Australian, Flying Officer Ross Stanford, in order to get some idea of what was involved. Following this up, on 4 March he flew in a Lancaster piloted by Flight Lieutenant Joe McCarthy, an American who had joined the RCAF and was a veteran of the Dams Raid, to attack the La Ricamerie needle-bearing factory at St Etienne, near Lyons. The raid was unsuccessful due to heavy cloud over the target, but Sam had by then established a good relationship with the squadron, which he would renew later in the year, and a much better understanding of its target-marking techniques.

In the early spring of 1944 it became clear that Berlin was proving to be too tough a nut to crack, and Harris moved on to other targets, mostly smaller German cities. During the course of March, however, French targets began to appear more frequently on the bombing programme, such as the one which Sam had visited with McCarthy, and he also went on a small but successful raid on an aircraft factory at Marignane, near Marseilles, in one of his own aircraft, piloted by Squadron Leader Arthur Doubleday,[5] a flight commander in 463 Squadron. This, however, turned out to be Sam's swansong at Waddington, as he was unexpectedly summoned back to Bomber Command HQ by Harris, for reasons directly connected with a change in strategy.

Chapter 8

Overlord and 5 Group

In December 1943 General Dwight D. Eisenhower was named Supreme Allied Commander of the Allied Expeditionary Force and charged with the implementation of Operation *Overlord*, the invasion of North-West Europe, as early as feasible in 1944. Air Chief Marshal Sir Arthur Tedder was appointed as his Deputy in January 1944 and given particular responsibility for the air forces in the invasion and the subsequent campaign. There was a dedicated air component, the Allied Expeditionary Air Force ('AEAF'), comprising the RAF's Second Tactical Air Force and the USAAF's Ninth Air Force, all under the command of Air Chief Marshal Sir Trafford Leigh-Mallory. However, it soon became apparent that the strategic bombing arms of both the RAF and the USAAF would also have to be incorporated into the plan.

Neither Harris nor Lieutenant General Jimmy Doolittle, who had succeeded Eaker in command of Eighth Air Force, nor Lieutenant General Carl Spaatz, the Commander of the US Strategic Air Forces in Europe, was happy about this. Harris wanted to continue with the area bombing of German cities, Spaatz and Doolittle with Operation *Pointbreak*, a directive issued in June 1943 for the two bomber forces to focus on crippling the Germans' fighter strength, largely by destroying aircraft factories. All of them still believed that the war against Germany could be won by their efforts alone, without the need for ground forces. By this time, however, their credibility on that score was very low, and the Combined Chiefs of Staff accordingly agreed to place the strategic bombing forces at Eisenhower's disposal for the run-up to Overlord, for the invasion itself and for an unspecified period thereafter.

At the beginning of March Leigh-Mallory produced an initial plan which, whilst it included attacks to destroy the Luftwaffe in line with *Pointbreak*, focused on the disruption of the railway network carrying essential supplies and reinforcements to the German forces which would oppose the invasion. Harris, Spaatz and Doolittle continued to voice their objections, with Spaatz in particular advocating attacks on German oil installations. Portal insisted on Bomber Command conducting a trial raid on a railway centre, and when this took place on the night of 6/7 March against Trappes in the western suburbs of Paris, it proved to be a great success. At the same time, the Oil Plan was widely perceived as requiring too much time to take effect. Thus the Transportation Plan, supported by Eisenhower, Portal, Tedder and a somewhat reluctant Spaatz, now served as a new directive for the heavy bomber forces. Not least because of Harris's personal antipathy towards Leigh-Mallory, these forces were placed under Tedder's direct control.

At Bomber Command HQ there were a number of consequential additions to the staff. On his promotion to Deputy AOC-in-C, Saundby had been succeeded as SASO by Air Vice-Marshal Robert Oxland, who had once commanded 3 Group and was now given responsibility for all matters dealing with the invasion. Air Vice-Marshal Hugh Walmsley, formerly AOC of 91 (OTU) Group, was brought in as an additional SASO to take over routine night bombing operations. There were now two Group Captains Operations, one of whom was Sam, who took up his appointment on 4 April.

As Sam knew well, the incumbent Group Captain Ops was his good friend and fellow New Zealander, Denis Barnett, with whom he had briefly overlapped at High Wycombe in 1942, so he was puzzled as to what his role might be. Harris explained that he would effectively become his own personal liaison officer to Eisenhower and Tedder and, as such, a member of the committee which had responsibility for delivering the overall plan. As much would depend upon Bomber Command's ability to deliver what the Supreme Commander wanted, and because there were likely to be some difficult moments in the relationships between the most senior officers, Sam's appointment was an emphatic confirmation of Harris's trust.

One problem still remained before the Transportation Plan could be fully implemented. Churchill remained highly dubious about it, fearful of the impact which civilian casualties would have on French public opinion. The detailed plan was required to assess the number of casualties expected for each target, and it soon became apparent that the most attractive targets were precisely those in which the most civilians were likely to be killed or wounded. If these were to be excluded, the value of the plan would be greatly reduced. Eisenhower became personally involved and was fully supportive. In Sam's words:

> Ike pointed out that he was not likely to get the plan approved in its original form because of the anticipated casualties, and when he suggested that perhaps we had miscalculated some of the figures, we took his point and re-worked the estimates. While we didn't exactly 'fudge' the figures we did do a downward revision of them because of Winston's arbitrary limit. Thus, the plan went through in an amended version, and, thank God, a survey taken later showed our amended figures to be more accurate than those we had originally calculated.[1]

There was, however, an agreement that key targets in some of the more densely populated areas in Paris, Lyon and Marseilles would be attacked last and as near D-Day as possible.

Sam now began a routine which would last for nearly five months, although there were occasional diversions. Every morning he attended 'morning prayers' at High Wycombe, at which he obtained full details on Bomber Command's dispositions for the night ahead. Whilst Barnett busied himself with preparing the operational orders for the groups, Sam then drove to the Main HQ of the AEAF at Bentley Priory in Stanmore to brief Leigh-Mallory, before setting out for the HQ of the Supreme Headquarters Allied Expeditionary Force (SHAEF) at Bushy Park, near Kingston, where he did the same for Tedder and, about three times a week, for Eisenhower. After spending the rest of the day there he returned to High Wycombe in the evening to deliver SHAEF's requirements for the following day. Once a week he would attend the Supreme Commander's regular update meeting with all his senior officers: Harris usually made a point of attending himself, whilst Oxland was always there.

Following the successful attack on the railway at Trappes there were a number of other raids on rail targets in March, but the activity stepped up several gears from April onwards, although still interspersed with raids on German cities. The latter were reduced to a mere five in May, with a corresponding increase in Transportation Plan operations. Raids also began on coastal batteries, almost all of which were in the Pas-de-Calais rather than Normandy, as part of the deception plan.

In addition to executing the Transportation Plan, Bomber Command was assigned a very active role in the invasion itself. By a month before D-Day the planning for this, in which Sam was very closely involved, had been completed and on 15 May he joined Harris, Saundby, Walmsley and Oxland at St Paul's School, Hammersmith, the HQ of General Sir Bernard Montgomery's 21st Army Group, for the presentation to the King of the complete plan for *Overlord*.

On the night of 5/6 June, as the invasion force sailed across the Channel, coastal batteries all along the landing beaches were attacked by over 1,000 aircraft of Bomber Command, with the largest tonnage of bombs dropped in a single night thus far. Diversion operations were also carried out, with 617 Squadron dropping *Window* to simulate a large convoy of ships approaching the French coast between Boulogne and Le Havre, whilst a force of Halifaxes and Stirlings dropped dummy parachutists and explosives in areas not under threat. Thereafter there was a heavy concentration on lines of communication, airfields, troop positions, ammunition dumps and harbours, as well as on railways.

There was one major diversion. Six days after the invasion, the first V-1 flying bombs were dropped on London and South-East England, and raids began immediately on the launch sites. 617 Squadron had recently been issued with Barnes Wallis's 12,000lb 'Tallboy' earthquake bomb, which was used with conspicuous success for the first time on the night of 8/9 June on the railway tunnel at Saumur, which was completely blocked. The squadron now began to use Tallboys against flying bomb sites, scoring a major success on 25 June in a raid on a site at Siracourt in which Cheshire himself used a newly delivered P-51 Mustang fighter as a low-level marker aircraft.

Harris, who had become friendly with Montgomery before the war[2] and had always considered him one of the Army's best officers, was keen to support major ground operations whenever requested. The first of these came on 7 July, when a force of 467 aircraft attacked the northern suburbs of Caen. Montgomery had originally expected to take the city on D-Day itself or shortly afterwards, but the Germans had defied all the attempts by his divisions to do so, either frontally or by encirclement. A new attack was now planned, preceded by the bombing. This was, for the most part, very accurately delivered, but the ruins thus created turned out to be both ideal for defence and obstructive to armoured vehicles. Notwithstanding this, the northern half of the city was taken by the attackers. In the next major operation, at dawn on 18 July, 942 aircraft attacked the German positions to the south-east of Caen in a prelude to Operation *Goodwood*, in which Montgomery hoped to break through the German defences into open country. This time the bombing succeeded in causing considerable damage to the defenders, although the British armoured divisions proved incapable of taking full advantage of their confusion.

On 14 August 805 aircraft launched an attack at short notice in support of First Canadian Army's advance towards Falaise in Operation *Tractable*. Although most of the bombs fell on German positions, 77 aircraft bombed inside the Canadian and Polish lines, with a concentration on a quarry in which a Canadian artillery regiment was sited. This was largely the result of the Canadians lighting yellow flares for identification, the same colours which were being used as markers by the Pathfinders. A number of men were killed or injured, and both guns and vehicles were destroyed.

In response to vociferous complaints from First Canadian Army, Harris instructed Sam to conduct an immediate investigation. Having been briefed at SHAEF on 15 August, two days later Sam took an Auster from the Bomber Command flight at Lacey Green and flew up to Yorkshire for meetings at the HQs of 1 Group at Bawtry Hall and 6 (RCAF) Group at Allerton Park, the aircraft of both of which had been involved in the incident. On 20 August he flew as a passenger in a Dakota to the RCAF airfield at Beny-sur-Mer in Normandy, from where he visited the HQ of 84 Group, which was located alongside that of First Canadian Army. There he met the SASO, Air Commodore Theodore McEvoy, and the Group Captain Ops, Fred Rosier, and raised the question of the yellow flares, to be told that these were the standard signal for all troops to indicate positions to aircraft, as set out in the Army's standing orders. He was also told that, due to some previous incidents, it was common for such signals to be displayed if the troops believed they might be attacked by their own tactical aircraft. Moreover, some Army Co-operation pilots had then fired red flares in an attempt to divert the bombers.

Sam went on to have a meeting with General Henry Crerar, the commander of First Canadian Army, and then to visit the site of the incident. He became very aware of how high feelings were running when he overheard some Canadians and Poles saying that they would like to put a bullet in him.

On his return to High Wycombe on 21 August, Sam delivered a report to Harris which provided the basis of the AOC-in-C's own report on the incident, sent to all interested parties three days later. In it Harris pointed out that Bomber Command had not been informed of the yellow flares being used by the Army, and that the error had been compounded by the red flares, which also resembled target markers. However, he also criticised his own crews, who had been provided with a precisely timed run check from the French coast, which they had ignored. Doubtless wishing to demonstrate to both the ground forces and his own command that he would not tolerate laxness in his crews, Harris took immediate action. He withdrew Pathfinder badges from the two Pathfinder crews which had been involved, reduced in rank the squadron and flight commanders in the two groups concerned and 'starred' all the crews as not to be employed within thirty miles forward of the bomb line without re-assessment.

The same day, 21 August, was actually Sam's last at Bomber Command and SHAEF, as he was off to another job. He had been summoned by Harris some days earlier, to be told to his astonishment that he was being promoted to Acting Air Commodore. This was a measure of the regard in which he was held by the AOC-in-C, as was the offer of three jobs from which he was invited to take his pick. One was as Deputy SASO at Bomber Command HQ, the second continuing as Harris's representative at SHAEF, which had recently relocated its Forward HQ to Normandy, and the third as SASO at 5 Group. There was no doubt about which one he would choose. He had spent quite enough time at High Wycombe and had never been really happy liaising with SHAEF, about which Charles Carrington, the Army Liaison officer, wrote subsequently: 'I had two long conversations with Elworthy which seemed to show that he was as little satisfied with his status as I with mine, a check in his brilliant career.'[3] SASO at 5 Group, on the other hand, was highly attractive, primarily because Cochrane was AOC, but also because it would be by far the most exacting, challenging and interesting of the three jobs. He never had any reason to regret his decision.

From having once been the oldest pilot officer in the RAF, at the age of thirty-three Sam was now very nearly its youngest air commodore.[4] After a brief leave in Cornwall, which he and Audrey spent with Paul and Babs Wright, he reported to Cochrane at Morton Hall, Swinderby, 5 Group's HQ. The main offices were in the substantial house, but others were in more recently constructed buildings, whilst accommodation, including married quarters for Sam and Audrey, was in Nissen huts in the grounds. There was an RAF airfield close by, which had once been part of 5 Group, but was now used for training. It housed the HQ flight, one of whose Proctors was available to Sam.

Sam was now in overall charge of the staff and responsible for the smooth running of the group. Since he had left it five months earlier it had been constantly in action, initially on area bombing and then in support of the invasion of Normandy and the subsequent campaign. Not long after his arrival, however, Bomber Command was released by SHAEF and reverted to the control of the Air Ministry, albeit with the proviso that it was likely to be required to support ground operations from time to time in the future.

Sam's appointment coincided with a modest change in structure of the group, prompted largely by Bomber Command's decision to move the Heavy Conversion Units, hitherto under the control of the individual groups, to the newly re-formed 7 (Training) Group, leaving 5 Group with four bases, which between them controlled eighteen squadrons. These were 53, still comprising Waddington, Skellingthorpe and Bardney, 54 with Coningsby, Woodhall Spa and Metheringham, 55 with East Kirkby, Spilsby and Strubby, and 56 with Fulbeck and Balderton. Other than the addition of Syerston to 56 Base in April 1945, the establishment would remain thus until after the end of the war.

A more significant change had also taken place. This was the growing independence of 5 Group from the rest of Bomber Command, the result of its highly successful development of target-marking techniques, which differed from those used by 8 (PFF) Group. Low-level marking, pioneered by 617 Squadron, was now carried out visually by the group's own Mosquitos. However, 5 Group had also invented 'time-and-distance' bombing, which provided an extra element of accuracy, and 'offset marking', in which a special plane, arriving ahead of all the others over a target, would lay a marker about 400yds upwind of the aiming point and notify the wind speed and direction to the Master Bomber, who would then broadcast a false wind for the main force to set their bomb sights accordingly. Whilst 617 Squadron carried out most of its operations by itself or in conjunction with 9 Squadron, the only other one equipped to carry the 'Tallboy' bomb, the remainder of the group now had their own Pathfinders. The Lancasters of 83 and 97 Squadrons and the Mosquitos of 627 Squadron, now employed respectively in high- and low-level marking, had joined 5 Group from 8 (PFF) Group in April 1944, supposedly on loan, but in practice permanently attached. The two Lancaster squadrons had both served in 5 Group before becoming Pathfinders, so were in a sense coming home.

Bennett, his monopoly on marking now at an end, was furious and complained bitterly to Harris, criticising Cochrane for his lack of personal operational experience and asking for the squadrons to be returned. He also disparaged 5 Group's techniques, notwithstanding that they were, if anything, proving to be more successful than 8 Group's. Harris, whilst wishing to mollify Bennett, whom he still rated very highly and whose Pathfinders were continuing to provide a vital service to the other groups, refused, seeing an attraction both in the development of a variety of techniques and in healthy competition. He would, in due course, also encourage 3 Group to develop its own marking techniques, using the new *Gee-H* blind bombing device, so many of the larger raids of the last year of the war were carried out by combining 1, 4, 6 and 8 Groups. In the meantime, according to Sam, the relationship between Cochrane and Bennett remained 'extraordinarily bad'.[5]

Sam had overall responsibility for all aspects of staff work, but inevitably took a personal interest in operations. Whilst there continued to be some raids in support of the Allied armies during September, notably on Le Havre, Boulogne and Calais, all of which came under siege by 21st Army Group, area bombing had resumed with a vengeance. One special operation, however, required Sam's direct involvement. For a long time the Admiralty had been deeply concerned about the presence of Germany's most powerful warship, the *Tirpitz*, in Kaa Fjord in Northern Norway, where it represented a considerable threat to convoys around North Cape. Attacks by both the Fleet Air Arm and midget submarines having failed to sink the ship, Bomber Command was now requested to take on the task of doing so.

This was a much more complex operation than usual, requiring a high level of staff planning, not least because the target was beyond the Lancaster's range from the UK and it would thus be necessary to mount the raid from Russia. Both 9 and 617 Squadrons were to provide as many aircraft as possible, and Sam had to spend time with them, but primarily with the latter at Woodhall Spa. By this time Cheshire had completed his tour, and the squadron was now commanded by Wing Commander J. B. 'Willie' Tait, whom Sam knew well as his former Wing Commander Operations at Waddington and respected greatly.[6]

On 11 September thirty-eight Lancasters took off in company with two Liberators carrying ground crews and flew to Yagodnik, an airfield on an island in the River Dvina about 20 miles from Archangel. One had to turn back and six crash-landed in Russia, albeit without loss to their crews; the remainder arrived safely. The raid took place in clear weather on 15 September. Six aircraft carrying 'Tallboys' attacked first as it was essential that they should take aim visually before a smoke screen was fully deployed. They arrived just before smoke covered the ship, whilst the rest had to drop their 2,000lb bombs through the smoke. Subsequent photo-reconnaissance showed a hit to the bows and intelligence later revealed that the engines were also badly damaged. Five aircraft were written off in accidents on the return to Yagodnik, but the rest made a safe journey back from there, apart from one which crashed in Norway with the loss of its crew.

Unable to make more than 10 knots, the *Tirpitz* was moved to a mooring near Tromsø for repairs. With the installation of more powerful engines in the Lancasters and the attachment of drop tanks, the battleship now lay just within range of an attack from the UK, which was duly mounted from Lossiemouth on 29 October. Thirty-seven Lancasters, this time all carrying 'Tallboys', mounted the attack but were foiled at the last minute by cloud cover; all returned safely, other than one which force-landed in Sweden, where the crew were interned. The final attack by thirty Lancasters took place on 12 November, once again with all aircraft carrying 'Tallboys'. As on the second raid, they were accompanied by a 463 Squadron Lancaster with a film crew aboard, who managed to capture the ship capsizing, later confirmed by photo-reconnaissance.

Sam attributed to Cochrane 90 per cent of the credit for the final success, on account of his determination to override the orders of the Air Ministry that the attacks should be carried out exclusively with 2,000 lb armour-piercing bombs. The AOC approached Barnes Wallis directly to find out if his new bomb would do the job. The immediate answer was, 'I don't know, but I'll go and work it out.'[7] Wallis came back to say that there was a better than even chance that it would penetrate the ship's armour, on the strength of which Cochrane made his decision. The Admiralty was delighted with the result.

The last three months of 1944 saw 5 Group engaged on a wide range of operations. Medium-sized German cities were regular targets, but the group was also involved in attacks on Walcheren Island in preparation for and support of amphibious landings there by First Canadian Army. This formed one part of a major offensive to open the River Scheldt to shipping bound for Antwerp, soon to become the Allies' most important port. The objective was to break down the dykes around the coast of the island, letting in the sea to flood the interior, with adverse consequences for the defenders. These raids began on 7 October and continued to the end of the month, with considerable success. Attacks were also mounted against the Dortmund–Ems Canal and the Mittelland Canal, which were major transport arteries from the Ruhr, to the port of Emden and to Berlin respectively. These were to continue into the New Year, the canal banks being breached on numerous occasions, with water spilling out into the countryside and barges being stranded.

Meanwhile, 9 and 617 Squadrons continued to carry out special operations with their 'Tallboys', including an attack on 7 October on the Kembs Barrage, governing the flow of the Rhine between Basle and Strasbourg, in which one of the sluice gates was demolished, causing the river to fall by over 11ft, with an adverse impact on shipping. On 15 October the two squadrons attacked 617's old target, the Sorpe Dam, which remained resistant to destruction but was weakened enough for the Germans to have to reduce the height of the water behind it. 'Tallboys' were also dropped on E-Boat pens in Ijmuiden and Rotterdam, which were severely damaged.

The year ended with a pinpoint raid mounted from RAF Peterhead by twelve of 627 Squadron's Mosquitos against the Gestapo HQ in Oslo. Whilst initially thought to have been successful, it was subsequently revealed that the target had not been hit and that instead seventy-nine Norwegians had lost their lives.

The year 1945 began with ground support for First US Army's offensive in the Ardennes, where the Battle of the Bulge had been raging for some weeks. Attacks on German cities continued, and on the night of 13/14 February 5 Group led the raid on Dresden, hitherto untouched, with 245 aircraft out of a total of 796 from Bomber Command. The group's aircraft attacked first and alone and were only moderately successful, due to persistent cloud. By the time of the second raid, three hours later, the cloud had cleared and marking was extremely accurate. A firestorm was created similar to that in Hamburg in July 1943, and it is thought that upwards of 25,000 people lost their lives. On the following day 311 American B-17s bombed the city. No other raid was so controversial and it had a disproportionate impact on Harris's reputation, which was to come in for considerable post-war criticism.

This was the penultimate raid for which Cochrane was responsible, as on 15 February he was appointed AOC-in-C Transport Command. With the end of the war in sight, Harris was keen to bring forward some of his younger officers, whilst Cochrane's new appointment was a tribute to his organizational skills, which would be needed in the only command likely to see growth in peacetime. His successor was Air Vice-Marshal Hugh Constantine, whom Sam had known well as Deputy SASO at Bomber Command, prior to which Constantine had been station commander at RAF Elsham Wolds and then SASO at 1 Group. They thus understood each other very well and, particularly as Constantine was only three years older than Sam, became good friends. The organization worked like clockwork, as Tedder found when he came to visit the Group in late February, writing subsequently to Sam:

> I can't say how much I appreciated my visit to the grand team you've got in 5 Group. It was a magnificent tonic. Incidentally the soldier I brought with me was tremendously impressed & has been telling all & sundry over here what a terrific show it all is – which is all to the good.[8]

A combination of factors meant that, whilst dropping more and heavier bombs than ever – in March 1945 alone the tonnage was nearly as much as that for the whole of the first three years of the war – Bomber Command could now do so without incurring heavy losses. The growing impact of the Oil Plan, the destruction of much of the German aircraft industry and the shortage of trained night-fighter crews, together with the increasing success of counter-measures by 100 Group and the shrinking territory of the Reich, meant that Allied aircraft could operate almost at will. On the night of 23/24 March, 5 Group led without loss the attack on Wesel which preceded 21st Army Group's crossing of the Rhine there, prompting a warm message of thanks from Montgomery to Harris.

In the meantime, an even larger bomb had been invented by Wallis, known initially as the 'Tallboy Large' and later as the 'Grand Slam', which was designed to penetrate deep beneath the surface before exploding. At 22,000lbs this was the largest bomb in the world and was used for the first time by a single aircraft in 617 Squadron's third raid of March 1945 against the Bielefeld Viaduct, which carried a key railway line from Cologne and the Ruhr to Minden and Northern Germany. Together with 'Tallboys', its use resulted in a 100yd gap being created in the viaduct. This was one of a series of successful raids against railway bridges, and the two specialist squadrons also began to use 'Grand Slam' against U-Boat pens.

The final raid of the war by 5 Group took place on the night of 25/26 April, when 119 aircraft bombed the oil refinery and storage installations at Tonsberg on the Oslo Fjord. In this raid a Lancaster of 463 Squadron was the last to be brought down in the war, crash-landing in Sweden without loss to the crew.

A heavy price had been paid by Bomber Command over the past six years, with the loss of 55,573 of its aircrew, some 44 per cent of the total. The only other force whose losses could be compared was Germany's U-Boat fleet. The command had carried the fight to Germany during the years when no other method of attack on the Reich was possible. It had denied significant resources to the Eastern Front because of the demands for night-fighters and anti-aircraft defences. Together with Eighth Air Force, it had so degraded the Luftwaffe that the Allied ground forces in North-West Europe were only rarely subjected to serious attack from the air. Yet it received little recognition relative, say, to Fighter Command during the Battle of Britain, in which the total losses of fighter pilots amounted to considerably less than those of aircrew in the Nuremburg raid of 30/31 March 1944.

Bomber Command's operations during the war have been the subject of considerable debate ever since. Area bombing, in particular, has come in for severe criticism, not only because of the huge number of civilian deaths, but also because it was seen by many as ineffective at destroying Germany's war industries. Harris himself bore the brunt of the criticism: too valuable and, in many ways, too powerful to be sacked whilst hostilities continued, he was retired in September 1945 and made a marshal of the RAF by way of some compensation. He was desperately upset that his ground crews and non-flying staff were never awarded a campaign medal, unlike those who had served with the RAF overseas. In spite of the fact that he had only rarely visited his groups, he remained enormously popular with those who had served under him.

Sam's own views reflected those of most of his comrades. In retrospect he deeply regretted the killing of women and children, but at the time he had not questioned the morality of area bombing. Like Churchill, the War Cabinet, the Chiefs of Staff and the British people generally, he saw no other means of attacking Germany directly. He remained a great admirer of Harris and Cochrane, whom he regarded as the two most important influences on his career.

On the day after its last bombing raid 5 Group was diverted to Operation *Exodus*, the repatriation of prisoners of war back to the UK from France, Belgium and Germany. By the end of the operation on 15 May 18,133 PoWs had been carried by the group without loss. In order to see what was happening, Sam himself flew on one of these operations on 8 May, VE Day, in a Lancaster piloted by Wing Commander Ian Hay, the CO of 467 Squadron, from Waddington to Frankfurt and back.

Sam went on a longer foreign trip in the following month, this time to Italy for discussions about using Bomber Command aircraft for the repatriation of British service personnel there. The great majority of them were expecting early demobilization, but the logistics of getting them back to the UK were proving troublesome, due to limited capacity on the railways and a shortage of shipping. He flew on 20 June in a Lancaster to Foggia, where he was briefed by Air Vice-Marshal Andrew 'Square' McKee,[9] AOC of 205 Group,

Edward Elworthy, Sam's paternal grandfather and the progenitor of the Elworthys of Pareora.

Sarah Elworthy, the matriarch of the family and Sam's paternal grandmother.

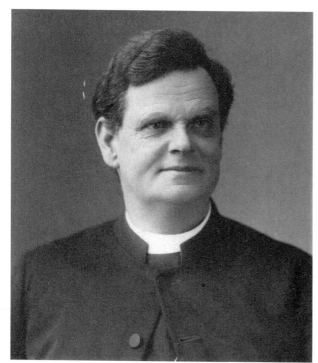

Churchill Julius, Bishop of Christchurch, Sam's maternal grandfather.

The house at Gordons Valley, built by Percy Elworthy on land inherited from his father.

Percy in England during the Great War, with Janet, Sam, Tony and Anne.

Sam and Tony at Gordons Valley with their tutor, Frank Ivey.

Percy Elworthy in the mid-1920s.

Bertha Elworthy, Sam's mother, in the mid-1920s.

Forbury, one of the houses in England rented by Percy.

Corporal Elworthy in the Marlborough College Officers Training Corps.

Percy with Sam, Tony, Anne and Di at Forbury, Christmas 1929.

The First Trinity 1st May Boat 1932 – Sam seated 2nd from right, Peter Kenrick 2nd from left and Pat Beesly standing 2nd from right.

Pilots of 600 (City of London) Squadron relaxing in front of their Hawker Harts at RAF Mildenhall for the Silver Jubilee Review in July 1935.

Formation flying on the return from Mildenhall.

Sam with his cousin, John Elworthy, near Innsbruck in 1935.

Sam and Audrey, with John Elworthy, visiting Ernest and Daisy Hudson at Prosperous.

Audrey in November 1935.

5 June 1936 – Sam and Audrey's wedding
at St Saviour's, Walton Street.

Sam, in the foreground, supervising the recovery of a crashed Hawker Hind as Adjutant of XV Squadron.

King George VI (fourth from right) inspecting a Handley Page Harrow at RAF Harwell in April 1938: Sam is standing on the far left, Edgar Ludlow–Hewitt on the far right.

Sam and Ludlow-Hewitt leaving the levée at St James's Palace, as described in *Tatler*!

The Blenheim Mark Is of 108 Squadron at RAF Bassingbourne in August 1939.

The Handley Page Halifax on whose maiden flight from RAF Bicester Sam acted as co-pilot.

The all-too-frequent outcome of a first night flying solo in a Blenheim.

Sam's Blenheim Mark IV in 82 Squadron, T2165.

Sam in the pilot's seat with 'Duggie' Douglas, 82 Squadron Intelligence Officer.

Bill Collins, Sam's navigator/ bomb-aimer.

Sam in the HQ at
RAF Watton.

Photo taken from
the turret of T2165
approaching a German
convoy off Heligoland.

As T2165 pulls away after
dropping its bombs, the aircraft
behind has lost much of its port
wing and is about to crash

The portrait of Sam by Eric Kennington.

Queen Elizabeth on a visit to RAF Watton accompanied by Sam, Air Marshal Sir Richard Peirse, AOC-in-C Bomber Command, and Air Commodore Bill Williams, SASO 2 Group.

'Bundles for Britain' – Audrey in a group including Janet Murrow, who is talking to Lord Nuffield.

'SAM'S TWO GREAT MENTORS'

Air Marshal (later Marshal of the Royal Air Force) Sir Arthur Harris, AOC-in-C Bomber Command.

Air Vice Marshal (later Air Chief Marshal Sir) Ralph Cochrane, AOC 5 Group.

Audrey presents prizes at a sports day at RAF Waddington, 1943.

Sam cuts the cake at a party at Waddington celebrating the fourth anniversary of the founding of the Women's Auxiliary Air Force.

Sam, on the right, planning a 5 Group operation.

A Lancaster of 617
Squadron releases its
'Grand Slam' bomb
over the Bielefeld
Viaduct in March 1945.

A 'Grand Slam'
embedded in the lawn
at Morton Hall, HQ 5
Group, for the garden
party celebrating the
end of the War.

Sam in Italy in July
1945 to plan Operation
Dodge with Air
Commodore Jarman
(left) and AVM McKee
(centre), respectively
SASO and AOC 205
Group.

Sam and the crew of the Avro Lincoln *Excalibur* at the start of the Central Bomber Establishment mission to the Far East and Australasia.

Rear Admiral Jefford, Major General Akbar Khan and Sam stand behind Mohammed Ali Jinnah, Governor-General of Pakistan, taking the salute at a review.

Audrey, second left in the front row, Sam, second right, with Tim and Anthony in the row behind, watch a football match at RPAF Drigh Road.

Sam as CO RAF Tangmere in 1952.

The AOC 11 Group, AVM the Earl of Bandon (3rd from left) inspects 29 Squadron at Tangmere with Squadron Leader Joe Bodien (4th from left), Sam (far right) and Wing Commander Barney Beresford (2nd from right).

Percy and Margaret Bowen on a picnic with the family on the South Downs.

and his SASO Air Commodore L. E. Jarman, both fellow New Zealanders and both formerly of Bomber Command. McKee flew Sam to Marcionese and then to Ciampino, from where he visited Rome. On his return journey to Coningsby he also managed to land at Treviso and spend some time in Venice. The visit resulted in a number of 5 Group's aircraft being allocated to Operation *Dodge*, each of them bringing back about twenty passengers at a time.

There was, of course, still the war against Japan to be won, and 5 Group was selected to be in the forefront of the final push on the Japanese Home Islands. Together with 6 (RCAF) Group, it was to form Tiger Force, equipped with Lancasters and new Avro Lincolns and based on Okinawa, from where it would carry out night-time raids on Japanese cities. Initially, it was proposed that the majority of the group's squadrons would be so employed, divided into five wings, one of which was for special operations by 9 and 617 Squadrons. However, Tiger Force was already in the course of being scaled back by the time that atomic bombs were dropped on Hiroshima and Nagasaki and the Japanese capitulated, although it was not formally disbanded until the end of October.

Although there was a strong sense of relief that the war was finally over, celebrated at a garden party at Morton Hall in August, the centrepiece of which was a 'Grand Slam' bomb with its nose embedded in the lawn, this was also a period of extreme frustration as the Group was progressively wound down. A new programme of training was introduced, covering the bare essentials to maintain operational efficiency. Squadrons were given a monthly quota of 800 flying hours, plus or minus 50 hours, satisfied in part by participation in Operation *Dodge* and also in Operation *Spasm*, whereby 'Cook's Tours' were organized to Germany for ground crews, many of whom had never flown before, to see the results of their work.

Sam had already been to Berlin. This followed a demand by the Russians, in the person of Marshal Zhukov, to be able to use Gatow, the airfield allocated to the British, on the grounds that there were very few aircraft there, whilst the Russians were short of space. Sam received an order from Bomber Command to get as many Lancasters as possible to Gatow in the shortest amount of time and decided to accompany them himself in an aircraft piloted by his old friend and the former CO of 9 Squadron, Pat

Burnett. After a rather drunken evening they set out to look round the city. They went first to the Chancellery, where they saw Hitler's desk and Burnett took his lavatory seat as a trophy! They then moved on to the bunker where Hitler met his end. This was guarded by Russian soldiers, but an air commodore was a general in their eyes, so the pair were admitted. Burnett picked up some photograph albums from Eva Braun's room, but as they were leaving there was an altercation between the guards and some other Russians who had come to do blood tests on the furniture, during which all the lights went out. Sensing trouble, the two men dropped the albums and made their escape. They had, however, already liberated an enormous carpet from the Chancellery which they persuaded some German workers to carry out and put on their truck. It was then stowed in the bomb bay of the Lancaster for the return journey!

By the beginning of October 5 Group was diminishing fast. The three Australian squadrons, 460, 463 and 467, had already been disbanded, as had a more recent arrival, 75 (RNZAF) Squadron, and 627 Squadron was re-designated as 109 Squadron. Two squadrons had already moved to other groups and six more were due to follow them in November, whilst 9 and 617 Squadrons were scheduled to move to India. There had also been major changes in personnel as large numbers were either demobilized or posted elsewhere. Constantine departed in late October, leaving Sam to wind up the group, which disappeared into history at the end of the following month.

Chapter 9

Going East

Sam had had a 'good' war. He had achieved fast promotion for his age, been awarded the DSO, DFC and AFC and been mentioned in despatches three times. One further distinction was bestowed on him in the New Year's Honours List of 1946, in which he was appointed a Commander of the Order of the British Empire. With his job as SASO at 5 Group now at an end, however, he was reduced to his war substantive rank of group captain.

It was possibly this reduction in rank which caused Sam to give some serious thought to his future. Holding a permanent commission, he could remain in the RAF if he wished, but it was clearly going to be a very different organization from that which had been such a powerful component of the British armed services during the war. Prospects for promotion back to air rank were not immediately encouraging, as it was clear that demands for cost savings by a country which was effectively bankrupt were likely to require radical reductions in personnel, and there were plenty of other good people available. He briefly thought about returning to the Stock Exchange, but very quickly decided that there was nothing he was likely to enjoy more than continuing his Air Force career.

Audrey was supportive, but she had another priority, to bring Tim and Anthony back from New Zealand. Moreover, she was pregnant with a third child, so time was of the essence. She sailed in the MV *Port Jackson* before the end of 1945 and arrived in Auckland in time for another son, Christopher Ashton Elworthy, to be born there on 21 February 1946. As soon as she had recovered she returned with all three children and a nurse on the MV *Akaroa* and was back in England in the late spring.

Sam had been in Bomber Command since he joined XV Squadron ten years earlier and he was to remain in it for the immediate future. On 1 December 1945 he was appointed to command the Tactical Wing of the

Central Bomber Establishment ('CBE') at RAF Marham, about ten miles south-east of King's Lynn. Marham had started the war as a 3 Group airfield for a squadron of Wellingtons and had later come under first 2 Group and then 8 (PFF) Group, both of which operated Mosquitos from there. In the late spring of 1944 it had closed for concrete runways, perimeter tracks and dispersals to be installed, following which it became suitable for the operation of heavy bombers.

The CBE was formed in the autumn of 1945 under the command of Air Commodore Geoffrey Spencer, with whom, as Assistant AOA at Bomber Command HQ, Sam had been dealing for much of that year. It comprised a Tactical Wing, a Development Wing, commanded by Group Captain J. H. T. Simpson, a Tactical Training Wing and a Servicing Wing. At the same time the Central Fighter Establishment, the Central Signals Establishment and the Central Servicing Development Establishment were also set up. Together they had an identical purpose, to consider and begin to prepare for the future. In the case of the CBE, the objectives set out by Norman Bottomley, who had succeeded Harris as AOC-in-C of Bomber Command, were as follows:

(a) To develop tactics and operating procedures, including target finding and target marking for day and night attacks by heavy, medium and light bombers, primarily for strategic operations but additionally for sea and land warfare, using information, experience and Intelligence gained in all theatres.

(b) To study the progress of bomber development, in collaboration with the appropriate Research and Development Establishments, and to make recommendations for the improvement of aircraft and equipment so as to increase the striking power of the bomber and to lessen its vulnerability in the face of all forms of enemy action.

(c) To undertake tactical trials of aircraft and all ancillary equipment, so as to assess their tactical value and define their best tactical employment.

(d) To form a Tactical School where potential Commanders and Specialist Leaders can be given a sound appreciation of current and future tactics, with practical demonstrations and exercises.

(e) To advance proposals and recommendations on bombing procedure, bombing methods and training methods, either for specific operations or for general adoption in the Royal Air Force.[1]

The Tactical Wing was to take the lead in the work of the CBE, comprising 'a specially picked corps of officers, including navigation, bombing and gunnery specialists who would be responsible for directing the work of the Development and Tactical Training Wings. This staff should not be burdened with detail, but should be free to debate, co-ordinate and direct the work of the Establishment.'[2]

The works on the airfield were only completed in January 1946, shortly after which the first three Lancasters arrived from the Bomber Command Development Unit at RAF Feltwell, to be followed in due course by other aircraft, Mosquitos and Avro Lincolns. The latter was a development of the Lancaster and had, indeed, begun life as the Lancaster IV. With a completely new wing and a longer fuselage, it could fly higher, faster and further than its predecessor and was armed with 0.5in machine guns instead of 0.303s. Sam, who had been up to the Avro airfield at Woodford in April 1945 for a demonstration of the aircraft by the company's chief test pilot, Captain Sam Brown, nevertheless believed that the Lincoln's advantages over the Lancaster were trifling. It was, in any event, seen as an interim solution whilst a completely new type of bomber was developed, the initial specification for which had been issued by the Air Ministry in 1944 as a requirement for a replacement for the Mosquito. This would be a high altitude, high speed and, as to defensive weaponry, unarmed bomber powered by jet engines. Several aircraft manufacturers submitted proposals, and in January 1946 English Electric was awarded a contract to develop four prototypes. Although the first of these would not fly until 1949, and it would be 1951 before the Canberra, as it was named, would enter service, it was clearly understood what the characteristics of the aircraft were likely to be, and the CBE's own trials were designed accordingly.

There were two more highly relevant developments which had taken place in the last year of the war. The first was the deployment by the Germans of the V-2 rocket, which had demonstrated how attacks might be made at a range of hundreds of miles via a medium which was evidently immune to defensive measures. In Great Britain, the USA and the Soviet Union scientists were already working on the development of guided missiles, to be launched both from sites on land and from aircraft. The second development was the atomic bomb, which had opened up a major debate about its future use, with not only strategic but also tactical implications. Together these were sufficient to cause the Air Ministry to issue a specification in January 1947 for a much larger and faster four-engined jet bomber, which would carry nuclear weapons: this was the genesis of the first of the V-Bombers, the Vickers Valiant.

There was thus a great deal of thinking to be done on the design and operation of bombers of the future, which Sam found both challenging and stimulating. Because such bombers would be unarmed except for their bombs, early detection and evasion would have to take the place of defensive weaponry. A lot of time was thus spent by both the Tactical and the Development Wings on considering the future use of the various navigational aids which had been developed during the war – *Gee* and its successor *Gee-H*, *Oboe*, *H2S* and *Rebecca*, the last of these a short-range transponder – as well as the electronic counter-measures which had been used by 100 Group. It became increasingly clear that the new generation of bombers would require even more sophisticated equipment, and trials began immediately on updated versions. Among other issues considered was the layout of cockpits for the new bombers, in respect of which an early assumption was made that Flight Engineers would no longer be required, Army support tactics, target marking and high-altitude fighter escorts.

There was a great deal of exchange of ideas with other experimental and technical establishments, specialist schools and the RAF staff colleges, as well as with the Air Ministry. In addition to visiting the other three central establishments, all of which were based in nearby RAF stations in Norfolk, Sam also undertook a number of overseas trips, including to Germany to both the British Air Forces of Occupation and the USAAF, which enabled him to see at first hand more of the damage wrought by Bomber Command in its long campaign. In September 1946, moreover, he embarked on a much more ambitious journey, which took him back to New Zealand for the first time since 1932.

Each of the Dominions had played a large part in the air war, and the Air Ministry was keen that they should be kept fully up to date with new developments. A programme was therefore devised to send a team to the Far East, Australia and New Zealand, where they would brief their local colleagues by way of lectures and face-to-face meetings. The tour would also be used to study the problems associated with long-range reinforcement flights.

Sam was to lead the tour personally, with Wing Commander Richard Ayling as his deputy and Wing Commander David McKinley as captain of the aircraft. McKinley was a renowned long-distance flyer. In 1944, flying a Lancaster named 'Aries One', he had carried out the RAF's first full circumnavigation of the globe, during which he had stopped in both Australia and New Zealand, and in May 1945 he had flown from Reykjavik to the North Pole and back, another first in the RAF. As he was also a former chief instructor at the Central Navigation School, he was a useful man to have on board. The three of them, with Wing Commander R. H. Winfield, a medical officer who had accompanied McKinley to the North Pole, comprised the staff mission and lecture team, whilst three other officers completed the aircrew and four NCOs were responsible for the maintenance of the aircraft and its equipment.

The Lincoln in which they travelled, named 'Excalibur', was modified by the removal of the mid-upper gun turret and the installation of more powerful engines and extra fuel tanks in the bomb bay. With Sam at the controls it flew out of Marham on 8 September on a brief hop to Blackbushe, from where it left early on the following morning for a long flight to Lydda in Palestine. From there it flew on in one day to Mauripur, just outside Karachi, and thence to Changi, the airfield for Singapore. About eight hours out from Mauripur a leak was spotted on the starboard inner engine, which had to be closed down. It turned out to be a fracture of a high pressure line which necessitated spending an unplanned day in Singapore for repairs to be made. On 13 September Excalibur flew to Darwin and, on the following day, to Laverton, a major RAAF base close to Melbourne. Four days were spent there briefing and answering questions from their hosts, who included Australia's Chief of the Air Staff, before the party flew on to Mascot,[3] outside Sydney, for a similar programme of lectures and discussions.

On 23 September Sam flew Excalibur to Ohakea, the RNZAF airbase near Palmerston North on the North Island, where he was met not only by the official welcoming party, but also by his parents, his brother Tony,[4] Tony's wife Gertrude, always called 'True', whom he had married in 1938 and his sister Di, with her husband, Hamish Wilson. On 26 September Excalibur flew down to the RNZAF base at Wigram, outside Christchurch. Before leaving for Whenuapei, the RNZAF base at Auckland, Excalibur 'showed the flag' over Timaru and Sam flew the aircraft at a low level over Gordons Valley and the surrounding area, causing the stock grazing there to bolt in all directions; the farmers were mollified when they discovered that the pilot was a local man! Back in the North Island, Sam was able to take a two-day break with his family at Ngaio-iti, the Wilsons' property not far from Ohakea, in between briefing and being entertained by his New Zealand colleagues.

After further briefings for RNZAF officers, Excalibur left New Zealand on 1 October, bound for Amberley, in Queensland, and then retraced its steps via Darwin to Changi. This time the stay was extended to four clear days for the CBE officers to brief those in South-East Asia Command as well as to take some time off. On 8 October the party flew to Negombo, the main RAF station in Ceylon and, two days later, on to Palam,[5] outside Delhi, for two full days of briefings with the RAF in India. On 13 October Excalibur flew via Mauripur to Habbaniya, in Iraq, and then on to Luqa, on Malta, for the night. The party arrived back in Marham, via Blackbushe, on the evening of 14 October, just over five and a half weeks after it had left.

This journey had given Sam his first real experience of the RAF outside the UK, in which country, other than on short trips, he had spent his entire career. He was very conscious of the fact that many of his contemporaries could point to overseas service in their curricula vitae, whereas he had none, and this might well come to be seen as an impediment to his future progress. He was thus not unhappy to find himself sent out to India in early 1947, notwithstanding that this was an 'unaccompanied' posting, so that Audrey and the boys had to stay behind.

Sam reported for duty at Air HQ India in New Delhi on 22 February 1947. He was not looking forward to his new job as Group Captain Training but was pleased to find that the AOC-in-C was Air Marshal Hugh Walmsley, an old friend as SASO at High Wycombe in 1944. He was even more pleased, less than two weeks later, to be posted as SASO at 2 (Indian) Group, where the AOC was an even older friend and former CO at XV Squadron, Bill Adams.

Following the capitulation of Japan, the RAF in India had been rapidly run down from its wartime establishment. Four of the twelve wartime groups were re-designated as 1, 2, 3 and 4 (Indian) Groups, the last of which only survived until mid-1946. Based in Peshawar was 1 (Indian) Group, with responsibility for the North-West Frontier, where the RAF had been most active in the inter-war years, while 2 (Indian) Group covered an enormous area in Central and Southern India, with its HQ at Bangalore, and 3 (Indian) Group was at Barrackpore, near Calcutta.

When Sam arrived in Bangalore, 2 (Indian) Group consisted of only two front-line Royal Indian Air Force squadrons, 2 and 8, based respectively at Yelahanka and Kolar, both close to Bangalore, where they were in the process of converting from the Spitfire XIV to the Hawker Tempest II. However, it was decided in June 1947 that there should be a major reorganization of the Royal Indian Air Force: 3 (Indian) Group was disbanded and 2 (Indian) Group lost its two squadrons and its station at Poona to 1 (Indian) Group, receiving in turn most of the latter's Training, Maintenance and Administrative units. It also assumed responsibility for all the university units. RIAF Kolar was closed down.

All this meant a great deal of work for Sam, which by and large he enjoyed, and because of the enormous area which the group covered – extending at the outset from Bhopal in the north to Cochin in the south and expanding even further north into the Punjab, Rajasthan and the United Provinces after the reorganization – he did a great deal of flying in the HQ flight's Harvards and Ansons. These were difficult times for India as Partition approached, and morale was frequently affected by events far away. There was a certain amount of anti-British feeling amongst the RIAF NCOs and other ranks, particularly those whose families were located in what would become Pakistan.

Even before Independence was declared by India and the new state of Pakistan in August 1947, it became clear that the majority of the British officers and men would have to leave the sub-continent, although some would be able to transfer to the Royal Indian Air Force or the new Royal Pakistan Air Force. Sam was to remain in 2 (Indian) Group for some weeks after Independence but was told that thereafter there would be no job for him. Having been in India by that time for only eight months, he expressed his disappointment and requested that he should complete a full overseas tour in the Far East or Middle East. The response was that there was no appointment available in either, but that if he was prepared to volunteer to serve in either the Royal Indian or Royal Pakistan Air Force, he could put his name forward, although he could not choose which one. This he duly did and was informed in due course that he was to be seconded on loan to the Royal Pakistan Air Force, specifically as Station Commander at Drigh Road, on the outskirts of Karachi. He arrived there on 23 September, just over a month after Pakistan had achieved Independence, although his formal appointment did not take place until 1 November.

Drigh Road, now Pakistan Air Force Base Faisal, lies seven miles east of the city centre of Karachi, between there and Jinnah International Airport. Constructed to a high standard, with mainly stone or brick buildings and substantial hangars, it opened in 1922 as a maintenance base, one of its major functions being to receive and assemble aircraft which were shipped out to India in parts. One of those working there in the engine shop five years later was AC2 T. E. Shaw, better known as Lawrence of Arabia. When the Indian Air Force was created in 1933, its No. 1 Squadron was formed there.

Throughout the war Drigh Road operated as a major maintenance base, and its work included once again preparing for operations aircraft arriving in India for the first time. Construction began on a concrete runway in late 1943, the work taking place at night so as not to disrupt its activities. After the end of the war the station retained its functions, but it was the site of unrest amongst its airmen, initially as the result of slow demobilization, overcrowded barracks and inadequate rations, so much so that the visiting Inspector-General of the RAF, Air Chief Marshal Sir Arthur Barratt, was shouted down when he attempted to address a meeting. Subsequently, there had been further trouble in sympathy with a serious mutiny by the Royal Indian Navy in 1946. The unrest was satisfactorily defused, but Sam was to encounter more personnel problems later.

After Independence, Drigh Road continued its maintenance activities. There were, however, no operational squadrons on the station; indeed, Pakistan had little in the way of a functional air force. The new Dominion had inherited just two fighter squadrons, 5 and 9, both equipped with eight Tempest IIs and both in the North-West Frontier Province, the former at Miranshah and the latter at Peshawar; 14 Squadron, also deploying Tempest IIs, was formed in Peshawar during 1948. The only other operational unit was 6 Squadron, based at Mauripur on the other side of Karachi. It was equipped initially with a single C-47 Dakota, increased to eight by the end of March 1948 and twenty over the next twelve months. Equipment generally was split two-third/one-third between India and Pakistan, but the division of aircraft was closer to 80:20 and the practical implementation of transferring assets from one country to the other caused great bitterness between them. Sam later recalled that India held the store of boots in a depot near Madras; most Indian and Pakistani men had small feet, but when the boots arrived they were all size 10 or over!

Sam's immediate superior was AVM Allan Perry-Keene, who had, remarkably, been serving in the sub-continent since 1935. Most recently, as AOA at AHQ India, he had chaired the Reconstitution Committee which dealt with the division of assets. Because of his long experience, he had been nominated by the British Government as the first AOC-in-C of the post-Independence Royal Indian Air Force, but the Indian Prime Minister, Jawaharlal Nehru, had insisted that the appointment go to an air marshal, and Tommy Elmhirst, Sam's former station commander at Abingdon, who had been serving in New Delhi as Chief of Inter-Service Administration, was duly chosen. Muhammed Ali Jinnah, the new Governor General of Pakistan, was then offered Perry-Keene as his own Air Commander and had accepted him.

Perry-Keene's task was not an easy one. The new Royal Pakistan Air Force was deficient in assets, but even more so in men. Relatively few of those in the pre-Independence Royal Indian Air Force had opted for Pakistan and those who had were of relatively junior rank. On the Reconstitution Committee Pakistan had only managed to field a wing commander and a squadron leader against India's air commodore and group captain. Furthermore, the new service was very deficient in the ground services and the numbers had to be made up by a large contingent of officers and men from the RAF who had volunteered to stay. Because of this, the first new units established at Drigh Road were a Recruits Training Centre and a Technical Training Centre.

Perry-Keene decided to site Air HQ in Peshawar, close to his active squadrons and to the most likely areas of military activity, whether these would be along the North-West Frontier or on the border with India. This decision was justified to some extent by the First Indo-Pakistan War of 1947/8, which took place exclusively in the north-west, although neither Air Force had much involvement other than the RIAF's successful troop lift into Kashmir. Perry-Keene's location, however, led to an important additional role for Sam. The meetings of the Pakistan Defence Council took place for the most part in Karachi, close to the centre of government. Because it was usually inconvenient for Perry-Keene to attend, Sam was appointed as the Air Force member, alongside the Prime Minister, Liaquat Ali Khan,[6] for whom he had the greatest respect, the Defence Secretary, Iskander Mirza,[7] the Army member, Major General Akbar Khan,[8] and the Navy member, Rear Admiral James Jefford.

Sam did a certain amount of flying himself, usually in one of the Drigh Road Harvards, but occasionally in a Tempest. Flying in Pakistan was not always straightforward. He was asked on a number of occasions to lecture at the Army Staff College at Quetta and, on one of these, flew himself there in a Harvard, accompanied by a British NCO, Sergeant Baddeley. They called in at Mauripur for clearance to go further and then flew on to Jacobabad, where they intended to refuel, as Quetta was only just within the aircraft's range. It turned out that there was no aviation fuel available there, so they had to top up with petrol. Then the starter battery failed, so they attempted to wind up the engine. When this, too, proved unsuccessful, the resourceful Baddeley purloined a battery from an ambulance, which provided just enough of a charge for the engine to start and for them to continue on their journey. Some weeks later, Sam offered a lift to Quetta to Jefford, whose normal aircrew were sick. On this occasion the tail-wheel tyre burst at Jacobabad, so the tail had to be lifted up by coolies at the beginning of its take-off. Moreover, because of heavy cloud, the aircraft had to fly very low through the high passes, losing radio contact in the process. Unsurprisingly, Jefford opted for his own aircraft to fly him back to Karachi!

There were some compensations in what turned out to be a frustrating period in Sam's career, as he and the other senior RPAF officers struggled to get the new force into reasonable shape. Most importantly, Audrey was with him again. Whereas his posting to India had been 'unaccompanied', he was now permitted to bring her out and she arrived in early 1948, leaving the children in the care of either the Kenricks at their home at Blakeshall in Worcestershire, or other very old friends from Cambridge days, Peter and Elizabeth Garran, in Sussex. Sam and Audrey lived in a well-built and comfortable bungalow and made some good friends amongst the local British community, which was still a large one. The normal weekend's recreation was to go to Sandspit, a beach to the south-west of Karachi which formed a natural breakwater between the harbour and the Arabian Sea, either to swim or, if conditions were right, to sail.

Sailing was by no means a completely new activity for Sam. He had enjoyed the occasional outing in friends' yachts or dinghies before the war and had taken part more competitively whilst at the CBE, joining Brancaster Staithe Sailing Club and buying a Sharpie to race off the North Norfolk coast. Now he acquired an International 14 dinghy named *Vanessa*, which he raced regularly and quite successfully. The sport, like rowing in his university days, brought out the competitive side of Sam's character, usually well concealed beneath a calm exterior. He was always determined to win and demanded a great deal of his one-man crews, not all of whom lived up to his expectations and were duly told as much.

The other weekend activity was shooting. The quarry was usually duck and the shoots often required a night to be spent away, sometimes under canvas. Since his boyhood in New Zealand Sam had been a good shot and he had had plenty of subsequent experience in England and Scotland, so this was a very welcome diversion. Back in Karachi, there were frequent social events and Sam and Audrey played both tennis and bridge. They also managed to get away from Karachi on two occasions, once to the North-West Frontier Province, where they and the Jeffords were taken up the Khyber Pass to the border with Afghanistan, and once to the Nilgiris in Southern India to stay with Sam's sister, Anne, and her husband.

Anne's very difficult relationship with her mother had resulted in her being sent away to Paris and then to Sydney. On one of their frequent journeys in the 1930s from New Zealand to the UK, on this occasion with Anne in tow, Percy and Bertha had stopped off at Madras and had then driven up to Ootacamund in the Nilgiris to visit a former governess to the Elworthys, then running a boarding house for retired officers. They asked her if she would take in Anne and, on being told that she would, left the poor girl there. Shortly afterwards, however, Anne met Shaun Jeffares, an Irish lawyer, at a local tennis club, fell in love and married him in 1937, enjoying subsequently a happy family life in India and later in Ireland.

For their summer holiday of 1948, Tim and Anthony, now both at prep school in Sussex, flew out to Karachi by BOAC, spending their time largely swimming and sailing at Sandspit. Christopher, still only two years old, remained with the Kenricks. In the knowledge that Sam's tour of duty was likely to be ending in early 1949, Audrey returned home with the boys by sea, sailing in the Anchor Line ship, RMS *Caledonia*.

Shortly after the family had left, Sam became intimately involved in an event of both huge local importance and international interest. Muhammed Ali Jinnah, the founder and first Governor-General of Pakistan and the *Quaid-i-Azam* (Great Leader) to the country's people, had been ill with tuberculosis for many years and had recently developed lung cancer, the result of very heavy smoking. He stayed for a lengthy spell in Quetta during the summer of 1948, as the climate was more favourable to his condition than in Karachi. However, he became so ill that he was advised by his doctors to return to Karachi for more specialist treatment. On 11 September, accompanied by his devoted younger sister, Fatimah, he flew down to Drigh Road in a RPAF Dakota.

Sam was on the airfield to meet the aircraft and was surprised when, instead of taxiing to the usual apron, it parked on the far side of the airfield. To find out what had happened he radioed the pilot, who answered that he was unable to tell him over the air but asked him to come out to the aircraft, under the wing of which Sam met Fatimah. She told him that her brother had died on the flight. Sam immediately summoned an ambulance, luckily driven by a British NCO, and accompanied it to a nearby military hospital, where Jinnah was certified dead. Sam in the meantime had called Liaquat Ali Khan and, without telling him what had happened, requested that he come to the hospital as a matter of urgency. They decided that the body should be removed to Government House, where it would be placed in an open coffin for government and civic leaders and members of the Diplomatic Corps to pay their respects.

Sam was then asked by Liaquat to arrange an immediate funeral, as the Muslim faith demanded. Moreover, he instructed that it should follow the example of that of King George V, with soldiers lining the streets and the coffin pulled on a gun carriage by sailors from the Royal Pakistan Navy. At short notice this required organizational skills of a very high order, but Sam managed to achieve it, even carrying out a quick dress rehearsal, with almost none of those involved knowing why they were there. When the funeral itself took place, Sam and a Royal Navy Captain acted as escorts to the coffin, which was pulled along packed streets to the burial ground, where the emotion of the crowd was so great that they removed the coffin from the gun carriage and carried it over their heads to the grave.

Sam's reputation in funeral management was now such that he was automatically chosen to organize that of Sir Ghulam Hussain Hidayatullah, the Governor of Sind, less than a month later. He described it to Audrey as 'complete chaos',[9] even though the crowds were not as great as they had been for Jinnah.

Whilst Sam was in Pakistan he received a copy of an Air Ministry edict which stated that in future important staff posts could only be held by those who were graduates of the RAF Staff College or its Army or Navy equivalents. This came as an unpleasant surprise because, although Sam had passed the qualifying exams before the war and had held important staff positions thereafter, he had never been sent on the Staff College course and was now too old to attend it. He wrote immediately to the Department of the Air Member for Personnel to say how unfair this was, as he would now be doomed to hold only unimportant staff posts. He was gratified to receive an answer from the Director-General of Personnel, John Baker, to say that his point had been taken and that he could instead attend a course at the Joint Services Staff College. If he graduated satisfactorily, he would not be barred from any staff appointments. He immediately applied for a vacancy and was, after a nerve-wracking delay, accepted for a course beginning in May 1949.

Sam had by then become increasingly frustrated with his job. In addition to a heavy workload arising from the expansion and reorganization of the

RPAF, the main issue with which he was contending was the question of the RAF NCOs and other ranks being allowed to have their wives and children join them, as was already the case for officers. He was deeply irritated by Perry-Keene, who repeatedly dragged his heels on the issue, delaying a decision whilst at the same time not allowing any of those concerned to be repatriated. This caused a near-mutiny, which Sam had to defuse. When the matter was eventually sorted out, due to Sam's persistence, the aircraft carrying the wives broke down in France and they were badly delayed.

His other major problem was a more personal one. A new Senior Technical Staff Officer had been appointed to the RPAF and Perry-Keene told Sam that he and his wife and two children would be sharing his bungalow. They duly arrived, with an ayah and a bearer in tow, disrupting Sam's life completely. He complained bitterly to Perry-Keene, asking to be allowed to live in the officers' mess, but that was refused. In due course Sam reached an accommodation with his new housemates, but the affair had done nothing to improve his mood and he was more than ready to leave, in spite of attempts by the Defence Ministry and Liaquat Ali Khan to persuade him to stay. He sold *Vanessa* and the motorbike which he had acquired and sailed from Karachi on the RMS *Cilicia*, *Caledonia*'s sister ship, on 19 February. The fact that the Perry-Keenes were also on the ship did not spoil his delight at being on his way Home.

Chapter 10

Fighter Command

When Sam arrived back at Liverpool on 11 March 1949, he was able to look forward to the glorious prospect of more than two months of leave, due not only from his service in Pakistan but also by way of End of War Leave, which he had never taken, and the normal Disembarkation Leave. This allowed him to enjoy the whole of the two older boys' Easter holiday and a visit to England by his brother Tony.

The family was now living in the West Sussex village of Bury, near Pulborough, the result of an introduction by Paul and Babs Wright, whose own home was not far away and who were friendly with the local vicar, Bertram Davies. The Victorian vicarage was much too large for the Davies family, who were themselves to become lasting friends, and so the two upstairs floors were let out to the Elworthys as a self-contained flat. It was convenient for trips and, in due course, commuting to London by train, and was not too far from the boys' school near Battle.

The Fifth Course at the Joint Services Staff College began on 23 May. The JSSC was still a young institution, having opened at the beginning of 1947 on the initiative of Admiral of the Fleet the Viscount Cunningham. Although administered by the War Office, it came under the auspices of the Chiefs of Staff Committee, with the specific objectives of training officers for appointments on joint staffs, developing a common doctrine among the services and evolving a standardized system of staff work. The course lasted for six months and the syllabus consisted of the organization of the three services and their relationships with one another and with Government departments, the planning, execution and administration of joint operations, Imperial strategy, including co-operation with the Dominions, the problems of war production and economics and the influence of scientific and technical progress.

The syllabus was delivered by two methods. The first was a programme of lectures by senior officers, civil servants and managers from the services, politics, industry and international affairs, the second a series of visits to each of the services. As at the services' own staff colleges, the students were split into syndicates for further discussion and the preparation of papers, guided by the Directing Staff (DS). There were eighty-seven students from all three services, the Dominions, the USA and the civil service, and twenty-one on the DS. The Commandant was Major General Bill Stratton, who had commanded an infantry brigade in Italy and had then been Chief of Staff successively of British Troops in Austria and the British Army of the Rhine.

For those who had been at the staff colleges at Camberley, Greenwich or Bracknell, one unusual feature was that the students and the DS were of much the same rank; indeed, Sam was senior to most of the latter. On the day of his arrival at the college he had actually reverted to his substantive rank of wing commander, whose three rings he had last worn in May 1942, but on 1 July he was promoted to substantive group captain. As might be expected of a group of men who had mostly seen active service during the war, there was a healthy smattering of DSOs and other gallantry decorations among both students and DS, but few of either went on to achieve prominence. One who did and whom Sam got to know better many years later was an Army officer, Lieutenant Colonel John Hunt, a contemporary of Sam's at Marlborough, who had served in the Commandos and as a battalion commander in Italy. Hunt would go on to lead the successful Everest expedition of 1953 and later to join Sam in the Order of the Garter.

The JSSC was located in Latimer House, near the village of that name in Buckinghamshire. The original Elizabethan building had been destroyed by fire in 1830 and rebuilt in substantially the same style. Although many of the married officers preferred to live away from the college, accommodation was provided, and Sam and Audrey decided that he would stay there for the week and come down to Bury on his motor bike on each Friday evening, returning late on Sunday in time for a prompt start the following morning. Audrey did occasionally come up and stay nearby for social events, including most notably the JSSC Ball towards the end of the course.

Sam enjoyed the JSSC, saying subsequently that he had had an easy time there. Moreover, it achieved what he wanted, the letters *jssc* after his name, orders and decorations in the Air Force List and qualification for senior staff appointments. Following his graduation in late November he was expecting a posting to the Air Ministry, where he had never served before, and hoping for one to the Air Staff, but to his initial dismay he found himself in the Department of the Air Member for Personnel, as a Deputy Director in the Directorate-General of Personnel (II). However, he adhered to the principle that an officer should go wherever he was posted without complaint and settled down to make the most of his job. Before long he realized that he was actually in an excellent position to learn about the inner working of the Air Ministry, at the same time gaining valuable practical experience in personnel management. Moreover, his day-to-day work gave him a unique perspective on his fellow officers, as he was responsible for the postings of all officers below air rank – air commodores and above – and he handled group captains personally.

As part of his job he was required to read the confidential reports on those who had been identified as candidates for a particular posting. He was not responsible for promotions, but he felt strongly that these could not be made on the basis of the reports alone; indeed, the grading on a 'nine-to-nought' basis was, in his opinion, meaningless to Promotion Boards without some knowledge of the reporting officer. If such officers always gave high marks, as some did, their assessments had less value than those who were consistently more critical. He also expressed concern about the requirement that the recipient should read the report, on the grounds that many reporting officers were likely to pull their punches in such circumstances. He prepared a paper on the subject for Air Chief Marshal Sir Leslie Hollinghurst, the Air Member for Personnel, whom he rated very highly. The result was, in due course, a much fairer system.

If Sam's posting to the Air Ministry was a valuable but relatively unexciting period in his professional career, there was also a significant development on the family front. Clare Louise Katharine Elworthy was born on 15 April 1950. As the first and only daughter, she would be a much loved member of the family, to whom she was known as 'Missy'. Percy and Bertha were able to come over for the christening on 24 June.

In the early autumn of 1951 Sam prepared a minute for Hollinghurst on another subject about which he felt deeply:

> In the minute, I said that I was worried about Fighter Command, in that the C-in-C's policy was, as far as postings were concerned, not to have in his Command people who were not born and bred in Fighter Command. This was acceptable in the days when he could have all the 'cream' – which he did – but it was my impression that he had had all the cream, he'd had all the milk, but now he was down to the skimmed milk, and this in my view was going to diminish the effectiveness of Fighter Command. I thought he ought to be persuaded to take officers who did not have Fighter Command experience but nevertheless who would greatly improve the calibre of officers of his command. Well, for a while I heard nothing. The next thing I knew was, one day in my little cubby hole at the back of Adastral House, the door was flung open and there was Basil Embry waving a sheet of paper which he pushed under my nose and said, 'Did you write this rubbish?' I looked at it and saw what it was. Holly had obviously given him a copy of my minute. I admitted to being the author and he fairly berated me: 'What the bloody hell do you know about Fighter Command? You bloody well tell me how to run my command' et cetera, et cetera. He gave me a dressing down and stormed out of the office. Being typical Basil Embry, twenty minutes later in he came again and merely said, 'Would you like a station in Fighter Command?' I used my position in charge of postings to post myself to command at Tangmere.[1]

This was a significant development in Sam's career, bringing him back to a front line command role for the first time since leaving Waddington in March 1944. To be fully fit for his new appointment he had to demonstrate that his flying skills were up to the standard demanded of a fighter pilot. However, neither at the JSSC nor at the Air Ministry had he had much opportunity for flying, the one exception at the latter taking place during a week spent on a visit to the Middle East Air Force, during which flights to the RAF stations in the Nile Delta and along the Suez Canal and further afield to Nicosia had provided him with a few chances. His lack of recent flying hours therefore required him first to attend the two-week No. 92 Refresher Course at RAF Syerston, which he knew well as an old 5 Group station. The course was conducted on the Harvard, a type on which Sam had had over sixty hours of flying time. Nevertheless, he had to go through each of the stages, culminating in the Green Card Test, which rated his instrument flying skills. He passed the course rated 'above the average' and was duly awarded his Green Card on 6 November.

One week later, he reported to No. 205 Advanced Flying School at RAF Middleton St George, a former 6 (RCAF) Group station in County Durham, to attend a Jet Refresher Course. Having satisfactorily passed a test in the decompression chamber up to 40,000ft, he began instruction on the two-seat Gloster Meteor T.7 trainer. The Meteor, in its various marks, was the first operational jet aircraft flown by the RAF and had been, since shortly after the war, its most important front line fighter. It was not entirely new to Sam, who had flown one for the first time whilst still SASO at 5 Group and had tried out another earlier in 1951. Nevertheless, he now had to learn to fly the aircraft to a level of competence which would enable him to engage in combat. He therefore undertook a series of exercises over the next ten days, both dual on the T.7 and solo on the F.4, an early fighter version. He duly qualified and, after a short leave, assumed command of RAF Tangmere on 5 December 1951, taking over from Group Captain Tom Prickett.

With the possible exception of Biggin Hill, there has been no more famous fighter station than Tangmere. Some three miles east of Chichester in West Sussex, it was opened in 1917 as a training facility but mothballed after the Great War, only to be re-opened in 1926, briefly for the Fleet Air Arm and then for the RAF. Many squadrons were to spend time there, but those most closely associated with the station were No. 43, which arrived for the first time in December 1926, and No. 1, which followed closely behind in February 1927. Initially, the aircraft operated were bi-planes, Gloster Gamecocks, Armstrong-Whitworth Siskins, Hawker Furies and Gloster Gladiators, but by 1939 the incumbent squadrons were equipped with Hurricanes.

When the Battle of Britain began on 7 July 1940 with attacks by the Luftwaffe on shipping in the English Channel, Tangmere was operating as a Sector Headquarters in 11 Group, deploying 43 and 601 (County of

London) Squadrons and the Blenheim 1s of the Night Fighter Interception Unit at Tangmere itself and 145 Squadron at the nearby satellite airfield of Westhampnett.[2] A number of other squadrons made brief appearances during the battle, including No. 602 (City of Glasgow), the first at Tangmere to be equipped with Spitfires. On 16 August Tangmere suffered a disastrous air raid by German Ju-87 Stukas, with buildings and hangars largely destroyed and many casualties. It was not easy, however, to put a grass airfield out of action, and operations continued almost without interruption.

Following the Battle of Britain, the station housed the Tangmere Wing, which mounted fighter sweeps across Northern France. Numerous squadrons moved in and out and a number of highly distinguished aces flew from the station, including Johnnie Johnson, 'Cocky' Dundas and 'Dizzy' Allen. Most notable of all was Douglas Bader, who was shot down and lost one of his artificial legs – the replacement, as we have seen, being later provided by Sam – whilst leading the wing from Tangmere. One other incumbent unit, occupying separate buildings on the far side of the airfield from the Tangmere Wing, with which it had little contact, was a flight from the highly secretive 161 (Special Duties) Squadron, which operated Westland Lysanders, dropping off and picking up agents of the Special Operations Executive in Occupied France.

Tangmere continued as a fighter station after the war and for some time also housed the RAF High Speed Flight, an offshoot of the Central Fighter Establishment. In September 1946 a Meteor of the flight, piloted by Group Captain Teddy Donaldson, established a world speed record of 616 mph. When Sam arrived, the station was still home to two Meteor units: 1 Squadron, flying single-seater Meteor F.8 day fighters, was commanded by Squadron Leader John Ellacombe, who had flown Hurricanes in the Battle of Britain, for which he was awarded the DFC, and Mosquitos on intruder operations over France, for which he received a bar to his decoration. Ellacombe was followed in November 1952 by Squadron Leader Brian Morrison, who had won a DFC flying Beaufighter and Mosquito night fighters. The second unit was 29 Squadron, flying two-seater Meteor NF.11 night fighters, commanded by Squadron Leader H. E. 'Joe' Bodien, who had also flown Mosquitos during the war and had come away with a DSO and a DFC. His successor in June 1952 was Squadron Leader Peter Horsley, who somehow managed to hold this particular job down whilst combining it with another. Horsley was yet another former Mosquito pilot, who had had the misfortune of being shot down at night near the Cherbourg Peninsula, spending three days in a life raft in the English Channel, mostly in a gale, before being miraculously picked up by a rescue launch. He had gone on to serve in the Second Tactical Air Force Communications Squadron, finishing the war with an AFC. In 1949 he became an Extra Equerry to Princess Elizabeth and the Duke of Edinburgh and remained an Extra Equerry to the Queen after her accession to the throne. He thus spent only 70 per cent of his time on squadron duties but, as he was later to write, 'Both my Wing and Station Commanders were quite convinced that I would fall flat on my back, but they hadn't taken into account that No. 29 Squadron flew mostly at night, and there were after all still the daylight hours in which to perform my duties as an Equerry.'[3]

Tangmere was still part of 11 Group, forming one of the four RAF stations in the Southern Sector, the others being Odiham, with two more Meteor Squadrons, and Filton and Llandow, with one squadron each of lighter single-engined De Havilland Vampires. When Sam arrived, the commander of the Southern Sector, with his HQ at Box, near Bath, was Air Commodore Douglas 'Zulu' Morris,[4] succeeded in early 1953 by Air Commodore Gerald Keily. The group was commanded by Paddy Bandon, an old friend of Sam's from 1940/1,[5] who inevitably made his presence felt very visibly, carrying out regular tours of his command. There was a mutual admiration between the two men which would have an impact on Sam's career before very long.

In the meantime, however, his priority was on making Tangmere the best possible station and, aided by his Wing Commander Flying, Barney Beresford, optimizing the effectiveness of his two squadrons. In contrast to his time at Waddington, where he was constrained by the requirement to supervise operations from the ground, he flew a great deal himself, mostly in his personal Meteor F.8, participating in station and sector exercises. He also had responsibility for the RAF radar station at Ventnor on the Isle of Wight, which he was required to visit regularly, usually in his Tiger Moth.

On the ground Sam ran a tight but happy station and was generally much admired by his subordinates. He and the family had moved to the station commander's house, where Audrey acted very successfully as hostess at a number of social occasions. Paddy Hine, then a lowly pilot officer, but later to become a distinguished air chief marshal, said that Sam had the knack of putting everyone at their ease.[6]

By this time Tim had moved on from prep school and was boarding at Radley College. Sam had earlier noticed his lack of aptitude or enthusiasm for cricket and asked him if he would prefer to go to a rowing school, which Marlborough had never been. Radley, on the other hand, had a very good record and reputation at the sport, so the choice was made, and Tim went on to have an excellent career as a school rower, reaching the 1st VIII and in due course rowing for the school at Henley.

In later life Sam always recalled one particular incident at Tangmere. Early one morning, a Dakota carrying Field Marshal Montgomery, then the Deputy Supreme Allied Commander in Europe, landed there, having been diverted from RAF Odiham, which was fogbound. Sam, warned of Monty's arrival, was on the tarmac to meet him, with the news that his car was waiting to drive the field marshal to Odiham. At this Monty said that he had changed his mind and would prefer to spend his morning talking to Sam. Offered breakfast, he replied that he had already had it. The only place on the station which Sam thought might be in an acceptable condition for their meeting was the WRAF officers' lounge and he duly took the field marshal there. Sam was, at that time, a fairly heavy smoker, but he knew that Monty disapproved of the practice, to the extent of forbidding it in his presence. After two hours of conversation he was desperate to light up and brought out his cigarette case, silencing Monty in mid-flow. Sam had decided that, as it was his station, he would do as he liked. He lit up, initially to complete silence, then Monty suddenly said, 'You have my permission to smoke'!

In the spring of 1953 Bandon asked Sam to come to see him at his HQ at Hillingdon. He began by saying that he realized that he had recently given Sam permission to go on holiday to Yugoslavia, but he was now withdrawing it as he had an important job for him. As part of the celebrations around the Queen's Coronation it had been decided that there should be a RAF Review on 15 July, and Bandon wanted Sam to deal with the administrative arrangements on the ground. The venue was to be RAF Odiham, and Sam was therefore ordered to exchange commands with the CO of Odiham, Group Captain Johnny Kent.

The changeover took place on 13 March, when Sam flew to Odiham in his Meteor. Kent, a highly distinguished Canadian fighter pilot who had made his name commanding a Polish squadron in the Battle of Britain, was deeply unhappy about the situation, believing that he, and by extension Canada, had not been considered good enough to receive the Queen. He took his feelings out on Horsley in particular, as a member of the Royal Household. Bandon, however, had recognized that, whilst Kent was an inspiring leader, Sam was the more reliable manager for an occasion on which everything had to go exactly to plan.

The RAF Coronation Review had been in contemplation since October of the preceding year. The Government, conscious of the cost, had queried the need for one, but having agreed to a fleet review at Spithead for the Royal Navy, could hardly deny the RAF. The preferred venue initially was RAF Waterbeach, but it was quickly decided that this would be too far from London, so Odiham was nominated as the best alternative. It was agreed that the programme would be divided into three parts: first a ceremonial parade, then an inspection by the Queen of personnel and static aircraft and finally a fly-past. Flying Training Command would take responsibility for the parade and for the transport and accommodation of nearly 5,000 personnel, whilst Fighter Command would not only provide the venue but also organize the static review and the fly-past, responsibility for which Bandon allocated to other officers. All the rest of the arrangements, including lunch for the Queen, would lie with Sam.

It is likely that Bandon was aware that Sam already had some experience with such events. Whilst serving at the Air Ministry he had at short notice been given responsibility for the Royal Enclosure at the RAF Display at Farnborough on 7 July 1950. The event was much less formal than the Coronation Review, the King and Queen making a relatively brief appearance to watch the flying, but it involved a lot of work in a short time, including installing temporary toilet facilities for Their Majesties, which involved laying drains across the airfield. In the event, they were never used.

The Coronation Review was a much more complex affair. It had to work to a lengthy and very precise timetable, which began at 06.00, when the gates were opened to visitors, and ended with the Queen's departure at 16.15. A lunch for seventy, hosted by the Secretary of State for Air, Lord de L'Isle, was to be laid on in the officers' mess at Odiham for the Queen, the Duke of Edinburgh and other members of the Royal Family, together with equerries and ladies-in-waiting, the members of the Air Council, the most senior civil servants at the Air Ministry, the RAF commanders-in-chief and the marshals of the RAF, all with their wives. The danger of failure in front of almost everyone who mattered in Sam's career was accordingly immense. In addition, 1,000 other guests of the Air Council were to enjoy a cold buffet in marquees alongside the special enclosure, whilst up to 40,000 members of the public were also to be admitted.

Sam's task was thus a massive one, which involved not only welcoming and dealing personally with the royal party for as long as they were in the mess, and ensuring their security at all other times, but also making all the other arrangements, including those for the admission of the public and their accommodation whilst on the site. This and the arrangements for the press, television and film companies required close liaison with the local authority and the police. Catering had to be organized, carried out for the public by NAAFI, and other facilities provided, including temporary lavatories. When Sam investigated the possibility of laying drains as he had done at Farnborough, he was informed that the airfield lay within the catchment area for the local water supply and that such construction would therefore not be permitted; instead, he would have to install special tanks. He was advised to visit an official in the Home Office who was an expert on such things. This he duly did, and the man was extremely helpful, enquiring about the numbers involved, the proportions of males and females, the time Sam expected people to remain on site and the likely weather conditions. Based on this information he came up with the calculations on the spot and the tanks were duly installed. By the end of the day of the Review they were full, but not overflowing!

Sam's major concern was the reception and lunch for the Queen. He was far from sure that the RAF mess staff would be up to the task, especially when, during the dress rehearsal, champagne cocktails were produced which for some reason included bottled orange juice! He immediately went up to Claridges Hotel and asked the General Manager for the loan of two of his best men. This was readily granted and they duly arrived on the day, only for one of them, a Cypriot, to be arrested by the Provost Marshal. Sam's quick intercession enabled the man to be available to mix some excellent champagne cocktails.

As the day of the Review approached, the event took over Sam's life completely, with briefings for the two responsible C-in-Cs, the Air Council, Buckingham Palace and the Press and a series of rehearsals of every part of the occasion. One other duty for the Elworthys was to act as hosts to Pamela, Lady Rathdonnell, who had been an official war artist and had now been commissioned by the Air Council to produce a painting of the Review. She later gave them a pastel sketch which she had produced as a preliminary to her final work.

Although the weather was indifferent, windy, cloudy and unseasonably cold, the day itself went off without a hitch, both on the ground and in the air, where 700 of the RAF's many types of aircraft were involved in the fly-past, which included the first public appearances of the prototypes of two new V-Bombers, the Handley Page Victor and the Avro Vulcan, neither of which had yet entered squadron service. Just before she departed, the Queen admitted Sam as a Member of the Royal Victorian Order (4th Class).[7] Bandon received the CVO, and Air Marshal Sir Dermot Boyle, Embry's recently appointed successor as AOC-in-C of Fighter Command, received the KCVO.

Boyle, whom Sam had known, albeit not well, in the AMP's Department at the Air Ministry as Director-General of Manning, was to become one of the most significant influences in his future career. He wrote to Sam on the following day:

My dear Sam

I think you possibly know how much I appreciate the extent to which the success of yesterday's Review was due to your efforts and those of your Staff.

2. I fully realized the tremendous load we were putting on you, and as we all knew you would, you rose to the occasion.

3. The day could not have gone better and in fact probably that fact more than anything else will be the greatest compensation for all the hard work and careful organization you have applied to the task for the last couple of months.

4. Again my very heartiest congratulations on the honour which you received from Her Majesty the Queen yesterday.[8]

Sam also received a letter of thanks from the Queen's Assistant Private Secretary, saying that, in addition to enjoying the excellent luncheon, she had been impressed by the mess decorations, with flowers both inside and out, and one from Lord de L'Isle, who was particularly grateful to Sam and Audrey for having looked after his family.

With an undoubted triumph behind him, it was now time for Sam to get back to his day job, running Odiham. Like Tangmere, it housed two squadrons of Meteors, Nos. 54 and 247, commanded respectively by Squadron Leader P. J. Kelly DFC and Squadron Leader H. G. Pattison DFC. Both squadrons were redeployed during the Review but returned as soon as the airfield had been vacated by the aircraft on static display. The pattern of Sam's working life as a station commander resumed, with flying, which had come to a halt as a result of the Review, becoming a regular feature. His right-hand man was the Wing Commander Flying, Denis Crowley-Milling, who had earned a DFC as one of 'The Few' in the Battle of Britain and a bar after being shot down over France and escaping back to the UK via Spain. One regular visitor was Montgomery, who used Odiham frequently for his travels to and from the Continent. In spite of Sam's smoking habit, the field marshal clearly approved of him and sometimes stayed with the Elworthys overnight.

Sam's period of command was a short one, however, as on 1 December he was appointed to succeed 'Zulu' Morris as Commander of the Metropolitan Sector of 11 Group, with promotion to Acting Air Commodore, a rank which he had last held exactly eight years earlier.

The Metropolitan Sector was by some way the largest of the six sectors in Fighter Command at that time and accounted for about 30 per cent of its squadrons, so Sam's appointment there was a measure of the high regard in which he was held by Boyle. By this time, the Cold War was well established, with the Soviet Union a fully-fledged nuclear power. Fighter Command's primary role was thus, once again, what it had been in 1940 and 1941, the interception of enemy bombers, although this time they were jet-powered and carried atomic bombs. The role of the Metropolitan Sector was to protect London and South-East England from attack from the East, its airfields positioned from north of Cambridge to south of London. From north to south they were: Wattisham (257 and 263 Squadrons), Waterbeach (56 and 63 Squadrons), Duxford (64 and 65 Squadrons), North Weald (72, 601 and 604 Squadrons), West Malling (25, 85 and 500 Squadrons) and Biggin Hill (41, 600 and 615 Squadrons). Of the sector's fifteen squadrons, five – 500, 600, 601, 604 and 615 – were manned by pilots from the Royal Auxiliary Air Force, but Sam knew better than anybody the high standards and overall efficiency of their enthusiastic part-time flyers, and was particularly pleased that 600 (City of London) Squadron was numbered amongst them.

At the time of Sam's appointment all the squadrons were equipped with Meteors, except for No. 25, which still had Vampires, which it exchanged for Meteor NF.11s in March 1954. No. 25 and its fellow squadron at West Malling, No. 85, were the only night fighter squadrons until February 1955, when 153 Squadron was re-formed, also at West Malling, and equipped with NF.12s and NF.14s, which by then were replacing the old NF.11s. Subsequently, 64 Squadron at Duxford also converted to Meteor night fighters, whilst 253 Squadron was re-formed at Waterbeach in April 1955 and equipped with De Havilland Venom NF.2s.

One other new aircraft to make an appearance in the sector early in Sam's period of command was the Supermarine Swift, which replaced the Meteors of 56 Squadron in February 1954. This was the RAF's first swept-wing fighter and was ordered as a safeguard against the possible failure of the Hawker Hunter, which was due to enter squadron service for the first time six months later. In the event, it was the Swift which proved to be the disappointment, under-armed and with an inadequate engine and poor control characteristics, which led to a number of bad accidents. It lasted in 56 Squadron for just over a year before being rejected as totally unsuitable in an interceptor role, although a subsequent fighter-reconnaissance variant performed satisfactorily for the RAF in Germany.

Sam's HQ was at none of his operating stations, although his own personal Meteor and the aircraft of the Metropolitan Sector Communications Flight, with its Oxfords, Austers and Chipmunks, were based at North Weald. It was instead located in an underground bunker at Kelvedon Hatch,[9] nine miles from North Weald, between Chipping Ongar and Brentwood. With the threat of a Soviet bomber attack using nuclear weapons, the Government ordered the construction of a large network of underground facilities, not only for radar early warning systems, which were initially based on the Chain Home technology used during the war and subsequently upgraded, but also for plotting and interceptor control by Fighter Command. Nearly eighty of these so-called ROTOR installations were constructed, all those to the east and south of the country deep underground, some of those to the west only partially so. The majority were used for early warning radar, but six acted as Sector Operational Commands for the RAF.

The only visible sign of the bunker was the radio mast and an insignificant bungalow which served as the entrance, from which a 130yd tunnel ran to the bunker itself. The nerve centre was the plotting room, 80ft below the surface and protected by blast doors. There were plant rooms to provide power and keep the air fresh, offices for the staff and living facilities in case the bunker had to be closed up during a nuclear attack. To Sam it was actually quite familiar. Not only did it have many of the characteristics of Bomber Command's 'Hole' at High Wycombe, but he had on a number of occasions visited the equivalent facility at Box, which housed the Southern Sector HQ, and the radar station at Ventnor, constructed on exactly the same principle. Nevertheless, it was not a particularly pleasant environment in which to spend much of his working life, and he took every possible opportunity to get out and about.

Sam flew a great deal during his period of command at the Metropolitan Sector, but the pattern of his flying was quite different from that at Tangmere and Odiham. Whereas previously he had taken part in station and sector exercises in the air, now those exercises required him to be at his underground HQ, controlling what was happening. His flights instead took him to visit not only his more faraway stations, but also the neighbouring sectors, the Central Fighter Establishment at West Raynham and the operational conversion units at Pembrey and Stradishall. One other regular destination was Manston, the home of the 406th Fighter-Bomber Wing of the USAF, with which the Metropolitan Sector frequently co-operated on exercises.

One unusual flight in June 1954 was to visit 601 (County of London) Squadron during its annual fortnight's summer camp, which was being held in Malta. Sam flew initially to Tangmere, refuelled at the French Air Force base at Istres, near Marseilles, and flew on from there to Takali, one of the airfields on Malta. The return flight two days later took in not only Istres but also El Alouina in Tunisia, then a French possession. It was a far cry from Sutton Bridge in 1935!

Sector Exercises took place every month and Group Exercises rather less frequently. Sometimes the former were what were named 'Rats and Terrier' exercises, which pitted the 'rats' – North American F.86 Sabre fighters from Manston – in dogfights against the 'terriers' of the sector's aircraft. Most, however, were air defence exercises, with raids being simulated by Canberras from Bomber Command, which had entered squadron service in 1951, only five years after Sam had been considering their future deployment at the CBE, or B.47 Stratojets from the USAF. These exercises showed up very clearly the inadequacy of the Meteors against jet bombers, which were now able to fly at much the same speed and a greater altitude, an embarrassing hark-back to the early days of the Hart, and later the Blenheim, which had outpaced the fighters of the day when they first went into service. The situation became so dire that the Canberras were required to fly at reduced speeds and altitudes to ease the task of the interceptors.

Salvation, however, was at hand in the shape of the RAF's new fighter, the Hawker Hunter, which began to be introduced into the sector's regular squadrons in September 1954, when 257 Squadron at Wattisham received its first aircraft. The Hunter proved to be one of the most successful fighters in the RAF's history. Although subsonic in level flight, it was appreciably faster than the bombers of the day and was able to carry out interceptions at 48,000ft. Armed with four 30mm Aden canon, it packed more punch than the Meteor and had much more sophisticated communications and navigation systems. Over the next two years, 41, 63, 65, 111, which had replaced 72 Squadron at North Weald, 257 and 263 Squadrons were all equipped with Hunters. There was no night fighter variant, so the Meteor and Venom night fighters remained in service until the introduction of the Gloster Javelin in the late 1950s, whilst the Meteor F.8 continued to equip the RAuxAF squadrons until they were disbanded under the defence cuts of 1957. Sam was allocated his own Hunter in November 1955.

During Sam's tour at the Metropolitan Sector, Audrey and the family moved to Wing House, the sector commander's residence at North Weald.

With Sam now a relatively senior officer, the social aspect of his job was becoming more important, and Audrey was a vital part of this. She invariably shone in such circumstances, able to hold her own with anyone and, moreover, to do so regardless of rank or importance; there was no snobbishness in either of them. In the meantime, the children were growing up fast. Christopher started at prep school during this time, whilst Anthony had gone on to the King's School, Canterbury. There was no family connection with the school, but Audrey had apparently been most impressed by a meeting with the headmaster, Canon Frederick Shirley, on the strength of which he was put down for a place there. Tim had joined the RAF section of the Combined Cadet Force at Radley and Sam was able to take him for local flights in an Auster and a Meteor T.7. Another regular visitor to Wing House was Robin Garran, the eldest son of Peter and Elizabeth Garran, who spent some holidays there whilst his parents were posted abroad, thereby repaying them for having Tim, Anthony and Christopher to stay whilst Sam and Audrey were in Pakistan.

At the end of September 1954 Audrey flew out to New Zealand for her first visit since she and Sam had married, taking Clare with her. Her intention was very specifically to see something of her mother, who had been widowed in 1948, and most of the two months there was spent with her in Auckland. Audrey and Clare returned by ship, arriving back in England just after Christmas.

Sam was continuing to impress his superiors. Shortly before his posting to the Metropolitan Sector, Bandon had been succeeded at 11 Group by Air Vice-Marshal H. L. 'Sam' Patch. The relationship was a cordial one, and after one particular air defence exercise Patch conveyed to Sam an extract from a letter from Boyle:

I have been reading your Group's report on Exercise 'Dividend' and have been struck by the thoroughness and clarity of the report submitted by the Metropolitan Sector Commander.

2. This does not mean that I necessarily agree with all his arguments, but would be glad if you could convey to him my appreciation regarding the excellence of his report.[10]

Dividend was the biggest exercise since the war, involving the whole of Fighter Command and designed specifically to test the defences against nuclear attack. About 6,000 intruder sorties were flown, not only by Bomber Command, but also by the USAF, Flying Training Command and the Fleet Air Arm. Boyle proclaimed it a success; Sam was more sceptical.

On 1 January 1956 Patch succeeded Boyle as AOC-in-C Fighter Command, whilst Boyle moved up to become Chief of the Air Staff. Sam wrote to congratulate the latter and received the following reply:

> Thank you very much indeed for your letter of congratulation and good wishes, which I greatly appreciate.
>
> 2. I would like to take this opportunity to thank you for the magnificent job of work which you have done in Metropolitan Sector, and I am sure that you will find when you look back on your tour in Fighter Command that it has broadened your outlook considerably, and therefore fitted you even better than you were already were, for appointment to higher rank.
>
> 3. Nor will I ever forget the splendid performance you put up at Odiham during the Coronation Review.
>
> 4. Do not work too hard at the I.D.C. Reserve your energies for greater and better things to come, in which with every confidence, I wish you success.[11]

Sam now had a strong supporter at the very top of his profession. Moreover, as the letter indicated, he was about to move on himself.

Chapter 11

Moving Up

Sam did not believe that he was being groomed for high office at the time of his selection to handle the Coronation Review, but there is little doubt that his appointment to command the Metropolitan Sector shortly afterwards was the beginning of just such a process. The next step, selection for study at the Imperial Defence College, confirmed this, and it is not difficult to detect the hand of Dermot Boyle behind it.

The IDC was opened in 1927 in Buckingham Gate on the advice of a Cabinet committee chaired by Winston Churchill, with the objective of instructing senior officers of the armed services in imperial strategy and bringing together those who would subsequently progress to the highest ranks in their respective armed services and the civil service. The initial intake of students included the future Field Marshals Viscount Alanbrooke and Sir Claude Auchinleck. The IDC was closed during the war, but re-opened in 1946 in Seaford House, Belgrave Square, where its successor, the Royal College of Defence Studies, is still situated. From then until the 1990s the commandant was invariably a four-star service officer or a top civil servant, and both General Sir William Slim and Air Chief Marshal Sir John Slessor, the first two post-war commandants, reached the top of their respective services. RAF graduates included Portal, Tedder, and William 'Dickie' Dickson, Boyle's predecessor as CAS and at this time Chairman of the Chiefs of Staff Committee, as well as Boyle himself.

Having handed over command of the Metropolitan Sector to Air Commodore Peter Hamley on 19 December 1955, Sam took some well-earned leave over Christmas before reporting at the Air Ministry on 2 January with his fellow RAF students for an extensive briefing by the Directorate of Staff Training. The course itself opened on 10 January under Admiral the Hon. Sir Guy Russell, a highly distinguished naval officer who had been in command of HMS *Duke of York* when it sank Sam's old bête noire, the *Scharnhorst*, in the Battle of the North Cape in December 1943. The senior RAF instructor was AVM Theodore McEvoy, who was succeeded later in the year by AVM Edmund 'Teddy' Hudleston. In addition to those from the three British armed services and civil service, there were students from Canada, Australia, New Zealand, South Africa, Rhodesia, Ghana, India, Pakistan and the USA. The course thus provided an invaluable opportunity for networking amongst contemporaries who were likely to rise to prominence in later years.

In the words of Fred Rosier, whose later career in the RAF would bring him into close contact with Sam and who attended the IDC in 1957, 'The year at the IDC was meant to be a respite from responsibility: a time when we would broaden our knowledge of world politics and recharge our batteries in preparation for those greater responsibilities which we confidently hoped would be thrust upon us.'[1] This was certainly consistent with Boyle's advice to Sam that he should not work too hard. The year, however, did not turn out to be quite as Sam expected, although it began as planned.

The course was high-powered in terms of the contribution made by both the participants and guests from outside, but it was relatively relaxed in other respects. The students and DS usually wore suits rather than uniform and, except when they were on trips abroad, worked normal business hours from Monday to Friday, with the weekends free. Moreover, it was divided into three terms, with holidays in between. There was the usual problem of accommodation for the Elworthys, but this was neatly solved by Paul and Babs Wright. Paul had joined the Foreign Office in 1951 and had just been posted to The Hague, so they offered Sam and Audrey the use of their own house, Coaters, in Bignor, West Sussex, not far from Tangmere and sufficiently close to London for Sam to commute every day by train from Pulborough. Babs's children by her first marriage, Tim and Pietie Rathbone, were both grown up but visited from time to time, whilst Faith, her daughter by Paul, was at boarding school. It was a convenient arrangement for all.

In addition to lectures by distinguished speakers and syndicate work on specific issues, the course included visits by the students to the three armed services and to industry, a short trip abroad to Germany and a much lengthier one to North America. Embarking on the latter, Sam and his fellow students and members of the DS flew to Ottawa on 1 August. The tour was designed to take them across Canada to the west coast, down into the USA and then over to Washington and other Eastern US locations before returning briefly to Canada. They were due to arrive back in England exactly a month later. However, on 5 August, with the tour barely started, Sam and a number of others were urgently summoned back to the UK.

The reason for this was the Suez Crisis, which had begun with the nationalization of the Suez Canal by President Nasser of Egypt on 26 July, taking the world by surprise and threatening Great Britain's strategic interests in the Middle and Far East. The initial reaction and continuing policy of the Prime Minister, Anthony Eden, was to take military action, a stance which was initially supported by most politicians at Westminster. Furthermore, France was, if anything, even more vigorously in favour, and work began immediately on Operation *Musketeer*, with an Anglo-French planning HQ established in the Montagu House Annex of the War Office. The designated commanders and their staffs began to gather there immediately, with the Army element under Lieutenant General Sir Hugh Stockwell, who had been summoned back from command of I Corps in Germany, bringing much of his corps staff with him, and the Royal Navy under Vice-Admiral Sir Maxwell Richmond.[2]

The RAF element was placed under the command of Sam's good friend Denis Barnett, a fellow New Zealander who, with his wife Pamela, had been a guest of the Elworthys less than two months earlier at the Henley Royal Regatta, during which Tim had rowed for the Radley 1st VIII. Barnett, some five years older than Sam, had worked closely with him at Bomber Command HQ in 1944 and they had served in the Air Ministry at the same time from 1949 to 1951. He had been pulled out of his job as Commandant of the RAF Staff College at Bracknell, largely on the strength of having recently commanded 205 Group, first in Egypt and then, following the agreement to withdraw all British forces from that country in late 1955 and early 1956, in Cyprus. The last RAF station had been handed back to Egypt only three months before the crisis erupted, and Barnett was thus, without question, the most knowledgeable officer about the Egyptian Air Force and its bases.

Two other RAF officers were taken off the IDC course at the same time as Sam to join Barnett's staff, Tom Prickett in charge of Plans and Group Captain Edward Jones heading Operations, whilst Teddy Hudleston left the Directing Staff to become Chief of Staff (Air) to the Allied Supreme Commander, General Sir Charles Keightley, who was appointed on 11 August.

Barnett, Sam and their burgeoning staff started work immediately. The main principles of Operation *Musketeer* were established very quickly. The RAF's objective was very simply the destruction or grounding of the Egyptian Air Force in preparation for Anglo-French landings; Barnett, in a draft of the basic ingredients of the air plan presented to the Chiefs of Staff on 9 August, thought this would take two to three nights. The core of the plan would be the deployment of a large force of Canberras and Valiants flying out of Cyprus and Malta to bomb the Egyptian airfields, but fighter protection would be required, as would transport aircraft for airborne forces. Coordination was vital not only with the land forces, but also with the Royal Navy, whose carrier-borne aircraft would supply much of the ground attack capability against the Egyptian Army.

This was not a happy time for Sam. The Montagu House Annex, constructed deep underground at much the same time and for much the same purpose as the Cabinet War Rooms, was an unattractive environment in which to work, a maze of offices on three floors, with nothing but artificial light so that there was no sense of day or night. The work itself was intense, up to fifteen hours a day with little time off, so that those of the staff who did not live in Central London slept on camp beds in the bunker.

Sam was later to describe it as 'a crazy operation'.[3] Even at his level he had meetings with senior politicians, including the Prime Minister, but mostly with Selwyn Lloyd, the Secretary of State for Foreign Affairs. On one occasion he was ordered by Lloyd to go to see Harold Watkinson, the Minister of Transport and Civil Aviation, in order to answer a query on the movement of shipping through the Mediterranean. When he used the code word for the operation, Watkinson did not have the remotest idea of what he was talking about. The one time he was able to return to Coaters, he was strictly forbidden to talk about what he was working on, but he was heard to say, 'Either I'm raving mad or the Prime Minister is.'[4]

Sam's involvement was brought to an end after little more than a week. On 15 August he became seriously ill, so much so that Barnett ordered him to go to hospital immediately. It became apparent very quickly that his condition was serious enough for him to be unlikely to return for some time, so Prickett moved up to SASO, his role on Plans being taken over by Group Captain Denis 'Splinters' Smallwood, the final IDC student to join Barnett's staff.

Sam's problem was an old one; indeed, it had sprung up initially during the war and he had been living with it ever since. The culprit was a duodenal ulcer, which for some years caused him to be sick every day but which he had been able to tolerate hitherto. Now it had blown up, possibly because it was perforated, and after a period of treatment with drugs failed to cure the condition, it became clear that more radical action was required and Sam underwent surgery. This was entirely successful, restoring him to full health, but it required a long period of hospitalization and convalescence, and it was late November before he was passed fit for return to duty, enabling him to attend the final three weeks at the IDC.

This could not have happened at a better time in Sam's career, as it did not take place during a command appointment. The IDC course, whilst valuable in many respects, had been interrupted anyway, and he had spent enough time on it to graduate with the letters *idc* after his name. Being removed from involvement in *Musketeer* did his longer-term prospects no harm, although, whilst the brief campaign proved to be a political and diplomatic disaster for the UK, from a military perspective it was highly successful, with the RAF performing its role to perfection.

As it turned out, however, *Musketeer* was the direct cause of Sam's next appointment. Barnett had been Commandant at Bracknell for only four months when he was called away to head the RAF element of the operation; had this not happened, he would probably have stayed on for another two or more years, the usual term of appointment. As the air operations of *Musketeer* were not launched until the last day of October, with the parachute and amphibious landings taking place on 5 November and the United Nations ceasefire coming into effect on a gradual basis thereafter, Barnett was in no position to return and, indeed, remained at his post until the end of January 1957. His deputy at the staff college, Air Commodore Roy Faville, had been there for about a year and was given the commandant's job on a temporary basis, with promotion to acting air vice-marshal. He was not, however, considered suitable for the permanent position and an alternative was sought, to be in place by the time the next course opened in January. Sam was readily available and matched the profile required.

The RAF Staff College had been formed at RAF Andover on 1 April 1922 under the command of Air Commodore Robert Brooke-Popham, the personal choice of the then Air Chief Marshal Sir Hugh Trenchard, the 'Father of the RAF'. It was one manifestation of 'Boom' Trenchard's fight for the RAF's independence after the Great War and played a vital role in distinguishing the new service from the Royal Navy and the Army, both of which still had designs on bringing its activities under their control. Its purpose was to provide training for the most promising flight lieutenants and squadron leaders, with a view to preparing them for staff and command appointments. It was closed down in May 1940 but re-opened at Bulstrode Park, near Gerrard's Cross, in early 1942. In 1945 the main part of the staff college was transferred to Bracknell, whilst certain elements, including the training of overseas officers, remained at Bulstrode Park. The latter was subsequently moved back to Andover, which continued to provide more specialist staff training, its commandant holding the rank of air commodore.

Before Sam took up his new appointment he was presented by the Air Ministry with six names as prospective Assistant Commandants and asked to make his choice. To the surprise of all he selected Air Commodore James Gordon-Finlayson, who was regarded as something of a maverick and difficult to control. Like Sam, Gordon-Finlayson was a Cambridge graduate and a barrister who had elected not to practise but to join the RAF. Moreover, he had also been a Blenheim pilot, in his case in the Western Desert and Greece in 1940 and 1941, where he had won the DSO and the DFC and bar, so they had much in common. Sam had met him later in the war, when Gordon-Finlayson was serving at the Air Ministry and they had gone up to Woodford together to look over and fly in the new Avro Lincoln, and subsequently when Gordon-Finlayson was on the Directing Staff at the JSSC. Sam wanted him not because he was reliable – indeed, he was the opposite – but because he had ideas. It turned out to be an excellent partnership.

After an enjoyable leave, some of which was spent with the Kenricks at Blakeshall but which also included one alarming episode when Sam and Clare were trapped on a broken-down Ferris Wheel at Olympia and had to be rescued by the fire brigade, Sam took up his appointment on New Year's Day 1957 and was simultaneously promoted to acting air vice-marshal. No. 47 Course opened at Bracknell two weeks later, with an intake of seventy-four RAF officers, fifty-five of whom were from the General Duties Branch, together with three officers from the Royal Navy and Royal Marines, four from the British Army, seven from Commonwealth Air Forces, four from the USAF and four from the Civil Service, a total of ninety-six students, divided into sixteen syndicates of six each. In addition to Sam and Gordon-Finlayson, the DS numbered twenty-four, composed of three group captains and seventeen wing commanders from the RAF and one officer each from the British Army, Royal Navy, RCAF and USAF. The RAF members of the DS were still substantially veterans of the war and included two Battle of Britain aces, Denis Crowley-Milling, Sam's former Wing Commander Flying at Odiham, and Al Deere, a fellow New Zealander, who, with his wife, were to become regular bridge partners of Sam and Audrey.

The Elworthys moved into the commandant's spacious house, which had been acquired at the time that Bracknell was selected to house the staff college and was called Broad Acres. Sam thought this a terrible name and changed it to Brookham House, an amalgamation of Brooke-Popham, the name of the first commandant. Audrey was in her element there as a hostess and was particularly good at entertaining the numerous distinguished visitors to lunch or dinner, inviting on such occasions both members of the DS and students, with their wives. The house also made a good family home during holidays from school and, in Tim's case, from Cranwell, where he was now a cadet, having decided to follow his father into the RAF.

As Commandant, Sam found himself in an unparalleled position for one of his rank in terms of his exposure to the great and the good. Visitors to the college in the first year alone included the CAS (Boyle), the VCAS (Hudleston), the Air Member for Supply and Organization (AM Sir John Whitley), the Secretary of State for Air (George Ward), the CIGS (Field Marshal Sir Gerald Templer), the First Sea Lord (Admiral of the Fleet Earl Mountbatten), the AOC-in-Cs of Fighter, Bomber and Transport Command (respectively ACM Sir Thomas Pike, ACM Sir Harry Broadhurst and Sam's old friend, AM Sir Andrew 'Square' McKee), the Commandants of the Royal Naval Staff College at Greenwich and the Army Staff College at Camberley, the Director of the British Employers Confederation and the General Secretary of the Trades Union Congress. Those in the next two years were of similar quality and importance.

One other lecturer whom Sam knew well by this time was Montgomery, still Deputy Supreme Commander of NATO; the frequency of his visits, some said, was influenced by the fact that he used to receive a brace of pheasants when they were in season!

It was not entirely one way. Sam himself delivered a lecture to both of Bracknell's fellow staff colleges on 'The Place of Air Power in Modern Strategy', which he was to repeat in the following years there and at similar overseas institutions. He developed a particularly good relationship with Major General Nigel Poett, a distinguished airborne soldier during the war and now his opposite number at Camberley, who would go on to very senior appointments in his own service.

As it only lasted for a year, the course at Bracknell was highly intensive, comprising lectures, not only by visitors but also by the DS and the students themselves, syndicate work and visits. The lectures covered a wide range of subjects, including the RAF Home and Overseas Commands, the organization of the Royal Navy and the British Army, the forces of the Soviet Bloc, the USAF, British defence policy, scientific advances and intelligence. There was an extensive menu of exercises for the students to work on in syndicates, comprising, inter alia, appreciations, staff papers, letters, reports, signal messages, orders and instructions. Visits took place within the UK to the staff colleges at Greenwich and Camberley, with which joint study weeks were held, and to the sister staff college at Andover, the RAF Technical College at Quigley, the RAF College at Cranwell, Bomber Command stations, naval units at Portland and elsewhere and the USAF, as well as to aircraft manufacturers and sub-contractors.

Sam participated in some of the visits, one of which began less than two weeks after the beginning of his first term. Unusually, this one comprised only himself and six members of the DS on a lecture tour of the USA and Canada, his first experience of both countries other than his interrupted visit to Canada during the IDC course. Flying via Paris on 26 January, the tour began in Washington, before going on for four days to the Air Command and Staff College at Maxwell Air Force Base near Montgomery, Alabama, and then for another five days at the RCAF Staff College in Armour Heights, Toronto, both of which provided valuable connections for the future. The second overseas tour in which Sam participated in 1957 was by both DS and students to Allied Air Forces Central Europe, beginning with its HQ at Fontainebleau and moving on to various other locations in Germany and the Netherlands. The C-in-C of AAFCE was traditionally a RAF officer, who at the time was ACM Sir George Mills.[5]

All this might seem very intense, but it was in fact a fairly relaxed period of Sam's career. There were plenty of social occasions, some of which were at the Staff College itself, which laid on an Annual Summer Garden Party attended by the members of the Air Council and all the Home AOC-in-Cs as well as by past commandants, a Summer Ball, an End of Course Ball, a Mess Cocktail Party and a number of dining-in nights. However, Sam and Audrey were still able to entertain friends and, during the holidays, to visit them. Sam was appointed a council member of both the Royal United Services Institute and the RAF Benevolent Fund and joined the committee of the RAF Rowing Club. He even found time to play both golf and tennis.

Sam spent his first year at Bracknell learning how to run the college. He had very little input into the curriculum for 1957, but by the end of that year his influence was already being felt. This was certainly the conclusion of Mountbatten, who wrote after his own visit to the college:

I have given a number of lectures over the years at Bracknell and I was struck by a change in the atmosphere and approach during question time by the present Course.

Howes,[6] with whom I discussed the lecture afterwards, told me he noticed exactly the same thing. At first we thought it might be due to a different composition of the Course, but on reflection it must be due to a change in leadership and direction.

The result was that the questions I was asked were noticeably more broadminded, higher level and understanding than in the past and shewed [sic] an notable appreciation of the problems of the other services.

I shall mention this to the C.A.S. when I see him at the Chiefs of Staff Meeting this afternoon, as I do feel that the other Services should express appreciation of what you have evidently brought about.[7]

Whilst Mountbatten's views were not always respected by his colleagues from the other services, his report to Boyle would have done Sam's prospects no harm at all. Moreover, Mountbatten himself now had his eye on Sam.

In the following year Sam thought that he knew enough to be able to make some alterations and improvements to the course, although the basic framework had to remain the same. It is clear from Mountbatten's comments, however, that it was not only these, but also Sam's overall leadership, which were making the difference. He was particularly concerned about the workload of the DS and arranged for them to be relieved of setting and marking promotion papers. As far as the students were concerned, there was an improvement in the assessments of those from the RAF over the period and a particularly marked improvement amongst the naval and military students: on the other hand, the standard of the majority of the students from the Commonwealth and the USAF and civil service was below that expected of them, almost certainly the result of poor selection rather than poor teaching.

During 1958 Sam went once again on the tours of North America and Europe, but in the summer holiday of that year he also visited New Zealand in a personal capacity. It was the first time that he had been there since 1946. Although his parents had been frequent visitors to the UK in the post-war years, Sam may have decided to go in the knowledge that he would not able to join them for their golden wedding anniversary, which was to take place that October, whilst it would also enable him to catch up with other members of his large family. He took advantage of an 'indulgence' passage with the RAF, which enabled service personnel to take up empty seats on Transport Command aircraft when they were available. The disadvantage was a slow journey relative to a commercial airline, due to having to make overnight stops on the way: Sam left London on the evening of 23 July and only arrived at Whenuapai five days later. He spent most of his first week with his parents at their house, Ringstead, near Havelock North, where they were joined by his brother Tony, before moving on to his sister Di's home at Ngaio-iti. On 7 August he flew down to Christchurch and drove on from there to Gordons Valley. The next few days were spent visiting relatives around Timaru and being taken on a tour of Gordons Valley by the manager, Robin Johnston, who had succeeded his father Bob in 1955. Sam then returned to Christchurch for more family reunions, notably with his cousin John, before flying back to the North Island for further meetings and meals with friends and relations and a courtesy call on the Air Department. After another week at Ringstead he finally left New Zealand on 22 August, travelling via Singapore and Karachi, where he spent a whole day renewing acquaintances, and eventually arriving back at Stansted on 27 August.

Having learnt and achieved much during his first two years at Bracknell, Sam felt that he would be freewheeling professionally if he stayed there much longer, although he was still enjoying himself. He was therefore both delighted and surprised to be told by Boyle that his next appointment, to take effect in November 1959, would be as Deputy Chief of the Air Staff, bringing with it promotion to acting air marshal. He would, moreover, be leaving Bracknell before the end of August, handing over temporary command to Gordon-Finlayson and spending the next three months as a supernumerary at the Air Ministry, preparing himself for the job.

First, however, he had to endure an interview with Duncan Sandys, the Minister of Defence, who insisted on vetting all higher appointments. Sam had encountered Sandys as a boy and his mother had been a bridesmaid at Sandys' mother's wedding, but he did not know him well. The interview was not a happy one. Sandys behaved as if they had never met and immediately asked Sam for his views on the nuclear deterrent. These Sam gave, only to be told that he was absolutely wrong. He held his ground, and an argument developed, with the two men at cross purposes throughout the interview. After it had finished, Sam went immediately to see Boyle to say that he might as well forget about the appointment, but much to his surprise it was waved through.

The post of DCAS was created in 1920, in the early days of an independent RAF. In its first two decades the holder had been effectively what the title implied, the deputy to the CAS, although the latter focused on the outward-looking face of the service, whilst the DCAS dealt with its internal affairs, other than those which came under the auspices of the Air Member for Personnel (AMP) and the Air Member for Supply and Organization (AMSO), who handled, respectively, human resources and logistics. In 1940, however, with the extra demands imposed by the war, a new office was created, that of the Vice Chief of the Air Staff, and it was the VCAS who became effectively the deputy to the CAS, with the DCAS regarded, if anything, as the most junior member of the serving officers on the Air Council. The post had nevertheless been held by some notable RAF officers, including Ludlow-Hewitt, Harris, Bottomley, Walmsley and Baker. Perhaps most importantly, it had also been occupied from 1953 to 1956 by Tom Pike, currently the AOC-in-C Fighter Command but already designated as Boyle's successor as CAS from the beginning of 1960.

After the war the responsibilities of the VCAS and the DCAS became more clearly defined, and by the time of Sam's appointment the former was responsible for Operations and Intelligence, whilst the latter dealt with Operational Requirements, Training and Signals. It was in the field of Operational Requirements that most of the work lay, and it was to bring Sam up to speed on this that he was to spend nearly three months learning about a highly complex subject.

The RAF had changed dramatically in the fourteen years since the end of the war. For all combat aircraft, jet propulsion had replaced piston engines by the early 1950s, although the latter and turbo props were to remain widely in use for transport, maritime reconnaissance and *ab initio* training. Even the first generation of jet aircraft had been entirely replaced by the time of Sam's appointment as DCAS, with both the Hunter and the Javelin also facing retirement over the next few years. The first truly supersonic British jet fighter, the English Electric Lightning, was due to enter service within a year. Perhaps even more significantly, however, there had come a realization that even very fast aircraft would not be able to intercept every enemy bomber and that an additional measure was needed to bolster the UK's defences in depth in the shape of guided missiles. The first squadron of Fighter Command to be equipped with Bristol Bloodhound missiles rather than aircraft was No. 264 in December 1958. Furthermore, the Thor intermediate range missile, manufactured in the United States, entered service with 77 Squadron of Bomber Command in August 1958 to supplement the V-Bombers.

The whole future of the RAF came under scrutiny in Sandys' Defence White Paper in 1957. This proposed amongst other things, such as the disbandment of the RAuxAF,[8] that there should be no further development of interceptor aircraft, but that they should in due course be entirely replaced by missile systems. Boyle fought hard against this, with considerable success, not only saving the Lightning but effectively ensuring that aircraft remained at the core of the country's defences against airborne incursions. In the meantime, the newly created strategic V-Bomber force remained intact, although considerable thought was being given to a replacement for the Canberra in its tactical bomber and reconnaissance roles.

Sandys also proposed the rationalization of the British aircraft industry. This led in due course to the creation of the British Aircraft Corporation through the merger of English Electric, Bristol and Vickers-Armstrong and the acquisition by Hawker Siddeley, which already owned Armstrong Whitworth, Avro and Gloster, of De Havilland, Blackburn and Folland. Westland became focused entirely on helicopters, and of the major fixed-wing aircraft manufacturers only Handley Page remained independent.

It was to come up to speed with these developments and to understand how the aircraft industry might serve the RAF's requirements in the future that Sam began a programme of meetings with the leading directors and managers of the companies concerned. After briefings by the current DCAS, Air Marshal Sir Geoffrey Tuttle, and the Defence Research Policy Committee, which reported to the Minister of Defence and the Chiefs of Staff on new technical developments, he began his programme with the Royal Aircraft Establishment at Farnborough, which was particularly concerned with the design and testing of missiles. Thereafter he had meetings with Vickers, Handley Page, English Electric, A. V. Roe, Bristol and Hawker Siddeley, together with Rolls-Royce, one of the largest sub-contractors through its aero engine division, and the Atomic Weapons Research Establishment.

His programme then took him on a round-the-world tour, beginning on 2 October in Canada, where he re-established his contacts with the RCAF and visited Avro Canada, moving on to Washington after five days. There he met General Curtis LeMay, the USAF Vice-Chief of the Air Staff, before embarking on a coast-to-coast tour. His first visit was to the Air Research and Development Command, the USAF's primary centre for the development of new aircraft and missiles; it was followed by a flight to Florida to see the ARDC's Air Force Missile Test Centre at Patrick Air Force Base, and then a visit to Cape Canaveral, where missiles and other rockets were tested for both the USAF and the National Aeronautics and Space Administration

(NASA). It was here that the Thor missile proving trials had been carried out.

Sam then flew from Patrick AFB to Wright-Patterson AFB at Dayton, Ohio, which housed a number of development units as well as one of the air defence control centres for NORAD (North American Aerospace Defense Command). On 15 October he flew from Dayton to Seattle and then on to Los Angeles. Whilst on the West Coast he visited three of the major US defence contractors. The most significant of these at the time was Douglas, the main contractor for the Thor and subsequently for the Skybolt air-launched nuclear missile, which was also expected to be deployed by the RAF, but Sam also visited the facilities and met senior executives of North American and Lockheed. At the time it was the policy of the British Government to buy British for military aircraft, but the contacts made by Sam would prove invaluable when change came in the mid-to-late 1960s.

Sam flew from San Francisco to Auckland on 23 October, arriving there two days later after crossing the International Date Line. He spent a week in New Zealand, almost all of it on official business, although he managed to see some of his family on the North Island. On 2 November he flew from Auckland to Sydney for a week in Australia, much of it spent at the Weapons Research Establishment at Salisbury, South Australia, and the Woomera Rocket Range, which had been the testing ground for the Bloodhound and was now conducting trials on the Blue Steel air-to-ground guided missile, which would begin to equip Victor and Vulcan squadrons in the early 1960s. It was also gearing up to test the Blue Streak missile, although this was later scrapped in favour of the longer-range US Skybolt.

On 9 November Sam left Sydney by BOAC to fly to Karachi, where he spent a whole day, catching a Qantas flight back to London, where he arrived on 11 November. Four days later he assumed his appointment as DCAS.

The DCAS had two roles, the first as a member of the Air Council, which was responsible for taking collective decisions and providing advice to ministers on all matters concerning the RAF, the second as a senior member of the Department of the Chief of the Air Staff. The political and civil service members of the Air Council were the Secretary of State for Air, George Ward, always known as 'Geordie', and the Permanent Under-Secretary, Sir Maurice Dean. Tom Pike relieved Dermot Boyle as CAS at the beginning of 1960, whilst the other RAF members were the AMP, AM Sir Arthur McDonald, the AMSO, ACM Sir Walter Dawson, followed in April 1960 by ACM Sir Walter Merton, and the VCAS, Teddy Hudleston.

Pike was a very different character to the extrovert Boyle and was described by Henry Probert, the long-serving Head of the Air Historical Branch, as 'a somewhat remote, austere man. But for those who knew him well, he was a sensitive, delightful companion.'[9] Sam knew him from his visits to Bracknell whilst AOC-in-C Fighter Command, but not well, as they had never served in related appointments. It would seem from future developments in Sam's career that there was at the very least a mutual respect, but perhaps not the warm relationship which he had enjoyed with Boyle.

Sam's own immediate subordinates were three Assistant Chiefs of the Air Staff, all of whom he knew from his time at the Metropolitan Sector of Fighter Command. John Worrall, the ACAS (Training) had commanded the neighbouring Eastern Sector of 12 Group, whilst Robert Bateson, the ACAS (Operational Requirements) and Geoffrey Eveleigh, the ACAS (Signals) had been Station Commanders at Duxford and North Weald respectively.

As Sam had been expecting, it was Operational Requirements which was to take up the largest part of his time. This was, in many ways, the most forward-thinking part of the air staff, charged with looking at what the RAF would require many years ahead. However, it also dealt on a day-to-day basis with the minutiae of specifications, prototype evaluations, ordering and commissioning of all new aircraft and missile systems, working alongside the Ministry of Supply, with which the Ministry of Aircraft Production had been amalgamated. Of all the specifications under consideration during Sam's tenure, the most time-consuming was General Operational Requirement 339, originally issued to manufacturers in March 1957, which called for a new bomber to deliver tactical nuclear weapons, bombs or rockets and to engage in photo reconnaissance at low and medium levels at a speed of Mach 1.2, with either VTOL (Vertical Take-off and Landing) or STOL (Short Take-off and Landing) capability. This aircraft would be an immediate replacement for the Canberra and in due course possibly also for the V-Bombers.

A number of manufacturers responded with proposals, and a contract, with a number of amendments to the original specification, including Mach

2 capability at high altitude, was awarded in January 1959 to Vickers, with English Electric in a subordinate role. The new plane was called the TSR-2 (Tactical Strike and Reconnaissance Mach 2). This was a highly ambitious project from the outset and, as the two manufacturers had to refine the designs set out in their responses to the specification with a view to having aircraft ready for testing in 1963, it required a great deal of involvement by Sam and his colleagues. Sam, with his experience of the Central Bomber Establishment in 1946/7, when the Canberra first appeared on the drawing board, was well suited to dealing with the complex issues which arose.

Whilst Sam was serving at the Air Ministry, he and Audrey bought a flat on Lyndhurst Terrace in Hampstead, from where there was a relatively short commute to the Air Ministry. It also proved to be highly convenient for their very active social life. By this time Christopher had moved from prep to public school, but the latter was neither Radley nor King's Canterbury. On this occasion, as with Anthony before him, Audrey had been highly impressed by a meeting with a headmaster, this time Tony Chenevix-Trench of Bradfield, so Christopher was packed off there. Anthony himself left school in the summer of 1958 and joined the tea department of the large trading company, Harrisons & Crosfield, staying with Sam and Audrey at Bracknell before moving into London, both living at and rowing for the London Rowing Club, as, like Tim, he shared Sam's love of the sport. He was a member of the LRC's crew at Henley in both 1958 and 1959.

Sam, who had become a Companion of the Bath in the New Year's Honours of 1960, possibly by way of a parting recommendation from Boyle, much enjoyed his time as DCAS. He learned a great deal about the higher governance of the RAF, found his job challenging but interesting, and expanded his list of senior contacts, not only within the RAF but also in business, government and overseas. He did, however, say later that he upset his colleagues on one or two issues, possibly because he was never backward in expressing an opinion, even if it was an unpopular one. He was referring in particular to one paper which he wrote for Boyle early in his appointment.

By the end of 1958 Sam's own flying days were over. He had flown very rarely whilst Commandant at Bracknell, and then only to use one of the college's Chipmunks to fly from RAF White Waltham. During the War Harris had always been opposed to senior officers in Bomber Command flying on operations, a policy with which Sam had agreed. Sam now went a step further, suggesting that they should not fly themselves at all, as they were too valuable. Whilst he was at the Metropolitan Sector, the then CAS, Dickie Dickson, who maintained that it was good for morale that everyone should see that their senior officers still flew, had kept a couple of Vampires for his own use at North Weald, each with the five stars of his rank emblazoned on its side. Whenever he flew from there on an inspection, Sam, who was far from confident about Dickson's flying ability, made sure that he was present and would strap in the CAS himself and set the controls trimmed for take-off. He always felt that if anything went wrong Dickson would not have a clue what to do, and it worried him greatly. With this in mind and in his capacity as the member of the Air Council responsible for safety, he wrote a paper for Boyle suggesting that senior officers should no longer fly themselves and maintaining that, rather than gaining respect from junior officers, those air officers who flew were actually losing their respect for taking unnecessary risks. This did not go down particularly well with Boyle, who flew his own Canberra on every possible occasion, although Sam admitted that he, at least, kept in practice.

Sam was fully expecting to be DCAS for about three years. It therefore came as a considerable surprise in the summer of 1960, after a mere eight months in the job, when he was selected without any warning to relieve Sam Patch as C-in-C British Forces Arabian Peninsula.

Chapter 12

Vantage

In July 1959 Earl Mountbatten became Chief of the Defence Staff in succession to 'Dickie' Dickson. Dickson, the first CDS, had originally been appointed in October 1955 as Chairman of the Chiefs of Staff Committee and Chief of Staff to the Minister of Defence, but the title had changed in July 1958 as the result of a White Paper published by Duncan Sandys on 'The Central Organisation of Defence'. This set up a new Defence Board under the Minister of Defence, consisting of the three service ministers, the CDS, the three service chiefs of staff and a Permanent Under-Secretary.

The changes to the way in which the whole apparatus of Defence was handled were modest at the time, but they formed part of the longer-term objective of Sandys and Mountbatten, which was to unify the three armed services. This was supported to some extent by Dickson, but strongly resisted by Boyle, the CAS, and Field Marshal Sir Gerald Templer, the CIGS. The Prime Minister, Harold Macmillan, was against wholesale integration, which he believed would be highly disruptive, but he was not opposed to arrangements being made along such lines at a more local level. The elevation of Mountbatten, the retirement of Boyle and Templer, replaced respectively by Pike and General Sir Francis Festing, the latter a distinguished soldier but a neophyte in Whitehall, and the appointment of a close friend of Mountbatten's, Admiral Sir Charles Lambe, to succeed him as First Sea Lord, meant that there was little opposition to such initiatives on the Chiefs of Staff Committee.

Denied unification on a grand scale, Mountbatten turned overseas, where there would be much less controversy. The first tri-service command was set up in Aden in October 1959 as HQ British Forces Arabian Peninsula. Since the interwar period the RAF had been the most prominent of the three services in the area, with the responsibility of keeping the peace in

Aden itself and the Aden Protectorate, and thus it was a RAF officer, Sam Patch, who was appointed as Commander-in-Chief, with a subordinate two-star officer in command of each of the three services. Two of them, Air Vice-Marshal David Lee and Major General Bobby Bray, already had their HQs in Aden. The Royal Navy, however, historically the strongest of the three services in what was then called the Persian Gulf, argued that it should retain its HQ in Bahrain. This had hitherto been under the command of a Senior Naval Officer, who did not hold flag rank, but the appointment was upgraded with the appointment of Rear Admiral Fitzroy Talbot as Flag Officer Arabian Sea and Persian Gulf.

In the summer of 1960 Patch fell ill, to the extent that he became unable to perform his duties and was compelled to retire not long afterwards. It was important that a successor should be appointed as quickly as possible and it was accepted that he should come from the RAF. As it was a tri-service command, however, and thus under the direct control of the CDS, Pike was invited to propose a candidate on the clear understanding that he would have to be approved by Mountbatten. Sam always believed that this had duly happened, but that Mountbatten had rejected the officer concerned, of whose identity Sam was unaware. As he was to say subsequently:

> If it hadn't been for Mountbatten I'd never have got where I did. It was he – and he alone – who sent me out to be Commander-in-Chief of the Middle East. He, and he alone, against the advice of the then CAS and everyone else.[1]

However, it seems that the story may have been somewhat different. The alternative version of events is that Pike's choice fell initially on Teddy Hudleston, a highly capable officer who was a good friend of Sam's and his close colleague as VCAS. Hudleston, however, was experiencing serious marriage problems at the time, and his wife, when told about the posting to Aden, flatly refused to go. After considering the implications of this, Hudleston turned down the appointment, recommending that Sam should go in his stead. Pike accepted the recommendation and put it to Mountbatten, who had not only admired Sam at Bracknell but had followed his career subsequently and approved of his work as DCAS. Mountbatten accepted the recommendation without hesitation, and Sam was duly informed of his new appointment.[2]

Whichever account is the correct one, it is clear that it was in Mountbatten's interest for Sam to believe that it was the first; indeed, Sam always attributed this immense boost in his career to the CDS. Either way, Sam stepped down as DCAS on 18 July and left by air for Aden eleven days later. In between, he had numerous briefing meetings, including with representatives of the other two services, culminating in an appearance before the Chiefs of Staff Committee. He had met Patch for dinner some two months previously and already knew something of the background.

Sam's new command was geographically vast. His directive from the Chiefs of Staff defined the operational area as the Aden Colony and Protectorate, the Sultanate of Muscat and Oman, the Trucial Sheikhdoms, the Sheikhdoms of Bahrain and Kuwait, the Arabian Sea and the Persian Gulf, plus East Africa for the purpose of air operations only. The area of more general interest covered in particular the countries in the Horn of Africa. The strategic aims were the security of the oil producing areas in the Persian Gulf, the security of bases and sea and air communications, the security against attack on British territories and protectorates and territories with special treaty relationships and support for the Central Treaty Organization (CENTO), of which the United Kingdom was a member.

At the heart of the command was Aden itself, since the mid-nineteenth century a key staging-post of the British Empire by virtue of its excellent harbour. It retained its strategic importance as a Crown Colony after the Second World War, serving both as a bunkering port between Europe and South and East Asia for ships travelling through the Suez Canal and as an air staging post. RAF Khormaksar was the busiest RAF station in the world, handling both internal movements and staging. At the time of Sam's arrival no fewer than five squadrons were based there, No. 8 with Venoms but about to re-equip with Hunters, No. 37 with Avro Shackletons, used primarily for maritime reconnaissance but with a bombing capability, No. 78 with Twin Pioneers for local communications and light transport work requiring short take-offs and landings, No. 84 with Blackburn Beverleys for heavier transport work and Bristol Sycamore helicopters for army communications, air ambulance work and search and rescue, and No. 233 with Vickers Valettas and Douglas Dakotas for longer-distance communications. There was also a large RAF hospital providing facilities for all three services.

The Army was the next best represented service in Aden, with two armoured regiments in the colony at any one time, subject to fairly frequent rotation. When Sam arrived, these were the Royal Dragoons and the Queen's Own Hussars, equipped respectively with tanks and armoured cars. Both were to be relieved before very long, the former by the 3rd Carabiniers, the latter by the 11th Hussars. There was also an infantry battalion of the Royal Highland Fusiliers. The Royal Navy had a shore establishment HMS *Sheba*, but no warships were permanently based there, although there were frequent visits. However, 45 Royal Marine Commando had arrived in April 1960, for what would turn out to be a seven-year stay, and took the primary responsibility for internal security in Aden itself.

The Army was also responsible for the Aden Protectorate Levies of four rifle battalions, whose HQ was in Khormaksar but the bulk of whose forces was deployed in garrisons in the Eastern and Western Protectorates, from which they established smaller outposts and mounted regular patrols, often supplied from the air. Primarily responsible for all internal security in the Protectorates and the defence of the external frontiers, it was armed with nothing more substantial than mortars and occasionally called on the RAF and the Army for more significant support. Following the creation of the South Arabian Federation in 1961, the APL changed its name to the Federal Regular Army. To complicate matters further, there was also the Federal National Guard in the recently established Federation of Arab Emirates of the South within the Western Protectorate, the Hadhrami Bedouin Legion in the Eastern Protectorate, under the control of the Adviser and Resident Agent, and lightly armed paramilitary forces maintained by the individual rulers.

Bahrain was the other main base in the command area and was the 'home' port for the Royal Navy, whose HQ was in a shore establishment, HMS *Jufair*. Three frigates were based in Bahrain, although one or even two might be away at any time. There was also an amphibious warfare squadron, consisting of an HQ ship, HMS *Meon*, itself a converted frigate, two tank landing ship (LSTs), one of which was operated by the War Department, and three tank landing craft (LCTs). One of the LSTs carried permanently a half-squadron of tanks from one of the armoured regiments in Aden, whilst the other was used for bringing up replacements on a six-monthly rota. The army was only modestly represented in Bahrain, whilst internal security in the Trucial States was conducted by the British-officered Trucial Oman Scouts. RAF Bahrain (later RAF Muharraq) was mainly a staging post, but it also housed 152 Squadron, flying Twin Pioneers. Like RAF Sharjah in the Trucial States, the airfield was shared with commercial airlines.

Sam's other direct responsibility in the Arabian Peninsula arose in respect of the Sultanate of Muscat and Oman, an independent state but one with which Great Britain had certain treaty commitments, notably the provision of a number of officers for the Sultan's armed forces and of men and equipment for a very small air force. In addition, Great Britain had a 99-year lease on the island of Masirah, on which an airfield had been constructed, and the use of another airfield at Salalah on the coast of Oman, close to the Aden Protectorate border.

In addition to being directly responsible for air operations in East Africa, Sam had another interest there. This was the theatre reserve, which was based in Kenya in the shape of 24 Infantry Brigade Group, comprising the 2nd Battalion Coldstream Guards, the 1st Battalion The King's Regiment and the 1st Battalion The Royal Inniskilling Fusiliers, together with supporting artillery and engineers, all under the command of Brigadier Derek Horsford. There was much opportunity for confusion here, since the GOC East Africa, Major General Dick Goodwin, was in command of land forces in the area. The solution was to make him responsible for all internal security and local defence and for the activities of the King's African Rifles, but to act as Sam's subordinate in the event of any outside threat to British territories in the region and in any major land force operations. As it turned out, both Sam and Goodwin were men of eminent good sense who got on well together, so no friction arose. Sam, in the meantime, became a member of the East African Defence Committee.

He was, however, through his subordinate AOC, in operational command of the RAF in East Africa. The principal station was RAF Eastleigh, on the outskirts of Nairobi, which housed 21 Squadron, operating Twin Pioneers, 30 Squadron, with Blackburn Beverlys, and 208 Squadron, which was about to exchange its Venoms for Hunters.

Sam and Audrey arrived in Aden on 29 July in a Handley Page Hastings, a spacious and comfortable, albeit rather slow, four-engined aircraft, which was to be his personal transport, other than on short journeys, for the duration of his tour. He was accompanied not only by Audrey and by Christopher and Clare, who were in the middle of their summer holiday, but also by his newly appointed aide-de-camp, George Norrie. This was the first time that Sam had been accorded the privilege of an ADC, and he was to have one for the rest of his career. Norrie was the son of a distinguished general of the Second World War, Lieutenant General Lord Norrie, who had been Governor-General of New Zealand from 1952 to 1957, and it may be because of this connection that he was selected. Sam had decided that his ADC should come from one of the services other than the RAF, and Norrie was an officer in the 11th Hussars, which was due to arrive shortly in the colony. His job was essentially to smooth Sam's path at a personal level, by supervising the staff in his residence, making travel arrangements, ensuring that the C-in-C was well briefed on all those whom he would encounter, meeting and greeting the many visitors, making sure that they were well looked after and even taking their wives shopping! Norrie lived in the officers' club at Tarshyne but had an office close to Sam's in the HQ building.

Sam's office was in the same corridor as those of David Lee and Bobby Bray, so that they could use this proximity to engender the greatest possible co-operation between their services. Talbot was still resisting being moved from Bahrain, but was a frequent visitor. In addition to his ADC, Sam had two other members on his personal staff, the Head of Secretariat, Commander Brown of the Royal Navy, primarily charged with organizing, recording and following through the meetings between the senior officers, and a Personal Staff Officer, initially Squadron Leader Philip Lagesen, followed in August 1962 by Squadron Leader Don Arnott, who handled the military aspects of the office. At a lower level, but vital to his heavy schedule, was his driver, Sergeant 'Ginger' Herbert, who invariably delivered him on time for any appointment.

After his military subordinates, Sam's immediate priority was to establish good relationships with his opposite numbers on the civil side. In Aden itself this was Sir William Luce, the Governor and Commander-in-Chief, an Arabist who had had a highly distinguished career in the Sudan Political Service, beginning in 1930 and ending with the independence of Sudan in 1956. His familiarity with the Arabs had stood him well in Southern Arabia, where the politics of and relationships between the Colony of Aden, the states of the Protectorate and the Kingdom of Yemen were, to say the least, highly complex. He was in the last months of his appointment as Governor but was of inestimable help in easing the path of the Elworthys, with whom he and his wife, Margaret, were to become great friends. Margaret Luce and Audrey shared one particular characteristic, in that they were acute observers of people and places, as the former was to record in her diaries, subsequently published, and the latter in her private record of the various journeys which she and Sam undertook.

It was vital that Sam should get round the other areas within his command as quickly as possible. He flew to Nairobi on a two-day visit on 8 August, staying with the Governor of Kenya, Sir Patrick Renison, meeting the army commanders, Goodwin and Horsford, and inspecting 24 Brigade and RAF Eastleigh. On 16 August he carried out a similar two-day visit to Bahrain to meet Talbot and the Political Resident in the Persian Gulf, Sir George Middleton, who was responsible for British interests in the area. Through political agents in the major sheikhdoms Middleton also handled their external affairs, whilst the rulers themselves dealt with internal matters. In contrast to Luce, and although the personal relationship was perfectly cordial, Sam found himself completely at odds with Middleton on matters of policy, finding that the Political Resident held the view that the British Armed Forces were 'an embarrassment to Her Majesty's Government'.[3]

His next visit was more encouraging. In mid-October, accompanied by Audrey and following visits to Bahrain, Abu Dhabi, Dubai and Sharjah, he flew to Muscat and Oman, where he called on Sultan Said. The two men got on exceptionally well and the Sultan invited Sam to become Inspector-General of his armed forces. At his first inspection he discovered that it would take place with the troops in the position of 'present' throughout, with rifles held in front of them. When he stopped to talk to a soldier, however, the man would immediately ground his rifle and shake hands! Sam spoke no Arabic, but many of the soldiers were Baluchis from Pakistan and he was able to use the few words of Urdu which he had picked up there, much to the admiration of the Sultan.

Bill Luce's term as Governor of Aden, extended once, came to an end in October 1960. To Sam's pleasure and relief, he learnt that Luce would be succeeding Middleton as Political Resident Persian Gulf. Sam knew that he would see him frequently, although he had no idea at the time of how intense their relationship would become in the following summer. Luce's successor was Sir Charles Johnston, an unusual choice as he was a member of the Diplomatic rather than the Colonial Service. He was serving as British Ambassador to Jordan, and it was agreed that Sam and Audrey would fly up to Amman in the Hastings on 22 October, staying at the Embassy for two nights for a visit to Jerusalem and the Dead Sea and an audience with King Hussein, and then bring the Johnstons back to Aden. Thus began another strong friendship, between the Elworthys and Johnston and his wife, Natasha. The latter's father was a member of the Bagration family, which had ruled Georgia from the Middle Ages until the early nineteenth century, and her mother belonged to the Russian Royal Family. There were more than enough problems in Aden for Johnston to deal with following his arrival, but they were not, at this time, of a military nature, so Sam was not drawn into them in a big way. Instead, his attention was diverted to a much more likely potential scene of conflict.

Since 1899 the Sheikhdom of Kuwait had been a British Protectorate, originally to prevent its formal annexation by the Ottoman Empire, which claimed it as part of the *casa*, or province, of Basra. Kuwait was already an important entrepôt between the Near East and India, but its fortunes were changed by the discovery of significant reserves of oil in 1938, although the war prevented them from being exploited at the time. From the late 1940s onwards these were developed by the Kuwait Oil Company, of which a predecessor of British Petroleum owned 50 per cent. The country was thus both rich and strategically important, and by 1960 it was providing a significant percentage of Great Britain's oil imports. It was also keen to assert complete political independence, to which the British Government was wholly agreeable. The only issue between the sides was the extent to which the British were prepared to defend Kuwait subsequently. This was duly resolved, and on 19 June 1961, in an Exchange of Letters between

Kuwait and Great Britain, the full independence of the former was declared, whilst the latter agreed to come to its assistance if requested to do so.

Over the years before this a number of plans had been produced on possible British military intervention in Kuwait, and shortly after his arrival in Aden Sam was ordered to produce a new Reinforced Theatre Plan in the light of the move towards independence and of the forces which would be available in the immediate future. In consultation with his service commanders, he and his staff not only drew up Plan *Vantage*, which first saw the light of day in November 1960 and was updated thereafter in minor respects to meet changing circumstances, but also designed a tri-service training regime to implement it. *Vantage* had two objectives, to deter any threat to Kuwait from outside the country, with the focus specifically on Iraq, and to provide internal security should this be requested by the Emir, Sheikh Abdullah Al-Salim Al-Sabah.

The major problem was distance. No British forces were to be maintained in Kuwait itself. The nearest elements of all three services were in Bahrain, 225 miles away by air or sea, whilst Aden was over 1,500 miles away by air and Nairobi nearly 2,000 in a straight line and much more via Aden. The plan thus involved the movement of significant resources in the potentially very short time between a request for assistance being received from Kuwait and an attack on the country being mounted. As it was not possible to maintain significant ground forces in Bahrain for an unlimited period of time, these were limited to the half squadron of tanks already loaded on to HMS *Striker*, one of the Royal Navy's LSTs, together with their ammunition, and two companies of 2nd Coldstream Guards from 24 Brigade. However, it was decided to build up on the island's stockpiles of vehicles, including armoured cars, and artillery, ammunition, rations and tents.

The Plan was divided into three parts to respond to differing scenarios. Plan A(i) assumed that there would be a four-day warning period followed by a request for intervention by the Ruler, enabling a build-up in Kuwait within 24 hours of the issue of an executive order, the initial force comprising a tactical HQ from Kenya, a parachute battalion from Cyprus, 45 Commando from Aden, an armoured squadron from Bahrain, a half-armoured car squadron from Aden and a Hunter squadron from Aden, supported offshore by two frigates from the Persian Gulf. Additional units from all three services would be committed subsequently as required. Plan A(ii) was to be activated in the event of an internal security emergency and assumed that there would be no warning and that the priority would be to get two infantry or parachute companies from Aden or Cyprus and one Hunter squadron from Aden into Kuwait immediately, supported by one frigate. Plan B assumed that no request for assistance would be received from the Ruler, but that intervention would take place after a five-day consultation period: it envisaged much the same build-up as Plan A(i).

On 25 June 1961, six days after the Exchange of Letters between Great Britain and Kuwait, General Abd Al-Karim Qasim, Prime Minister and Defence Minister of Iraq, who had seized power there in a coup against the monarchy in 1958, claimed publicly that Kuwait was part of Iraq by virtue of its status as part of the Ottoman Empire, of which Iraq was a successor state. This claim was followed by evidence of movement of troops and armour southwards from Baghdad towards Basra, and thus Kuwait.

Sam heard the news on the BBC on the morning of the following day, just as he and Audrey were about to depart for Rhodesia, where he was to discuss supporting that country in the event of internal or external threats. Leaving instructions with his subordinate commanders and staff that they should prepare to activate *Vantage*, he flew first to Nairobi to brief and be briefed by Goodwin in respect of preparations for the deployment of 24 Brigade, before flying on to Salisbury on the following morning.

After three productive days in Rhodesia, during which the Rhodesians offered whatever support they could provide in the event of an operation in the Gulf, most notably transport aircraft and airfield facilities during the build-up period, Sam received a message that *Vantage* was imminent and left immediately, arriving in Nairobi on the evening of 29 June. He had originally intended to stay the night with Goodwin, but, following an update on developments and discussion with those on the spot, he decided to fly on immediately to Aden, taking with him Brigadier Horsford, Horsford's Brigade Major and Group Captain L. J. Joel, a fellow New Zealander who was station commander at Eastleigh and now designated as air forces commander in Kuwait. Sam was in his office by 07.00 on the morning of 30 June, where he met all his commanders, including Talbot, who had flown down from Bahrain.

As Sam was later to write to Mountbatten, 'We have had some good strokes of fortune and, of course, some misfortunes.'[4] The first of the former was that HMS *Bulwark*, one of the Royal Navy's Commando carriers, was about to leave Karachi for hot weather trials in the Persian Gulf, with both 42 Royal Marine Commando and the Whirlwind helicopters of 848 Naval Air Squadron aboard. Talbot now ordered the ship to proceed to Kuwait with all despatch. The second was that RFA *Empire Gull*, the War Department LST with the other half squadron of the 3rd Carabiniers' tanks aboard, was in the Gulf about to effect the six-monthly exchange. The tank crews for a full squadron were flown up to Bahrain to be reunited with their vehicles and both LSTs were ordered to sail towards Kuwait together with HMS *Meon*, which would act as the HQ ship until *Bulwark* arrived.

On the RAF side, Lee ordered both 8 Squadron from Khomaksar and 208 Squadron from Eastleigh to fly to Bahrain, the latter refuelling in Aden. Two Shackletons from 37 Squadron were also ordered to Bahrain, whilst a squadron of Canberras from Germany flew into Sharjah, due to lack of space elsewhere.

On the evening of 30 June the British Government received a request from the Ruler of Kuwait for forces to help defend his country from a potential incursion by Iraq, and an order was sent from London to implement *Vantage*. At this point the most serious of the misfortunes hit the British and Kuwaiti Governments, when both Turkey and the Sudan refused permission for RAF aircraft to overfly their territories. This was a potentially major setback, in particular for the arrival of the parachute battalion from Cyprus, but also for the complex reinforcement arrangements requiring an airlift from the UK, which now had to be diverted via West Africa. Thankfully, the Sudan lifted its ban very quickly, but not before major disruption was caused, whilst the Turkish ban remained in place for another day and was only then lifted for overnight flights, first closing and then severely limiting the quickest route from Cyprus.

The first landings took place early on the morning of 1 July, when a succession of Whirlwind flights lifted in 42 Commando from *Bulwark*. These were followed by the Hunters of 8 Squadron, whilst the tanks of the Carabiniers and the two companies of 2nd Coldstream Guards arrived over the beaches. As the airlift of the parachute battalion was severely delayed, it was decided, pending its arrival on the night of 2/3 July, to bring up 45 Commando and the 11th Hussars[5] from Aden via Bahrain, joined by a detachment of Royal Marines from HMS *Loch Alvie*, the only frigate on station in the Gulf. Of the other two frigates, HMS *Loch Ruthven* was at Mombasa and HMS *Loch Fyne* was at Karachi carrying out a self-maintenance programme; both were ordered to sail for Kuwait with all despatch. The aircraft carrier HMS *Victorious*, in the Indian Ocean on its way to Hong Kong via Singapore, was also diverted to the Gulf with its accompanying destroyer and frigate escort, adding a further powerful ground attack element and an air defence capability which was otherwise lacking. Further naval forces were despatched from the Mediterranean, notably a squadron led by the carrier HMS *Centaur*, which was allowed through the Suez Canal by Egypt, a supporter of Kuwait, and ordered to make for Aden and remain there pending developments.

Sam flew to Bahrain on the morning of 2 July with Major General Jim Robertson, who had relieved Bobby Bray as GOC earlier in the year, to join his advanced HQ in HMS *Jufair* and to link up with Luce. On the following day Sam, Luce and Robertson were in Kuwait for a day of meetings with John Richmond, formerly the Political Agent in Kuwait and now the newly appointed British Consul-General, the Ruler and his army commander, Brigadier Mubarak Al-Sabah. As always, Sam and Luce saw eye to eye on everything, but Richmond was out of the same mould as Luce's predecessor as Political Resident, disliking any military involvement. He was, moreover, very tired after the events of the last few days and was thus eased out of the picture, with Luce and Sam taking over all discussions with the Kuwaitis as well as Richmond's residence, where an operations room was set up in the dining room.

The build-up of forces in Kuwait, involving primarily 208 Squadron and the remaining elements of 24 Brigade, plus a Royal Artillery field regiment from the UK, was not completed until 9 July, by which time the total strength of British personnel in Kuwait was just short of 6,000. The main defensive line, also manned by two Kuwaiti brigades, was formed along the Mutla Ridge north-west of Kuwait City, with a screen of British and Kuwaiti armoured cars in the desert towards the Iraq border and a mobile reserve in the rear. Conditions on the ground were atrocious. This was the middle of summer, when both heat and humidity were at their highest. There were also frequent sandstorms, closing down visibility to yards and making flying difficult to impossible. Instances of heat exhaustion occurred, but were fewer than expected, and *Bulwark* was able to take in 200 men at a time for recuperation in the ship's air-conditioning. The Kuwaitis themselves were not at all helpful on accommodation and other administrative matters, but the Kuwait Oil Company and a number of its fellow commercial businesses provided refrigeration equipment and soft drinks for the troops.

In the meantime there had been significant political developments. Kuwait immediately applied for membership of and was subsequently admitted to the Arab League, and a mixed force from the League began to arrive in the country many weeks later, which allowed the British forces to be relieved. The last withdrawal, however, did not take place until mid-October. In the meantime, Sam's staff had prepared *Vantage*'s successor Theatre Reinforcement Plan, *Sodabread*.

Sam maintained subsequently that he and his team had 'got away with it'[6] as far as Kuwait was concerned. The most important factor in *Vantage*'s success was, of course, the lack of an Iraqi attack; indeed, there remains considerable doubt that Qasim ever intended one. Had he acted decisively shortly after his declaration that Kuwait was part of Iraq, the British would have been powerless to stop him. Nevertheless, Sam was being overly modest. The positioning of a large number of troops, aircraft and ships, ready for immediate action, into and off the shore of a faraway country over a matter of a few days, was a considerable feat, requiring a very high standard of command and staff work. Mountbatten was in no doubt about this, writing to Sam on 5 July:

> You have exceeded all our plans and, indeed, expectations in the way you have got your forces built up and have enormously enhanced the prestige of the Services and yourself in particular.[7]

Mountbatten compared Sam's achievement with his own circumstances, 'struggling with the woefully inadequate staff and organization to run the London end on behalf of the Chiefs of Staff'.[8] In fact, once the ball had been set rolling, the influence of the Defence Staff in London was minimal.

If nothing else, however, Vantage fully justified the decision to establish tri-service commands, as it is difficult to conceive how such a complex operation could have succeeded under the control of three separate service HQs with no experience of working together.

Vantage dominated Sam's life during a short period of his appointment as Commander-in-Chief, but it highlighted as nothing else could have his qualities both as an organizer at his HQ and as a commander on the ground, and in particular his skill at dealing simultaneously with military and political issues whilst under extreme pressure. He had no need to convince Mountbatten of his abilities, but his performance did no harm to his standing with both the British Government and the other two services.

There was, however, much else to keep him fully occupied for the three years of his appointment.

Chapter 13

Middle East Command

T wo changes in Sam's circumstances took place in early 1961, prior to the initiation of *Vantage*. From his personal perspective the less important one came on 1 March with the renaming of British Forces Arabian Peninsula as Middle East Command. This was a consequence of the change in name of the second tri-service command, which had been formed in Cyprus in 1960 under an army officer, General Sir Dudley Ward. Ward's HQ took responsibility for all British forces based in Cyprus itself, Malta and Libya, whilst its area of interest covered the Eastern Mediterranean, Egypt and the Levant. Originally called Middle East Command, it was now renamed Near East Command.

Mountbatten had less immediate success with his proposal for a third tri-service command, to be based in Singapore. He was strongly opposed on this by the Commander-in-Chief Far East Land Forces, General Sir Richard Hull, who maintained his opposition after he became CIGS at the end of 1961. Mountbatten persisted, but it was not until November 1962 that he was able to engineer the creation of a unified Far East Command under Sir William Luce's brother, Admiral Sir David Luce.

The other change, which was of a much more personal nature, came in the New Year's Honours of 1961, in which Sam was appointed a Knight Commander of the Order of the Bath. This caused an immediate difficulty. When asked how he wished to be styled, he naturally chose 'Sir Sam'. The relevant authority informed him that he would not be able to use the diminutive form of his first name. Sam replied that he had never been called 'Samuel' and positively disliked the name. As a compromise they agreed on 'Sir Charles', a name which he had never used before but would now become the one by which he was known formally and to the general public, although friends and colleagues all continued to call him 'Sam'.

The sequel to this took place a year later, when his membership of the Order of the Bath was upgraded to Knight Grand Cross, very likely in recognition of his performance on *Vantage*. As it was exactly two years since he had first been admitted to the Order as a Companion this was accelerated promotion indeed, and among the many letters he received was one from Mountbatten, congratulating him on getting from the shallow to the deep end of the Bath in record time! The investitures for the KCB and the GCB took place within two months of the respective announcements, during visits by Sam to London on other business, but he had to wait some years before his installation as a GCB in the Chapel of the Order in Westminster Abbey.

To add to his growing list of distinctions, Sam was promoted once again on 1 September 1962. From being the oldest pilot officer in the RAF in 1936, he was now its youngest air chief marshal.

High-profile though these changes may have been, they were relatively brief distractions. Both he and Audrey were later to say that the years they spent in Aden were the most interesting and happiest of their service life together. From a professional perspective there were constant demands on Sam's time, although none of them assumed the importance or urgency of *Vantage*. Notwithstanding the intervention of the Arab League, however, Iraq was believed to be still a potential threat to Kuwait, and the Theatre Reinforcement Plan had to be constantly updated, with a quicker response time being built in. There was one alarm subsequently when railway trucks, containing what were thought by local agents in Iraq to be tanks, were seen moving south. It was a Friday afternoon in London and nobody could be found to authorize any action. All aircraft movements were halted at Khormaksar and, very bravely, Sam took it on himself to order a photo-reconnaissance Canberra to fly over Iraq at 60,000ft. The results it brought back were negative, but if the aircraft had been identified, it would have probably caused an international incident.

As far as the Arabian Peninsula was concerned, a longstanding dispute between Saudi Arabia and Abu Dhabi over the ownership of the Buraimi Oasis rumbled on; it never became acute, although it was not finally settled until 1974. More worrying were the beginnings of what would become the Dhofar Rebellion, when insurgents began operations to 'liberate' the southern province of Dhofar from Muscat and Oman. The first attacks took place towards the end of 1962, and as these involved sabotage of the airfield at Salalah, which was operated by the RAF, they were of direct concern. However, they did not assume crisis proportions until after Sam had left Aden.

In Aden itself, most of the developments were of a political rather than a military nature. Charles Johnston had been appointed to continue the policy of the British Government, which was to move towards full federation of the Aden Colony with the states in the Eastern and Western Protectorates, a number of the latter having already formed the Federation of Arab Emirates of the South. Johnston and Sam worked hand in glove, as the former was later to write:

> The close harmony between all three services, and their admirable working relationship with the civil Government, were directly due to the lead given by the Commander-in-Chief. He and I used to meet regularly, and on both the military and the civilian side it was known that any disagreements which might come up at lower levels would be promptly stamped on by the Air Marshal and myself. During the whole of Sam's tour in Aden the Government never had a disagreement with the Services on any matter of significance.[1]

Apart from an ambush of part of the Hadhrami Bedouin Legion in the Eastern Protectorate in July 1961, prompting reprisals by the RAF on the tribe concerned, there was no significant military action until early 1962, when a revolt broke out amongst some of the tribes resisting federation. The RAF response followed the tactics adopted in the inter-war years in Iraq and on the North-West Frontier, dropping leaflets on the villages concerned and then bombing them, at first with little impact, but later achieving capitulation. In October of that year, following the overthrow of the Imam of Yemen and the installation of a republican government backed by Egypt and the Soviet Union, there were attacks mounted from that country by air. Patrols were stepped up by the RAF's Hunters, after which the border remained reasonably quiet apart from two incidents. One occurred during a training expedition by a mixed group from HQ Middle East Command which strayed across the border, where a number of participants were killed or captured, the latter only being released after a period of intense diplomacy. The other involved a forced landing in the Western Protectorate by a Yemeni helicopter. The members of the crew, who were found to be all Russian, were arrested by the Federal Regular Army and brought back to Aden to be interrogated prior to their release.

In April 1962 Johnston at last brought the remaining states of the Western Protectorate into what became known as the Federation of South Arabia and this was joined by the Aden Colony in January 1963, but the states of the Eastern Protectorate continued to reject integration. Republican sentiment and a desire for full independence grew strongly in the former Colony, encouraged by the new regime in Yemen and the Aden Trades Union Congress, and civil disturbances broke out from time to time. For the moment, however, these were capable of being dealt with by the civil authorities.

In East Africa the emphasis was on relief operations in the wake of drought in Northern Kenya and Somalia and floods in the Tana river basin and elsewhere. Uganda achieved independence in October 1962 and Tanganyika two months later, but Kenya had to wait another year.

Changes in the command structure were relatively few. David Lee was succeeded as AOC by Air Vice-Marshal Fred Rosier, who later wrote that 'This was probably the best AVM's job in the Royal Air Force.'[2] RAF Khormaksar was enlarged significantly to enable it to take both 8 and 208 Squadrons at the same time, together forming the Khormaksar Wing, although part of either one or the other was always on detachment in Bahrain. Moreover, they were joined by a third Hunter squadron, No. 43, in March 1963, whilst in the same month 26 Squadron also arrived to provide an additional lifting capability with its Westland Belvedere twin-rotor helicopters; 21 and 30 Squadrons remained at Eastleigh until well after Kenyan independence.

The army units in Aden were all relieved regularly, the 11th Hussars being followed by the Queen's Royal Irish Hussars and then the 17th/21st Lancers and the 3rd Carabiniers by the Royal Scots Greys. Two more infantry battalions were also to serve there, the Queen's Royal Surrey Regiment followed by the King's Own Scottish Borderers.

Towards the end of 1961 Talbot at last moved his HQ to Aden, to the accompaniment of a certain amount of grumbling, although he continued to be an excellent member of the team. He was relieved in late 1962 by Rear Admiral John Scotland.

Sam had by now developed a much admired method of conducting meetings: he would say very little for three quarters of the time and then produce an impressive summing-up, which invariably followed the line which he himself had taken from the start. In terms of binding his colleagues together, it helped that not only were the offices of Sam and his immediate subordinates now co-located along the same corridor in the Command HQ, but also that all their houses were nearby and close to each other, on the hill overlooking Steamer Point and Telegraph Bay, with fine views of the harbour and the opposite peninsula of Little Aden. Perhaps appropriately, Air House was at the top, with Flagstaff House, the residence of the GOC, close by and Command House, where Sam and Audrey lived, somewhat further down. Government House at Steamer Point was also nearby, with the Officers' Club just below it on the beach at Tarshyne. A new house had to be constructed for Talbot, causing some controversy in the press because of the cost; it was known as the Round House, because of its shape on the foundations of an old gun emplacement.

Aden might well seem to be remote and forbidding today, but in the early 1960s it was a hive of activity and a key hub of what remained of the British Empire. Its situation meant that it was on the direct route for trooping by air to the Far East, whilst it was also served by a small number of commercial airlines, although most of the latter ran their flights to India and South-East Asia through Bahrain. Although travel by air was now commonplace, a number of shipping lines still operated regular services across the Indian Ocean and through the Suez Canal, and almost all of these stopped at Aden, as did an increasing number of cruise liners. They usually carried passengers with friends ashore who were only too pleased to offer them hospitality. With visits by Her Majesty's ships and those of some friendly foreign navies, not to mention the tankers serving the busy oil terminal and refinery, the harbour was invariably busy.

The large, substantially British, foreign community took every opportunity for social engagements, amongst themselves and for the entertainment of visitors. Sam and Audrey were outstandingly good hosts; indeed, Audrey, who loved people, was in her element. Her task as a hostess was eased by having a household staff. Although Sam's ADC had some responsibility for its smooth operation, the nature of his other duties meant that, to all intents and purposes, it was under the day-to-day control of Flight Sergeant Ponsford from the RAF. Ponsford was always known as 'Flight', even after he had been promoted to Warrant Officer, and he distinguished himself not only by having an excellent sense of humour, but also by mixing very fine dry Martinis, Audrey's favourite pre-prandial tipple. He tended to spoil the children and once took Christopher off to the Sergeants' Mess, with strict instructions not to tell his father. There were three Arabs on the staff: Abdullah, who looked after Sam personally, Abdi, who was a Somali and an expert at cooking 'rumble-tumble' eggs, and Mohammed. Abdi was a regular source of amusement. At one party for a hundred or so guests he fell over whilst carrying a full tray of glasses. As he got back onto his feet, he re-assured Sam with the words, 'Don't worry, master, only RAF glass'!

The frequency of RAF flights meant that Christopher and Clare were able to come out for their school holidays, although Christopher spent the Easter holidays with a family in France to prepare for his A Level French exam. Another prominent member of the household was Adu, a black Labrador bitch acquired whilst Sam was at Bracknell. She was named after a Ghanaian friend of Sam's from the IDC, Yaw Adu,[3] who, on being introduced to his namesake, said that he was proud to be her godfather and, moreover, that if he ever acquired a white dog, he would name it Elworthy! On one occasion Adu trod on one of Abdi's feet, provoking ear-piercing cries that he had been stung.[4]

The strategic position of Aden meant that there was a constant stream of visitors on official business from both the services and government. Mountbatten himself came only twice, once in early 1961 and the other time shortly before Sam left in 1963, but the First Sea Lord, Caspar John, the CIGS, Dick Hull, and the CAS, Tom Pike, all made appearances, as did numerous of their most senior colleagues and a succession of Secretaries of State and other Ministers. These included Jack Profumo, the Secretary of State for War, who was an excellent visitor, although rumours were already circulating about his affair with Christine Keeler, the story breaking in the press just after he left. Sandys, by that time Secretary of State for the Colonies, was as difficult as ever and insisted on meeting late into the night, much to everyone's annoyance. Equally, Sam went to London two to three times in each year for a series of meetings, the visit in the summer coinciding with his home leave. In 1961 this allowed him and Audrey to be present at Tim's wedding to Victoria Bowring, the daughter of Sam's best friend at Marlborough and Adu's breeder, Kit Bowring.

Every time a distinguished visitor came to Aden there would be a series of lunches and dinners at Government House, Command House or the residence of the appropriate service chief, but there were also a great number of other, less formal, events. In addition to acting as the hostess at Command House, Audrey helped as much as she could with the events at Flagstaff House, as Jim Robertson was a widower. The nature of the unified command led to a much greater integration of the services on a social level than would normally be expected in an overseas posting. As Sam was to say much later:

> The whole of our social structure was quite different. You could go to an Army Colonel's dinner party and find a sailor there, an airman there, and a chap from the Civil Government there. There was never any semblance of Army parties, Air Force parties, or Navy parties. We really were wholly 'joint' and it worked admirably.[5]

Sam did not mention the members of the business community, but they were not excluded. Amongst them were a couple who were to become lasting friends of Sam and Audrey, Tony and Christiane Besse. Besse was the leading member of the mercantile community in the colony as the head of a company founded by his father, Sir Antonin Besse, a French-born businessman who had built up a commercial empire trading in Southern Arabia under its own name and as an agent for some major companies, including Royal Dutch Shell. The elder Besse's great wealth had allowed him to endow the foundation of St Antony's College in Oxford in 1950, and his son Tony, who took over after his father's death in the following year, funded the purchase of St Donat's Castle in Wales for Atlantic College, part of United World Colleges.[6]

Among those who came to stay at Command House were various members of the Elworthy family, notably Percy and Bertha for just over a week in November 1960. This was the last time that Sam saw his father, the news of his death on 10 July 1961 reaching him in the middle of the Kuwait Crisis. The two of them had been geographically separated for the majority of Sam's life, but his relationship with 'Willie' had nevertheless always been a close one. Other than during his service in the Great War, Percy had never worked, and this allowed him the luxury of frequent foreign travel to keep in touch with his family, without which the bond between him and his eldest son might have been more difficult to maintain. The source of his income was somewhat mysterious, but Sam always maintained that whenever he became short he sold off a parcel of land. Generous and extrovert, Percy was greatly missed by his family. Bertha, whom he had adored, was to live on for another thirteen years.

In addition to the formal occasions, there were also frequent opportunities for more relaxed social gatherings, sometimes taking the form of beach parties and barbecues. Sam himself did much of the work in preparation for one of these during a visit by Princess Alexandra of Kent, who turned out to be a delightful guest. The sea played a large part in Sam's extramural activities, the most important of which was sailing, which he took up with the same intensity which he had demonstrated in Karachi. He had kept his hand in whilst serving at Tangmere, hiring a clinker-built dinghy and a larger yacht at Bosham for family sailing in Chichester Harbour. Now he arranged for a 'Flying Fifteen', a racing keelboat for a crew of two, to be flown in a transport aircraft out to Aden, where he named her *Jambia*, the Arabic word for the short curved knife carried by men in Southern Arabia and the Horn of Africa. He raced as often as possible during the relatively cool weather of the winter and early spring.

Sam underwent something of a change in character on the water. He was hugely competitive, as demonstrated in one race when, with Christopher as his crew and leading by only a short head, he cut under the bow of a large Japanese tanker, telling Christopher that steam should give way to sail. With the crew of the tanker shouting down and its siren going at full blast, he got away from the rest of the fleet and won by a full fifteen minutes. He was also intolerant of any inefficiency on the part of his crew member. On two occasions when nobody more competent was available, Sam drafted in his ADCs. George Norrie had had no previous experience of sailing and had only just begun to learn from Sam when he was required to take part in a race as a substitute for the usual crew member, who was sick. After a good start, *Jambia* steadily lost ground until she lay second from last after rounding the fourth marker:

> The wind was getting up and Sam became more boot-faced by the minute. His orders to me came out in sharp staccato tones. For myself, the end of the race could not come soon enough. 'Get the bloody spinnaker up!' he yelled. In my haste I jammed it halfway up the mast, where it billowed hopelessly in one long distended line, failing to open. Sam screamed, 'Take the tiller!' I scrambled over to where he was and took control – I thought – but the boat seemed to have a mind of its own.
>
> We zig-zagged towards the finishing line in last place, the ignominious boom of the cannon signifying that the race was over ... Whereas he never ran me down in public as the most useless crew member with whom he had ever had the misfortune to sail, we hardly spoke until he was safely reunited with his first choice of crew member, who thankfully had now recovered. They won the next race and all returned to normal: it was as though our old relationship had never faltered.[7]

After Norrie had returned to his regiment towards the end of 1961, his successor as ADC encountered the same treatment. Richard Novis was a subaltern in the Coldstream Guards in Kenya when he was approached by his CO to see if he would be interested in the job. As he had no wish to return to ceremonial duties in London he agreed to have his name put forward and duly flew up to Aden for an interview. He was greeted on the steps of Command House by an imposing figure in half-moon glasses wearing 'Red Sea rig' – black tie attire with a cummerbund but minus the dinner jacket – and sporting a pink Leander Club bow tie. Sam was holding an informal birthday party for one of his staff, into which Novis was cordially invited, and after returning to Kenya he was chosen for the job. Unlike Norrie, he was quartered in an annexe of Command House, where he was instantly on call. He was, however, no more successful at crewing for Sam than Norrie, managing to drop a key item of equipment into the sea and causing great irritation at his incompetence. It was agreed that sailing duties should be handed over to the newly appointed Personal Staff Officer, Don Arnott, who proved to be much more satisfactory in the role.

It would be impossible to overstate Audrey's contribution as the C-in-C's wife; indeed, this was a partnership in every sense of the word. She had a number of interests of her own, notably in the work of the RAF Hospital and of the Soldiers, Sailors, Airmen and Families Association (SSAFA), in its way the archetypal tri-service organization, with which she was to have a close relationship for many years. However, she was also Sam's greatest asset socially. Highly intelligent, well read, lively and unpompous, she could hold her own at any level, from royalty to 'other ranks'. Whilst she was quick to spot any flaws in the characters of those she met, her instinct was always to recognize the best in them, and they responded accordingly.

It was whilst Audrey and Sam were in Aden that she began the practice of recording all their journeys together. She did so in notebooks which she kept in her handbag, taking the opportunity to write them up when she was flying or being driven or alone in her bedroom. The contents were personal and private and she never showed them to anyone, including Sam, although it became her intention in due course to use them one day as the basis for a book. Written in an idiosyncratic style and displaying a huge sense of humour, they were not just a chronology of events and a description of people and places, but an expression of what Charles Johnston called her 'acute curiosity about human nature and an extraordinarily detached capacity for psychological exploration'.[8] The notebooks eventually numbered twenty-seven, covering many more than that number of journeys, and were written over nearly thirteen years from shortly after their arrival in Aden to two years after Sam's retirement from active service.

Geography dictated that Sam should be a frequent traveller on command business, flying up to Bahrain or down to East Africa at least bi-monthly and frequently more often, to London at least twice a year and further afield to the Far East on two occasions. Audrey did not accompany him every time, but she was keen to do so as often as possible. The journeys which seem to have stimulated her most at this time were those up-country into the Aden Protectorate, to East Africa, sometimes for important occasions, but also on local leave, and those which were further afield outside Middle East Command.

Audrey's first trip into the interior of the Protectorate took place little more than a month after their arrival in Aden. Christopher and Clare were still on holiday and thus accompanied Audrey and Sam in a Twin Pioneer up to Mukheiras in the small state of Audhali. Accompanied by an armed guard, they were able to look out over the frontier into Yemen. Later that month, Sam and Audrey flew up for the day to Beihan, one of the larger Western Protectorate states, and in early December they were there for three nights as guests of the Amir, Sharif Hussein, who, according to Norrie, 'had distinguished good manners and an uncontrollable sense of humour',[9] which clearly appealed to Audrey. Sam and Audrey were driven personally by him to his pink and white palace. Ushered to their rooms, they found 'sinister stains'[10] on the sheets, whilst the bathroom and toilet were indescribable, the former without taps, the latter a hole with a long drop underneath, both exuding foul odours due to a strong upward draught from the sewers below. After a traditional dinner they were entertained to a film show. On the following day they were taken on a gazelle shoot on the edge of the Empty Quarter, with the Sharif driving them in his own Land Rover extremely fast over the dunes. Audrey, wedged on the front seat between him and Sam, described his technique: 'We approach banks with a rush – foot down Sharif mutters "Allah!" & over we go not knowing what is beyond & descending vertically with appalling crash but undamaged.'[11] After a lunch of roast gazelle they visited some salt mines and the ruins of the reputed palace of the Queen of Sheba.

Of even greater interest were the visits to the Hadhramaut, the first of which took place in March 1961. This began on the coast at the prosperous port of Mukalla, in the territory of the Qu'aiti Sultanate, where they met the Sultan and inspected his own troops and those of the Hadhrami Bedouin Legion, later staying in the palace. They then flew up to the Wadi Hadhramaut to visit the astonishing, densely populated and surprisingly clean cities of Sayun, Tarim and Shibam in the Kathiri Sultanate. Audrey was particularly impressed with Shibam, the 'Arabian New York', with its high-rise buildings constructed out of mud bricks. A second visit took place for two days in April 1962, with a flight directly to Ghuraf, near Sayun, this time with Clare.

Audrey's last trip of several more up-country took place over two days at the beginning of 1963, when she and Sam, with Christopher but without Clare, who was ill, flew up to the Wahidi Sultanate for two days, this time camping with friends. This was particularly dangerous country, with some of the tribesmen known to be hostile, so a large escort was provided by the Federal Regular Army, including three armoured cars. At least they managed to avoid some of the less appealing features of staying with the local ruler!

East Africa was the location of several visits of note, including to the Serengeti, Murchison Falls, Zanzibar and Rhodesia, the last of these taking in the Kariba Dam, Victoria Falls and the Great Ruins of Zimbabwe. The longest stay in Kenya itself took place in August 1962, when not only Christopher and Clare but also Tim and Victoria joined the party, first for fishing on Lake Rudolf and then to Nyerere and the Aberdare National Park to fish some more. In February 1962, although the trip took in Nairobi, it was more notable for a visit to Ethiopia. This included an audience with Emperor Haile Selassie and some days spent in Dire Dawa, in Harar in the Ethiopian Highlands and on Lake Langano, where Sam and Audrey camped and fished. At a dinner in Addis Ababa in the house of the military attaché, Sam encountered a number of coincidences. His hostess turned out to be not only a New Zealander but his second cousin through the family of his grandfather Bishop Julius, whilst one of the other guests had been born in Timaru and a third had been born and brought up in Christchurch, where they had mutual acquaintances.

In October 1962 Sam and Audrey were part of the official British delegation at the celebrations of Uganda's independence, giving rise in Audrey's notebook to some typical observations on some of those involved, including Evelyn Baring (the Governor of Kenya) – 'tired eyes, noble brow, sensuous, cynical and obstinate mouth', Milton Obote (Prime Minister of Uganda) – 'wise, humorous and seemingly humble', and Jomo Kenyatta (later the first Prime Minister of an independent Kenya) – 'smooth, sharp and sinful'![12] At one of the dinners Sam was placed next to the Sultan of Muscat and Oman, who by that time he knew well. The man opposite came from West Africa and spoke only French, with which Sam managed to engage him in conversation, yet again impressing the Sultan by his command of languages.

In November 1961 Sam set off on an official tour of Far East Command, taking with him Talbot, Robertson and some other officers, Audrey, Talbot's wife and George Norrie, who was nearing the end of his appointment and would return to the UK from Bahrain on the way back. En route to Singapore they landed at Gan, the southernmost of the Maldive Islands and a key British base, both strategically and as a stopover on the trooping route. In Singapore they stayed at Air House with Sam's old friend and the C-in-C Far East Air Force, Mark Selway and his wife, and were delighted to renew the friendship forged whilst at their respective staff colleges with the Poetts, Nigel Poett having taken over from Dick Hull as C-in-C Far East Land Forces. The other key service officer was to become Sam's opposite number as the first C-in-C of Far East Command, Admiral Sir David Luce, Audrey noting that he and his wife were unlike Bill and Margaret Luce and 'oddly indescribable but delightful and memorable'.[13] They flew on first to Hong Kong and then to Bangkok and Calcutta, where they were met by their second son, Anthony.

Anthony had been posted by Harrisons & Crosfield to Calcutta in 1960, staying with his parents on his way out there. Audrey described him at this time as 'a real business man, tough and resilient and opportunist, determined to get on and to equip himself to do so'.[14] He was to be physically the most distant of Sam's and Audrey's children, but the ties were never broken and they continued to see each other in the future whenever the opportunity presented itself.

Sam and Audrey were back in the Far East in March 1963. This journey differed from its predecessor in that it had little to do with Sam's role as C-in-C and much to do with his next appointment, which by this time he knew would be as Chief of the Air Staff. The focus was thus on the RAF rather than the armed services as a whole, although Richard Novis, an army officer, was asked to join the party 'if you've nothing better to do'.[15] The first stop was at the Indian Air Force base at Sulur in Tamil Nadu, taking Sam back to his time in 2 (Indian) Group, when it had been one of the group's stations. As well as re-establishing a link with the Indian Air Force, this was an opportunity to see Anthony again, as he had relocated to Cochin. During their stay, Sam crewed for Anthony in a sailing race, which they won.

Moving on, Sam and Audrey not only visited Singapore and Hong Kong but flew from the former to both Brunei and Sarawak, travelling upcountry in a Belvedere. Two months earlier, in the aftermath of a proposal to combine the independent Federation of Malaya, the self-governing state of Singapore and the British colonies of Sarawak, North Borneo and Brunei[16] into Malaysia, Indonesia, which claimed the whole of the island of Borneo as its own, announced a policy of Confrontation with Malaysia. No military action had been taken by the time of the Elworthys' visit, but tensions were rising and Sam was keen to understand the RAF's role in any response to Indonesian aggression. It was time well spent, as this would come to exercise him in the not too distant future.

Sam's tour as C-in-C Middle East expired on the last day of May 1963. The weeks before had been taken up with final visits to East Africa and to the Gulf states and Oman, as well as many farewell lunches and dinners in Aden, although there was no formal handover to his successor, General Sir Charles Harrington. On 30 May there was a ceremonial departure at Khormaksar, during which Hunters from the Khormaksar Wing flew over in the formation of a capital E.

Chapter 14

Chief of the Air Staff

I t was to be three months before Sam took up his appointment as Chief of the Air Staff. Pike would not be retiring from the service but moving on to become Deputy Supreme Allied Commander Europe, an appointment which he was due to take up on 1 January 1964. Seven months was doubtless considered to be too long a period for him to be unemployed, so he was to stay on for the time being.

Sam's first full week back in the UK was nevertheless taken up with meetings with Pike, Mountbatten, Air Chief Marshal Sir William MacDonald, the Air Secretary, Peter Thorneycroft, the Minister of Defence, and Sir Maurice Dean, the Permanent Secretary at the Air Ministry. On 11 June he and Audrey departed for a tour of Australasia, flying in a Bristol Britannia which was furnished with beds which converted to couches by day, providing much greater comfort than they had been used to in the Hastings. They took off from Lyneham, stopped briefly at Thule in Greenland and then flew on to Elmendorf Air Force Base near Anchorage in Alaska, where they were the guests of Lieutenant General George Mundy, C-in-C of NORAD. On the following day they left for Christmas Island, with a refuelling stop at Honolulu. After a day's fishing and bird watching, they arrived at Whenuapei in New Zealand on 14 June for three weeks' leave, spent on both the North and the South Islands. This was the first visit by Sam since 1959 and by Audrey since 1954. They had, of course received many visits themselves from relatives, both in the UK and Aden, most notably from Sam's parents, brother Tony and sister Di, but there was still a great deal of catching up to do with both relatives and friends.

The official business of the tour took place largely in Australia, following Sam and Audrey's arrival in Canberra on 5 July. Australia was seen to be a key military ally of the UK and, from the RAF's perspective, was regarded as particularly critical to its interests, bordering as it did on the Indian Ocean.

There were thus a number of meetings for Sam, with the air staff, politicians and civil servants, to discuss future co-operation and the purchase of British aircraft, notably the TSR-2, whilst Audrey was entertained by their wives. Five days later, they left for Adelaide, from where they flew up to Woomera for Sam to pay another visit to the Rocket Range, where tests were still being carried out for the RAF.

Sam and Audrey flew on from Woomera to Perth on one of the RAF's Comet IVs, an aircraft which had entered service with 216 Squadron of Transport Command a year earlier and provided yet another step up, not only in comfort, but also in range and speed. The pilot was Squadron Leader (later Wing Commander) Basil D'Oliveira, who would become a firm favourite over the next few years, particularly with Audrey. At their next destination, Perth, they were met by their good friend Air Marshal Sir Wallace 'Digger' Kyle, himself a native of the city, who had served in the RAF since 1928 and, like Sam, had spent the war years in Bomber Command, including a period as CO of a Blenheim squadron. He was in Australia on leave from his job as VCAS, in which he would be working closely with Sam in the future.

The next stop was Singapore, where Sam and Audrey stayed with Air Marshal Sir Hector McGregor, the C-in-C Far East Air Force, and his wife. Sam was also able to meet Admiral Sir Varyl Begg, who had succeeded David Luce as C-in-C Far East Command. On 16 July Sam and Audrey flew via Gan to Aden, where they were met by a large party, led by Sam's successor as C-in-C, Charles Harrington. They stayed with the Johnstons at Government House, where, following drinks with first the Scotlands and then the Rosiers, there was a large dinner party for all their old friends. On the next day, with Audrey feeling somewhat frail, they left for the UK.

There was still a month and a half to fill in before Sam began work as CAS, the first week or so of which was largely taken up by meetings in Whitehall, although there was also an audience with the Queen, who was constitutionally obliged to give her consent to his appointment. They then set off on a family holiday in the UK, spent first in Scotland and then with friends in England. They also concluded the negotiations for the purchase of a house of their own, although they would not move in for several months. Perseverance Cottage was acquired in the knowledge that they would be living during the week in an official residence in London, but would need a bolt hole in the country for weekends and holidays. Situated just outside Henley, the cottage was an easy drive from London and convenient for the Royal Regatta and for members of the family, who now included Sam and Audrey's first grandchild, Kate, the daughter of Tim and Victoria and born that year. It was to become a much loved home.

Sam spent the whole of Friday, 30 August being fully briefed by Tom Pike. He and Audrey then went to stay with Dermot and Una Boyle for the weekend, when he doubtless received more advice about what his new job entailed. On the following Monday he arrived at the Air Ministry for his first day's work as Chief of the Air Staff.

Quite how Sam was chosen as CAS remains something of a mystery, as the procedure was not recorded in any way. The nomination to the Queen would have come through the Prime Minister from the Secretary of State for Air on the basis of a recommendation from Pike, but Sam's name would have emerged during a process of consultation which had been going on for many years. Unlike the Royal Navy and the British Army, in which the offices of the Naval Secretary and the Military Secretary, responsible for monitoring the careers of officers with a view to their selection for the most senior appointments, went back to the early nineteenth century, the RAF had had no such position until 1957. Denis Barnett was appointed the first ever Air Secretary, after which the post tended to be held by a very senior, usually four-star officer, whose career was itself coming to an end and who thus had no axe to grind. He would be expected to submit a number of names for consideration for the most senior appointments, providing a justification for each. It is clear from Sam's own subsequent experience that former Chiefs, who would almost certainly have views on the candidates, were usually consulted on the issue of a future CAS. This would probably have played well for Sam, as Boyle was a strong supporter, and Boyle's surviving predecessors, Dickson, Slessor, Tedder and Portal, had all come across him and most of them knew him well.

Clearly, the views of both ministers and senior civil servants at the Air Ministry would have been part of the process of consultation, and it is likely that a short list was developed several years before the vacancy was expected to arise. In this case, however, there was a special consideration, in that it was already expected that Pike's successor would also become Chief of the Defence Staff in due course. It had been agreed by the politicians and the three services that this appointment would be held in turn by each of them. Mountbatten was still the CDS and was to be succeeded by General Sir Richard Hull, who in turn would be followed by an airman. This meant that the incoming CAS would have to be a relatively young man, able to serve a full term in both roles before retirement, which would normally be before he reached his sixtieth birthday. This ruled out candidates such as Denis Barnett, Teddy Hudleston and 'Zulu' Morris, all of whom might otherwise have been in contention. There were a number of talented air marshals of Sam's own age, such as 'Digger' Kyle, Kenneth 'Bing' Cross and Gus Walker, but none of them appear to have caught the eye of the selectors. Sam's promotion to air chief marshal in September 1962 would probably have been the signal to all of them that he was the chosen one.

The choice of the single service Chiefs was guarded fiercely by each service, albeit that it was subject to the approval of the relevant secretary of state and his permanent secretary. Moreover, the appointment had also to be approved by the Prime Minister. However, for someone who was to go on to become Chief of the Defence Staff, others would have been consulted, notably the Minister of Defence. Whether or not the incumbent CDS or his designated successor would have been involved is less certain, but it seems likely. It also seems that he did not have a veto, as Hull, the Army's choice to succeed Mountbatten, and Mountbatten himself did not get on at all well. In Sam's case, however, the CDS was a strong supporter and would probably have volunteered an opinion in his favour in any event.

If there is a considerable element of uncertainty as to how Sam was chosen as CAS, why he was chosen is easier to understand. Sam's contention that he was not being groomed for high office at the time of the Coronation Review was, in all likelihood, correct, but thereafter he was on a relatively steep curve. His selection as Commandant of the Staff College was fortuitous, a direct result of the Suez crisis and Sam's illness, but it was a highly suitable appointment, giving him exposure not only to senior RAF officers but also to members of the other two services and to politicians. Thereafter he was clearly fast-tracked into becoming DCAS and then a tri-service C-in-C. He was particularly valued for his intellect, which it was thought would be needed to fight the RAF's corner, but also for his ability to provide a bridge to the other services, which had been clearly demonstrated in Aden, particularly during *Vantage*. The latter quality was particularly important at a time in which inter-service rivalry between the RAF and the Royal Navy was high, as will be related later, and it was a tragedy yet to come that this would get worse rather than better on his watch; but it was clear to all that there was nothing personal in it as far as Sam was concerned, and he remained universally liked.

The service which Sam now commanded was structured much as it had been since the war, although it was significantly smaller, with an establishment of less than 150,000, compared with just over 1,000,000 at its peak in June 1944. Moreover, the ending of National Service in 1960 had caused some difficulties with recruitment, particularly in the ground trades.

In the United Kingdom the old command structure still held good, although a separate Signals Command had been formed in 1958. Bomber Command, under John Grandy, was divided into two groups, 1 and 3, both of which were equipped with the three V-Bombers, the Valiant, Victor and Vulcan. The Valiant fleet by this time had been largely converted to tankers for in-flight refuelling, but the aircraft had shown worrying signs of metal fatigue and would be withdrawn from service by the end of 1964. Its refuelling duties were taken over by the Victor, which also continued to be deployed in the bomber role, carrying both conventional and nuclear weapons, as did the Vulcan, which had preceded the Victor into service. The US Skybolt air-launched ballistic missile programme had been cancelled, so the British 'stand-off' missile, Blue Steel, which was already in service, remained the lynchpin of the UK's nuclear deterrent for the next few years, although its short range meant that the bombers would have to penetrate Soviet airspace at a very low level to have a chance of their missiles reaching their targets. Following the Cuban missile crisis the V-Bomber Force was effectively assigned to NATO.

Between 1959 and 1963 Bomber Command had also deployed the Thor intermediate range ballistic missile from fixed sites, but the development of intercontinental ballistic missiles had rendered it redundant. However, it had already been agreed between the Prime Minister, Harold Macmillan, and President Kennedy that the United Kingdom would deploy Polaris missiles in specially constructed Royal Navy submarines which would go into service in the late 1960s. Taken together with the cancellation of Skybolt, this would end the supremacy in long-range offensive warfare which had been the preserve of the RAF since the 1930s, something which was regretted by many in the service and resented by a few.

Fighter Command, under the leadership of 'Zulu' Morris, was still divided into two, but the nomenclature had recently changed, from 11 Group to 11 (Northern) Sector and from 12 Group to 12 (East Anglian) Sector. Although no fewer than nine squadrons were equipped with Bloodhound ground-to-air missiles, the proposal by Duncan Sandys in the 1957 Defence Review to replace fixed-wing aircraft entirely with missiles had not been implemented. The Javelin was still in service, but was due to be phased out by 1968 and was being replaced by the English Electric Lightning. This was the first truly supersonic British interceptor and was a wholly admirable aircraft in respect of its speed and manoeuvrability, but it had one major drawback, limited fuel capacity, which meant that it used up much of its fuel getting at full speed to its flying ceiling. It thus required in-flight refuelling to keep it on station. Its air-to-air missile systems, Firestreak and later Red Top, were never entirely satisfactory, but both were to remain in service until the late 1980s.

Coastal Command, led by Mark Selway, also comprised two groups, Nos. 18 and 19. It was equipped almost entirely with the Avro Shackleton, the last and by no means the least distinguished derivative of the Lancaster, which was to be in service for no less than forty years, from 1951 to 1991. The Air Staff was working on issuing a requirement in 1964 for an aircraft to replace the Shackleton, but it would be the end of the decade before the first Hawker Siddeley Nimrod, based on the airframe of the de Havilland Comet, entered service.

Transport Command, at the head of which Teddy Hudleston, soon to be appointed Commander, Allied Air Forces Central Europe, was succeeded at the end of 1963 by 'Bing' Cross, was effectively divided into three forces. The Strategic Force consisted of the more modern Britannias and Comets for trooping and long distance communications, with the Vickers VC 10 on order. The Short Belfast, for very heavy and long-range lifting, was also on order, due to fly before the end of the year and to enter service in 1966. The

Medium Range Force deployed Hastings and Beverleys, together with the lighter Armstrong Whitworth Argosy, which had entered service in 1962. The Short Range Force contained the RAF's helicopters, together with the Pioneers and the Twin Pioneers.

Flying Training Command, under the leadership of Gus Walker, deployed a variety of aircraft. Chipmunks were still in use to some extent for *ab initio* training, but even basic training had since the mid-1950s been carried out on jet aircraft, and specifically the Hunting Jet Provost, whilst a variety of other types were also on the strength.

The other UK Commands were Technical Training, under Alfred 'Tubby' Earle, Maintenance, under Norman Coslett, and Signals, under Walter Pretty.

The RAF retained a significant presence overseas. RAF Germany, of which Ronald Lees was simultaneously the C-in-C and the Commander of the Second Allied Tactical Air Force, occupied five stations in North Rhine-Westphalia and comprised twelve squadrons, deploying Canberras for tactical strike and photo reconnaissance roles and Javelins for air defence, with two Hunter squadrons used for tactical reconnaissance. The Near East Air Force, based on Cyprus under Denis Barnett, also deployed Canberras and Javelins, whilst Air Forces Middle East, now commanded by AVM Johnnie Johnson, a celebrated fighter ace of the war, retained the mix of aircraft with which Sam was very familiar. Finally, there were the Canberras and Hunters of the Far East Air Force in Singapore, where Sam had recently visited the AOC-in-C, 'Mac' McGregor.

It was three years since Sam had had the benefit of an overview of the RAF whilst serving as DCAS, and he needed to come back up to speed very rapidly. His immediate priority was to carry out inspections of each of the Home Commands, which he managed to achieve by the end of the year, together with a four-day tour of RAF Germany. His long service in Aden and two recent visits to Singapore had covered a significant proportion of the service's overseas activities, which was just as well, as in late 1963 Confrontation with Indonesia turned from threats into action, whilst in early 1964 an armed revolt broke out in the Radfan area between Aden and the Yemen.

Shortly after Sam had become CAS, Indonesian mobs had stormed the British and Malaysian embassies in Djakarta and the Malaysian consulates in Sumatra. The immediate requirement for the RAF was the evacuation of women and children, with some 400 flown out to Singapore over a 24-hour period. Hostile activity grew on the borders of Sabah and Sarawak, requiring the deployment of Javelins and Hunters to the territory, whilst Belvedere, Whirlwind and Wessex helicopters and Twin Pioneers were despatched to provide mobility in the jungle to the army units operating there. As tensions grew, Canberras and V-Bombers were sent to Singapore to act as a further deterrent. The tri-service organization once again worked well, under the leadership of Varyl Begg, although Sam had to deal with some criticism by the Army of inadequate helicopter support in the early days, as a result of which an additional twelve Whirlwinds were deployed.

At the beginning of 1964 trouble broke out in the Radfan, the mountainous area lying between Aden and the town of Dhala, close to the Yemen border. This was, as ever, stirred up by Egypt and the Government of Yemen, which had armed the rebels. Three battalions of the Federal Regular Army, supported by British armour, artillery and engineers, were airlifted on to a defensive position in the mountains by Belvedere and Wessex helicopters. Although they had some success, the permanent garrisoning of Radfan was beyond their resources. They were pulled out, and at the end of April British troops were sent in, supported by ground attack Hunters. A pitched battle in June saw the dissidents comprehensively defeated, and although Radfan continued to be a sore in the side of the Government of the Federation, the threat was greatly diminished, at least for the time being.

Sam knew that he could leave the RAF's operations in Borneo and South Arabia to very competent subordinates, although he monitored closely what was going on. He had other priorities, one of which was to get to know the members of the Air Council and the Air Staff. The Secretary of State for Air at the time of his appointment was Hugh Fraser, and the senior civil servant, the Permanent Under-Secretary, was the highly experienced Sir Maurice Dean, who had been in the post since 1955 and was well known to Sam. There were two Deputy Under-Secretaries, Sir Henry Smith and Martin (later Sir Martin) Flett, who would succeed Dean in the following year and go on to be Second Permanent Secretary at the Ministry of Defence. The service members were 'Digger' Kyle, the VCAS, Christopher Hartley, the DCAS, Walter Cheshire, the Air Member for Personnel and John Davis, the Air Member for Supply and Equipment. The Assistant Chiefs of the Air Staff included two of those who had been withdrawn with Sam from the IDC at the time of the Suez Crisis, Tom Prickett and 'Splinters' Smallwood.

Sam also had a small personal staff. His Private Secretary was a highly gifted career Air Ministry civil servant, Michael Quinlan, who would become a good friend and, many years later, go on to be the Permanent Under-Secretary at the Ministry of Defence. His Personal Staff Officer was Wing Commander Reg Bullen, who had originally trained as a navigator and had won the George Medal for pulling the wireless operator out of their burning Wellington following a crash landing, in spite of his own injuries. Bullen, who had later transferred to the Secretarial Branch, was responsible among other things for writing the briefs for Sam prior to his meetings and drafting his speeches. He was succeeded in 1966 by Wing Commander Ambrose Streatfield. The clerical side was handled by Warrant Officer Morrison, who ran the outer office.

Sam had a buzzer to summon his staff, one buzz for Quinlan, two for Bullen and three for his ADC. It was last of these who would become physically the closest to him over the next two years, accompanying him on all his journeys and getting to know Audrey very well. As CAS, Sam's first ADC was David Hawkins, who had been a National Serviceman in the RAF Regiment and had applied for a regular commission thereafter, going on to Cranwell and then to Sandhurst. Whilst serving in the Far East he was surprised to receive an order to report to the office of the CAS, where he was interviewed by Pike, as Sam was still in the Middle East. He was thus able to get his feet under the table before Sam arrived. His duties, as usual for an ADC, included making all the arrangements for travel at home and abroad, accompanying Sam on all formal visits, organizing official dinner and lunch parties and drafting the thank you letters when Sam had been entertained himself.

Hawkins, who would be followed in due course by Flight Lieutenants David Conran-Smith and Christopher Granville-White, was thus not only a member of the professional staff, but in some respects of the personal staff as well. The latter function required his frequent presence at 39 Hyde

Park Gate, the official residence of the CAS. This large and comfortable apartment came under the management of WO Ponsford, who, having proved indispensable to the Elworthys in Aden, accompanied them back to the UK. Assisted by a cook and Sam's batman, he ran a household which was both cohesive and relaxed, just as Sam and Audrey wanted. The establishment was completed by Sam's driver, Flight Sergeant 'Blackie' Blacklock, who drove the official car, an Austin Princess.

Having held his first C-in-C's conference in early November at his old stamping ground, Bomber Command HQ at High Wycombe, and visited all his Home Commands and Germany by the end of the year, Sam's next priority was to make a visit to the UK's closest ally. On 12 March 1964 he and Audrey boarded a Comet at Heathrow in company with Christine West, the wife of General Sir Michael West, the Head of the British Defence Staff in Washington, and Admiral Sir Nigel Henderson, who was to be West's successor, and his wife. Another passenger was Anthony, who was on leave from India and had taken up Sam's offer of a seat in order to visit the USA for the first time and to mix business with pleasure whilst there. After a refuelling stop at Gander, they landed at the newly renamed John F. Kennedy Airport near New York, to be met by Colonel Robert E. Gotchey, who had served on the Directing Staff at Bracknell whilst Sam was Commandant. Gotchey was now Commander of the Williams Air Force Base in Arizona but had been seconded to the Elworthys for the duration of their visit. After a day in New York they flew to March Air Force Base near Riverside in California, meeting Ed and Janet Murrow that evening in Riverside and spending the following day at the Murrows' house in La Jolla. Audrey was deeply concerned about Ed Murrow's health. A chain smoker, he had contracted lung cancer and had undergone surgery to have a lung removed a year earlier. Just over twelve months later he was to die from the disease.

The Elworthys flew to Edwards AFB on the following day. As usual Sam was on business whilst Audrey was being entertained by the wives of senior officers, but they both managed to spend a day in the Yosemite National Park. Sam paid a formal visit to the USAF Academy at Colorado Springs, before they flew to Miami for the weekend. A visit to MacDill AFB followed, where Sam was able to see the USAF's most versatile interceptor and fighter-bomber, the McDonnell Douglas F-4s of Tactical Air Command. On 23 March they landed in Washington, to be met with full military honours by the Chief of Staff of the USAF, General Curtis LeMay, whom Sam had last met on his round-the-world tour prior to becoming DCAS and with whom he and Audrey were staying. After three days of talks at the Pentagon, a visit to Systems Command for Sam and sightseeing and shopping for Audrey, they flew back to Heathrow with Anthony, who had had a most successful visit of his own.

Sam arrived back three days before one of two major events which were to take place in 1964. The first of these was the implementation of the project on which Mountbatten had set his heart many years earlier, the creation of a unified Ministry of Defence, which came into being on 1 April. From the beginning of his appointment as CDS on 1 May 1959, Mountbatten had been foiled by the united opposition of the service Chiefs and a lack of political will. In July 1962, however, the easygoing Harold Watkinson had been sacked in Macmillan's 'Night of the Long Knives' and succeeded as Minister of Defence by Peter Thorneycroft. Thorneycroft was much more open to the idea of a unified ministry, offering as it appeared to do a more streamlined and less costly organization. Moreover, Macmillan himself, initially wary of the idea, had swung in its favour. The three Chiefs at the time, Dick Hull, Tom Pike and Admiral Sir Caspar John, remained firmly opposed to the reforms, but the Prime Minister and Thorneycroft were now determined to see them through.

The first step was to extend Mountbatten's tenure as CDS. He had been First Sea Lord for four years and CDS for another four and, now into his sixties, was well past the normal retirement age. However, he was the only man who could do the job, so his tenure was extended by another two years from 1963 to 1965. Shortly afterwards, it was agreed by the Prime Minister and Thorneycroft that Mountbatten should write a brief paper setting out his ideas as to how a unified Ministry of Defence would look and operate. Working in conjunction with Solly Zuckerman, the Chief Scientific Adviser and a longstanding ally from the war years, Mountbatten produced his paper within two months. In it he rejected the organization adopted by the Canadians, of a single, wholly homogenous armed service, with common ranks, uniforms, training and doctrine, but nevertheless proposed some radical changes. These were that there should be a single Secretary of State, assisted by two Ministers who would have functional rather than single service responsibilities and three who would be responsible for the individual services. The three service staffs would be integrated into a single Defence Staff, responsible only to the CDS, whilst their Chiefs would no longer exist, other than as advisers.

Unsurprisingly, the three service Chiefs were viscerally opposed to the proposals and not only sought, and very quickly received, support from a number of their predecessors, but produced a paper themselves, accepting the principle of overseas tri-service commands and some strengthening of the central defence staff, whose deficiencies had been only too evident during *Vantage*, but totally rejecting any further integration. Macmillan, taken aback by the strength of opinion, opted for a well-established political expedient, an independent report. This was undertaken by two men who had made their names on Churchill's personal staff during the war, General Lord Ismay, later the first Secretary General of NATO, and Lieutenant General Sir Ian Jacob, a former Director General of the BBC. Ismay had also been Chief of Staff to Mountbatten when the latter was Viceroy of India.

The report took a mere six weeks to write. By selecting Ismay and Jacob, Macmillan and Mountbatten had effectively stacked the deck, as they had been two of a three-man committee which had reported to Clement Attlee on the subject in 1946, advocating greater integration of the services, whilst Jacob had also prepared a memorandum on the subject for Montgomery in 1948. They now advanced three possible alternatives. The first proposed some strengthening of the CDS's role and the choice of the best man for the position, rather than have it taken by the three services in rotation, but otherwise substantially accepted the status quo. The second proposed the co-location of the service staffs and the Defence Staff in a single building, the downgrading of the political head of each service from secretary of state to junior minister, the replacement of the Board of Admiralty, the Army Council and the Air Force Council with Navy, Army and Air Force Boards and the strengthening of the Defence Staff. However, the individual service Chiefs would retain their responsibilities as the professional heads of their services. The third option was similar to Mountbatten's proposal, the creation of a fully integrated ministry, with all officers of two-star rank

ACM Sir William Dickson (CAS), Lord de Lisle (Secretary of State for Air), the Queen and AM Sir Dermot Boyle (AOC-in-C Fighter Command) watch the flying display at RAF Odiham during the Coronation Review, whilst the Duke of Edinburgh talks to a WAAF officer.

Sam climbs into his personal Hawker Hunter at RAF North Weald for a visit to the USAF at RAF Manston.

Sam at the RAF Staff College, Bracknell with Admiral of the Fleet the Earl Mountbatten and Air Commodore James Gordon-Finlayson.

Sam with his immediate subordinates in Middle East Command: (clockwise from top left) Major General Jim Robertson, Air Vice-Marshal Fred Rosier, Vice Admiral Roy Talbot, Major General Derek Goodwin.

Audrey with the Sharif of Beihan.

Sam, Audrey, Christopher and Clare with Sir Charles Johnston, Governor of Aden.

Sam as C-in-C Middle East.

Sam sailing *Jambia* with his Personal Staff Officer, Don Arnott, as his crew.

Perseverance Cottage, Sam and Audrey's country retreat near Henley.

CAS Conference 1965.

Standing: (L to R) Tom Shirley (Signals Command), Paddy Dunn (Flying Training Command), Peter Wykeham (Far East Air Force), Donald Evans (Technical Training Command), Johnny Johnson (Middle East Air Force), Paul Holder (Coastal Command), Christopher Hartley (DCAS), Tom Prickett (Near East Air Force), 'Zulu' Morris (Fighter Command), Norman Coslett (Maintenance Command), Gus Walker (Inspector-General RAF).

Seated: (L to R) Ronald Lees (RAF Germany), Brian Burnett (VCAS), 'Digger' Kyle (Bomber Command), Ted Hudleston (Allied Air Forces Central Europe), Sam (CAS), Bill MacDonald (Air Secretary), John Grandy (Far East Command), David Lee (AMP), 'Bing' Cross (Transport Command).

The Chiefs of Staff Committee 1964: (L to R) Lord Mountbatten (CDS), Admiral Sir David Luce (First Sea Lord), Sam (CAS), AVM John Lapsley (Secretary COSC), Brigadier John Gibbon (Director of Defence Plans), General Sir Richard Hull (CGS).

Sam with the Queen and Lord Shackleton (Minister of Defence for the RAF) on the roof of the Ministry of Defence to watch the fly-past marking the 25th Anniversary of the Battle of Britain.

Sam about to board an Avro Vulcan for the annual fishing camp for senior NATO officers on the Eagle River.

'A way of living, not just a means of transport'! Audrey's beloved Comet at RNZAF Ohakea during their round-the-world tour in March 1966. To the right of Audrey are Christopher, Sam, Tony, True, Bertha, Di Wilson and James Wilson, with Hamish Wilson fourth from left.

George Thompson, Denis Healey, Sam and General Sir Michael Carver at the Five Power Conference in Kuala Lumpur in June 1968.

Sam meets President Nixon in the White House. General Earle 'Bus' Wheeler, Chairman of the US Joint Chiefs of Staff, is in the left foreground.

Sam inspects the Bundeswehr in Bonn with General Ulrich de Maizière.

Sam on the Rhine with two
of his key civil servants,
Ewen Broadbent and Frank
Cooper, during a meeting
of the Nuclear Power
Group.

Sam with WO 'Blackie'
Blacklock, his long serving
driver.

Sam takes the salute on
the steps of the Ministry
of Defence on his last
day of service, 8 April
1971. Behind him stand
his successor, Admiral
Sir Peter Hill-Norton,
with General Sir Michael
Carver, Air Chief Marshal
Sir Denis Spotswood and
(in suit) Brigadier Robert
Ford.

Sam and Audrey at Windsor Castle.

Sam's study in the Norman Tower with its round desk and portcullis.

Audrey launches the *British Prospector* in Nagasaki, November 1971.

Sam with his two supporters, Lords Carrington and Shackleton, at his Introduction to the House of Lords in June 1972.

Christopher, Tim, Clare Sam, Audrey and Anthony, together in 1977 for the first time in many years.

Knight Companion of the Most Noble Order of the Garter.

Garter Day 1977 – Sam and the Earl of Cromer lead the procession of Garter Knights.

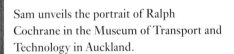

Sam unveils the portrait of Ralph Cochrane in the Museum of Transport and Technology in Auckland.

Sam talks to Arthur Harris at the dinner in his and Audrey's honour at the RAF Staff College, Bracknell in July 1978.

The new house at
Gordons Valley.

Sam about to take flight at a New
Zealand Air Training Corps
camp.

Audrey with Hester
and John Elworthy.

Sam with his beloved sister Di.

One of many visitors from the UK – Field Marshal Sir Edwin (later Lord) Bramall, at that time the CDS.

Audrey with Peter Kenrick.

Croquet at Gordons Valley.

Sam feeding his tame magpie, Maggie, and her friends.

Sam at the South Pole – 26 November 1985.

Sam with every one of his children, grandchildren, step-grandchildren and their spouses at Coates House, the home of Tim and Anabel, on 11 July 1992 during his last visit to the UK. All are Elworthy, unless otherwise shown.

Back: Edward, Mandy, Tracy, Caroline, Robert Churchill

Centre: Richard Block, Lucy, Anabel, Alexander, Annie, Anthony, Chris, Serena Churchill, Kate, Anthony Cary, Clare Cary, Tim

Front: Sam Cary, Arthur Cary, Tom Cary, Harriet Cary

'Just call me Sam' – in New Zealand in the late 1980s.

and above wearing a common uniform rather than the one specific to their service and being given tri-service responsibilities. Ismay and Jacob rejected the first proposal, recommended the second and suggested that the third might be a long-term objective.

Macmillan and Thorneycroft enthusiastically accepted the recommendation, which was endorsed by the Cabinet and was the subject of a White Paper published in July 1963. It did not go as far as Mountbatten wished, but he was realistic enough to accept that it satisfied most of his objectives. Equally, the three service Chiefs disliked much of what was proposed and managed to get some of the details changed, but were relieved that it did not go nearly as far as Mountbatten's paper and preserved both the individual identities of their services and their own authority. Whatever the arguments at the time, the basic structure has proved sufficiently robust to remain essentially the same today, although the status of the Chief of the Defence Staff, as adviser on matters of defence to the Prime Minister and the Secretary of State, has significantly increased, while that of the three service Chiefs has commensurately diminished.

One of the most important aspects of the new organization was co-location. There were few buildings large enough around Whitehall, other than those already occupied by powerful ministries such as the Foreign Office and the Treasury. One suitable building did exist, however, of largely post-war construction, occupying a large area between Whitehall and the Embankment, with its entrances at either end on Horse Guards Avenue and Richmond Terrace. To its relief, as disruption was minimal as a result, the Air Ministry was one of the existing occupants, along with the Board of Trade, which left to make way for the Navy and Army staffs. The building was subdivided in two ways, vertically between the three services, with the RAF continuing to occupy the Richmond Terrace end, the Navy at the other end and the Army in the middle, and horizontally by function. The sixth floor was the nerve centre, with offices for the Secretary of State and junior ministers, the CDS and other service Chiefs, the senior civil servants and the Chief Scientist. Whilst there was no overall integration, four integrated staffs were created, for Operations, Operational Requirements, Signals and Intelligence.

All of this had been effectively agreed in principle by the time Sam took up his appointment as CAS. A joint working party from the three services was set up to plan and implement the organizational changes and the move, and he had to appear before it from time to time. Field Marshal Lord Bramall, then closely involved in the reorganization as a staff officer, believed that Sam saw the changes as inevitable.[1] His experience as a tri-service C-in-C and his professional relationship with Mountbatten had probably resulted in a readier acceptance of the reorganization by him than by Pike or, for that matter, Hull, who continued as Chief of the General Staff, albeit with the word 'Imperial' removed from his title. Nevertheless, Sam was later to say that he found it 'a difficult and traumatic business'.[2]

Sam now had two major roles, as the head of his own service and as a member of the Chiefs of Staff Committee, which was the professional advisory body to the government on military strategy and operations; he was also a member of the Defence Council, which included the senior politicians and civil servants as well as the service chiefs, but in practice this met only rarely. His membership of the COSC brought him into frequent contact with Mountbatten. On a professional level Sam was wary of the CDS, notwithstanding that he continued to attribute to him, rightly or wrongly, all the credit for his appointment as C-in-C in Aden, a vital stepping stone on his path to becoming CAS. As far as the COSC was concerned, Mountbatten had an unfortunate habit of trying to get his own way by methods which many considered to be devious. His detractors were led by Hull, an orthodox and straightforward soldier who deplored some aspects of his behaviour, notably his practice of telling ministers that agreement had been reached between the Chiefs when this was not the case. Sam himself confronted Mountbatten in the strongest terms in just such an instance, going as far as to accuse the CDS of lying and expecting to lose his job as a result, only to be told to forget it by Mountbatten, who at the same time did not deny the charge. Mountbatten was totally shameless in such circumstances, even referring to the matter on a number of occasions subsequently, invariably maintaining that he had been in the right.

Sam's relationship with Mountbatten was cordial on a personal level, helped not a little by Audrey, who was both an excellent hostess herself and an amusing guest whenever she and Sam were invited to stay at Broadlands, the Mountbatten residence. In July 1964 Sam even extended an invitation to Mountbatten to join him on the first of what were to become annual trips during his time as CAS and CDS, a brief holiday during the salmon fishing season on the Eagle River in Labrador as a guest of his Canadian colleagues. Usually there were some senior American officers there as well, and it provided an excellent informal opportunity for networking. On the first occasion Sam and Mountbatten travelled by Transport Command, but subsequently, more often than not, Sam flew in a Vulcan, in which he had a camp bed installed, whilst the salmon were kept frozen in the bomb bay!

Sam's position also brought him into frequent contact with the Secretary of State for Defence and, if he was able to deal satisfactorily with Mountbatten for most of the time, he found it quite impossible to develop any proper understanding with Thorneycroft. The most difficult issue was the question of a new strike-cum-air defence fighter to meet the requirements of both the RAF and the Royal Navy. In Sam's words:

> Thorneycroft decided, with advice from Solly Zuckerman very largely, that they had to have the same aircraft. Although David Luce, who was then CNS or First Sea Lord, and I agreed in general, we were both equally agreed that there must be some variations. But Thorneycroft, to my mind, was quite blind to this issue. It had to be a standard aircraft for both services ... But to have the standard aircraft was operational madness for both the Navy and the Air Force. It was this thing that I could never get across to Thorneycroft, who insisted, 'I'm just saying flatly that it's going to be the same aircraft.' Well, it didn't matter very much because Thorneycroft, along with the Government, went out of office.[3]

Sam was, of course, referring to the second significant event of 1964, the General Election, which brought the Labour Party back to power for the first time since 1951.

Chapter 15

The Defence Review

Just over a month after Sam became CAS, Harold Macmillan resigned as Prime Minister due to ill health and was succeeded by Alec Douglas-Home, a compromise candidate chosen after support for the front-runners was split. After thirteen years in office the Conservatives were widely considered to be in decline, tarnished by, among other things, the Profumo affair. The General Election of 15 October 1964 brought the Labour Party to power under Harold Wilson, albeit with a slim overall majority of only four seats.

The new Secretary of State for Defence was Denis Healey, a very different proposition to Thorneycroft. Healey was possessed of a formidable intellect, as might be expected of a former scholar of Balliol College, Oxford who had achieved a double first in Greats. He had served as an officer in the Royal Engineers during the war, seeing action as a Military Landing Officer in Southern Italy and at Anzio, which gave him practical experience of combined operations. He was, in general, well disposed towards the armed forces. After the war he had entered politics as the International Secretary of the Labour Party, a post which enabled him to travel widely and to build up an impressive web of connections in both Europe and the United States. He was elected to the House of Commons in 1952 and rose up through the ranks as a supporter of the Leader of the Opposition, Hugh Gaitskell. From the beginning of his political career his main interests were international affairs and defence, and after serving as a front bench spokesman on the Commonwealth and the Colonies he was appointed Shadow Secretary of State for Defence when Wilson succeeded Gaitskell in 1963, following the latter's death.

Healey thus came to the Defence Ministry exceptionally well prepared. After Thorneycroft he was, in many ways, a breath of fresh air. Unlike his predecessor he was able to countenance different points of view, but equally unlike him, he would achieve his goals by force of argument rather than sheer obduracy. Right from the start he knew what he was talking about. Sam, himself possessed of no mean intellect, found him highly stimulating and soon recognized that he was a master of his brief. Moreover, on the purely personal front Healey was very accessible, often stopping in the corridors of the ministry to chat, even to secretaries and typists. He had a highly developed sense of humour, which added to his popularity.

Healey was, however, first and foremost a politician. He was impatient with the processes in the Ministry of Defence, in which most issues had to go through layers of staff work before a conclusion could be reached, and he took steps to ensure that the system was circumvented whenever he required, but was not receiving, a fast response. He could even, on occasion, be something of a bully in order to achieve his ends. Moreover, he was not above using tactics which some found unacceptable, one of which was the long established political practice of 'divide and rule', trying to split off one or more of the Chiefs against the others.

Healey and Mountbatten got along well together on the whole, although they held differing views about further integration of the Ministry of Defence, Healey firmly insisting on leaving the organization as it now was. On the other hand, to the CDS's delight, the Secretary of State was strongly in favour of retaining Great Britain's nuclear deterrent, unlike certain of his colleagues who demanded unilateral disarmament. At a meeting at Chequers from 22 to 24 November 1964, nicknamed 'The Crunch' by the Press and attended by ministers and the service Chiefs, the arguments were advanced by both sides, before Wilson came down in favour of continuing to build the Polaris submarines, albeit with their number reduced from five to four. It was quite clear, however, at this meeting and many others to follow, that the Treasury, which invariably outgunned the Ministry of Defence when push came to shove, had its eye on making substantial cuts to a number of other major defence projects and that the RAF, in particular, was in the line of fire.

During the early 1960s, with many of the post-war generation of aircraft approaching the end of their service lives, the RAF had a number of new models under development for introduction later in the decade. One of these was the Hawker Siddeley P1154, the aircraft over which Sam and Thorneycroft had so vigorously disagreed on the issue of the variations required respectively by the RAF and the Royal Navy. The P1154 was a supersonic strike and reconnaissance aircraft with a V/STOL (very short take-off and landing) capability, potentially suitable for use from carriers for air defence as well as from airfields. The impossibility of achieving the goals of both the services concerned had eventually resulted in a decision before the General Election that the aircraft, built to the RAF's specifications, should replace the Hunter by the end of the decade, whilst the Royal Navy should instead purchase the McDonnell Douglas F-4 Phantom. However, the P1154 now became the first casualty of the change of government, announced in the Defence White Paper of 1965, its replacement being once again the Phantom, modified for use by the RAF.

Sam considered the P1154 to have been a gamble and shed no tears at its cancellation. There were major problems associated with its plenum chamber burning technology, which was essential for supersonic flight, and the costs associated with resolving them had mounted unacceptably. This technology was not used in another aircraft under development at Hawker Siddeley, the P1127, named initially the Kestrel and later the Harrier. This incorporated the innovative Pegasus engine, whose vectored thrust used in VTOL was much simpler in concept, although it did not permit supersonic speed in level flight. Sam considered that the Harrier had inherent weaknesses, particularly its short range and modest bomb load, and believed that it was eventually ordered into production not because it was an essential part of the United Kingdom's defence requirements, but because the Labour Government could not face the political implications of abandoning it, including major redundancies in the British aircraft industry. In spite of its deficiencies, however, he was glad to see it added to the RAF's order of battle when it entered service in 1969.

Sam was also content with the decision to cancel another aircraft, the HS.681, at the same time as the P1154. The HS.681 was designed to be the replacement for the Beverley and the Hastings, Transport Command's tactical lifting workhorses, both of which were nearing the end of their service lives. The HS.681 was yet another complex project, once again using advanced engine technology to provide a STOL or even a VTOL capability. Sam thought it was over-ambitious, with a specification which bordered on the extravagant. In this case, therefore, the Air Staff was only too pleased, when asked to suggest an alternative, to point to the Lockheed C-130 Hercules, which had entered service with the USAF in 1956 and had subsequently been acquired by both the RAAF and the RCAF. It met all the RAF's operational requirements, so much so that, remarkably, it is still in service fifty years later. However, by so doing, and by also ordering the Phantom, albeit powered by the Rolls-Royce Spey engine and equipped with a Ferranti attack system, the Government had broken the 'Buy British' rule which had been in place since shortly after the war, establishing a clear precedent for the future.

This precedent was to be applied as a remedy for the third major cancellation, which took place some months later than the other two, in April 1965. The project under fire this time was the TSR-2 and this one was of greater personal interest to Sam, as it had been very much his ' baby' whilst he was DCAS and he had at the time been 'an immense advocate'[1] of the aircraft. The TSR-2 was always intended to be a replacement for the Canberra, which had been in service since the early 1950s. Following the introduction of the V-Bombers, the Canberra had lost its strategic bombing function, whilst remaining an important part of the RAF, particularly overseas, in the tactical strike and photo-reconnaissance roles.[2] It was in the former role, which continued to include a nuclear capability, that the TSR-2 was initially intended to fill the gap, although it could also replace the V-Bombers when they were retired.

The problem with the TSR-2 was once again the escalation of costs, largely associated with its highly advanced technology. On the original assumption that 150 aircraft were to be purchased, the estimated cost had risen to £750m. As the number actually required was significantly reduced, the cost per unit increased sharply, and when the RAAF, which had shown interest at first, pulled out in favour of buying the General Dynamics F-111 from the Americans, the situation became untenable. Sam had always been worried about the way in which the aircraft had been developed. He considered that the process had been lethargic, with the RAF often at odds with the manufacturer and the Ministry of Aviation over the specifications. Notwithstanding the criticisms of his many friends in the aircraft industry, some of whom were former colleagues, he had recommended to Hugh Fraser, the Secretary of State for Air, even before the election that it be cancelled and he now supported Healey's decision.

The question then arose of a replacement aircraft, for which there were three candidates. One was the Blackburn Buccaneer, the first model of which had been in service with the Royal Navy for just over a year, with a more powerful version on order. However, it failed to meet the RAF's requirements on range and speed, whilst in the strike role it would need very different radar and attack navigation systems. The second was the French Dassault Mirage, fitted with Rolls-Royce Spey engines. Quite apart from the difficulties of fitting the Spey into the airframe, the aircraft did not match up to the RAF's specifications in a number of other respects.

This left the aircraft which the Air Staff had wanted since the TSR-2 project began to falter, the General Dynamics F-111, a swing-wing supersonic strategic bomber which met all the RAF's requirements. According to Sam it was better than the TSR-2 in some ways, notably because of its excellent radar system, and less good in others, but overall it was broadly comparable. It was already flying and due to enter service with the USAF in 1967 and could be available to the RAF in the early 1970s. Moreover, the Americans were prepared to let the RAF have it at a fixed price, which worked out at about £2.3m for each of the fifty aircraft to be ordered, a fraction of the cost of the TSR-2. Healey was persuaded, and discussions on a potential order began with the manufacturer.

At the same time the British and French Governments signed an agreement to develop two further aircraft. One of these was a ground-attack fighter, also used as an advanced trainer, which would come into service nine years later as the SEPECAT Jaguar. The other was a much more complex project, the development of the Anglo-French Variable Geometry aircraft, which in RAF service would complement the F-111s and allow the retirement of not only the remaining Canberras, but also the V-Bombers.

The RAF was not the only candidate for defence cuts. The Army was the least badly hit, although it had to accept the reorganization of the Territorial Army into the much smaller Territorial Army and Volunteer Reserve. It was the Royal Navy, however, which now came under close scrutiny, and particularly its largest project other than the Polaris submarines and their missiles, the new fleet aircraft carrier, the CVA-01.

During the course of the Second World War the aircraft carrier had replaced the battleship as the capital ship of the world's two biggest navies, those of the United States and Great Britain. The Royal Navy ended the war with six fleet carriers, twelve light fleet carriers and over thirty escort carriers, but peace brought an immediate and very large reduction in the carrier fleet, and from the late 1940s onwards the number carrying fixed-wing aircraft stabilized at four to five. By 1964 only one of the wartime fleet carriers, HMS *Victorious*, remained in service, having provided a welcome reinforcement for Sam during Operation *Vantage*. Two more fleet carriers of post-war construction, HMS *Ark Royal* and HMS *Eagle*, along with two smaller carriers, HMS *Centaur*, shortly to be paid off, and HMS *Hermes*, comprised the remainder of those carrying fixed-wing aircraft, whilst HMS *Bulwark*, another veteran of *Vantage*, and HMS *Albion* had been refitted as commando carriers, carrying helicopters. All of these had a limited future life and would require very expensive refits and modernizations in order to remain up-to-date.

In the knowledge that *Centaur* was approaching the end of her life and that *Ark Royal* and *Victorious* were due to be scrapped in the early 1970s, leaving just *Eagle* and *Hermes*, both of which required modernization, in 1959 the Admiralty proposed that five new carriers should be built over the next twenty years as replacements. The proposal encountered strong opposition from both the Air Ministry and the Treasury. The former maintained that the East of Suez role could be carried out much more cheaply by land-based TSR-2s and other aircraft. The latter was deeply concerned about the price tag for each of the new ships, initially estimated to be £50m. Faced with such opposition, the Admiralty, in which the then First Sea Lord, Sir Caspar John, was the first naval aviator to hold this appointment, scaled down its proposals to four carriers in 1962 but continued to meet opposition from the Treasury, which now believed that each one would cost double the amount previously suggested. The upshot was an agreement in principle in mid-1963 to build one new ship, the CVA-01, and to modernise *Eagle* and *Hermes*, thus ensuring a force of three carriers into the 1980s. This plan, however, was thrown into uncertainty by the formation of the new Labour Government.

Before any further decisions could be made, however, Healey and the Chiefs of Staff took a step back to look at the air components of all three services, with a view to rationalization. In January 1965 a committee was set up comprising three senior retired officers, whose terms of reference were: 'To determine the most efficient and economical organization for the control and employment of air power in support of National Defence Policy'. As Chairman they chose Field Marshal Sir Gerald Templer, a former CIGS. Templer, who was well known to and much admired by Sam, was regarded by both the Royal Navy and the RAF as a good choice, as the Army was seen to be neutral on the subject matter; whilst the Army Air Corps actually deployed much the same number of aircraft as the Fleet Air Arm, these were substantially helicopters and light aircraft employed in communications and the close logistic support of ground forces and did not threaten the strategic roles of either of the other two services. The Royal Navy and RAF members of the Committee were, respectively, Caspar John, who had been succeeded as First Sea Lord by David Luce shortly before Sam became CAS, and Denis Barnett, who had recently retired. Three assistants were also appointed, one from each of the services, the RAF representative being AVM Andrew Humphrey, himself a future CAS and, albeit very briefly, CDS.

There was more to the remit of the Committee than the terms of reference might suggest. This was seen by some as an opportunity for the radical reform of Great Britain's air forces, and there was considerable speculation about its recommendations. A fortnight before the Committee's report was issued, the authoritative magazine, *Flight International*, wrote:

> The belief is prevalent in Whitehall, and in senior military circles, that the committee … is recommending that all military air activities, including those of the Fleet Air Arm and Army Aviation, be vested in the RAF.[3]

In fact nothing could have been further from the truth, as the Committee, in its twenty-five recommendations and its conclusion, came down firmly in favour of maintaining the status quo. In particular it dismissed both the two most radical alternatives, firstly that there should be a single unified air service, and secondly that the RAF should be abolished and its tasks and resources allocated to the Royal Navy or Army as appropriate. The Committee did include recommendations on the common training and cross-posting of aircrew, on the interoperation of aircraft, including the new Phantoms and the helicopters of all three services, on common systems for air stores, stock control, repairs and overhauls and on an integrated organization for flight safety, but these, whilst sensible enough, were far from radical.

There was one minority view on an important subject. The RAF had put forward a proposal for a Common Supplementary List, which would include all those aircrew, whether destined for the RAF or the Fleet Air Arm, who were on either a short service commission or a permanent commission up to the age of thirty-eight or sixteen years' service, whichever was earlier, or who had not otherwise been offered General List commissions in the RAF or Royal Navy, which guaranteed service up to the age of at least fifty-five. Under these proposals such officers would remain in the RAF throughout their careers, but would be available to fill posts in the FAA. Barnett supported this, but Templer and John were strongly opposed, largely because the Royal Navy was not prepared to accept a situation in which the majority of its aircrew would owe their allegiance to the RAF, a situation which had existed before the war and which was always highly resented.

The Committee's Conclusion ended with the following words:

> 137. ... none of our recommendations would be of the slightest avail unless the Chiefs of Staff and the Service Boards gave a lead to those who would be charged with the responsibility for carrying them out and made it unmistakably clear that they were determined to achieve a successful and growing partnership between the Royal Navy and the Royal Air Force.

> 138. We believe that the present state of feeling between the two services at the Whitehall level is deplorable.[4]

There was a vast amount of history behind the last paragraph; indeed, it went back to the very formation of the RAF in 1918 by the amalgamation of the Royal Flying Corps and the Royal Naval Air Service. Thereafter Lord Trenchard and his successors had been forced to fight hard to maintain its independence against the lobbying of the two other services, which regarded it as unnecessary. Of the two, the Royal Navy was by far the most determined, not least because it continued to deploy aircraft on its few carriers, manned by RAF aircrew. The fact that it had operational control of these was only partial consolation. After a long campaign, the Royal Navy did achieve full control over the Fleet Air Arm just in time for the outbreak of war in 1939 and clung on to it tenaciously thereafter. It also argued hard during the war itself for full control of Coastal Command and was given operational control from February 1941 until the end of hostilities, but this fell short of direct command, let alone of administrative control.

The rivalry rumbled on after the war, with the Royal Navy continuing to cast covetous eyes on Coastal Command, and the RAF believing that it should control all service flying. However, with the progressive reduction in the armed forces from 1945 onwards due to constant cuts in defence expenditure, the real battles were in the competition for scarce financial resources, set against a background of the growing threat from the Soviet bloc and the retreat from Empire. This now came to a head in the Defence Review which was carried out by Healey through 1965 and whose results were published in the Defence White Paper of February 1966.

Unfortunately, both the process and the result of the Defence Review were to exacerbate the antipathy which existed between the Royal Navy and the RAF. Sam was exceptionally worried by the bad feeling, although he believed that it existed primarily at the level of Captain RN and Group Captain, who 'thought they were doing their utmost for their own Services, when in fact on both sides they were damaging their own Services by being so implacably opposed to anything which the opposition might do'.[5] This bitterness did not exist at the junior level, whilst Sam himself, notwithstanding his very personal involvement in the debate, appears to have remained *persona grata* with senior officers of the Royal Navy. As evidence of this, in June 1964, before the General Election but at a time when the ordering of new carriers was already a contentious issue between the RAF and the Royal Navy, Audrey was invited by David Luce to launch HMS *Intrepid*, the second of two *Fearless* class amphibious warfare ships. She and Sam were also invited to the ship's commissioning in March 1967, and she retained a strong personal connection to the ship and its officers and crew thereafter.[6]

The Templer Committee had made some good suggestions, mostly in the interests of cost savings, but it had not altered the relative positions of the

RAF and the Royal Navy. The former nevertheless felt potentially vulnerable. The loss at the end of the decade of its position as the wielder of Great Britain's strategic nuclear deterrent and the spectre of new carriers carrying out any long-range strikes East of Suez left it with the prospect of becoming, on the one hand, a transport provider and, on the other, a defensive force within NATO. Nothing could be done to reverse the decision on Polaris, but there was still the opportunity to contest the long-range tactical strike role with the Royal Navy. This, the RAF believed, could be done with the right aircraft, initially the TSR-2 and, after this was cancelled, the F-111. What it needed was bases from which these aircraft could be deployed.

As it happened, bases East of Suez already existed to some extent. However, whilst the RAF still maintained a strong presence in Aden, Bahrain and Singapore, these would not be enough to provide coverage of the whole Indian Ocean, and thus a number of island airfields had to be incorporated into what, from 1961 onwards, became known as the Island Strategy. These were Aldabra, north-west of Madagascar, Masirah, off the coast of Oman and well known to Sam from his time in Middle East Command, Gan, the southernmost island of the Maldives, and the Cocos Islands, an Australian territory 1800 miles north-west of Perth. Of these, there was an existing RAF station on Gan and more primitive airfields on Masirah and Cocos, whilst an airfield on Aldabra would have to be constructed from scratch. Aircraft with the range of TSR-2 or F-111 based on these would be able to cover the whole of the Indian Ocean and much of the land mass around its perimeter. Moreover, they would be both unsinkable and very much cheaper than the two aircraft carriers required to be on station in the Indian Ocean and Far Eastern waters at any one time.

The promotion of the Island Strategy by the RAF went back to the beginning of the decade, but it had not achieved much traction with the Conservative Government as a whole, although it was viewed favourably by the Treasury. Although the demand for new carriers had been progressively scaled down from five to just one, the Air Ministry remained resolutely opposed to them and in 1963 built a case not just in favour of the Island Strategy, but also against the carriers, whilst the Admiralty did the exact opposite. The decision at the time to go ahead with CVA-01 was a defeat for the former. However, with the installation in the following year of a Labour

Government intent on defence cuts, the whole issue came up for debate again.

Following the cancellation of TSR-2, which had been essential to the Island Strategy, and before going ahead with an order for the F-111, Healey set up a Joint Service Group to look at the issue yet again. It was chaired by Vice Admiral Sir Frank Hopkins, the Deputy Chief of the Naval Staff, who had had a long career in naval aviation, culminating in his appointment as Flag Officer Carriers. The group's report, produced in April 1965, was equivocal: it did not rule out land-based air power, but noted that there were many uncertainties about its employment, not least the availability of suitable aircraft, in the absence of which it continued to support the use of carriers.

The RAF representative on the Joint Service Group was Air Vice-Marshal Peter Fletcher, the ACAS (Policy & Plans). Fletcher was a Rhodesian who had read Law at university in South Africa and then qualified as a lawyer before joining the Southern Rhodesia Law Department. He had come to the UK in 1940 to join the RAFVR and had been granted a permanent commission in the RAF at the end of the war. He had an analytical mind and an extraordinary ability to marshal arguments, both verbally and on paper. Alongside Sam, who was to remain personally involved in every aspect of the argument, and Michael Quinlan, who remained in the background but was a crucial member of the team, Fletcher would now become the RAF's leading advocate in the ensuing debate. Having been on the directing staff of the wartime RAF Staff College in Haifa, the JSSC and the IDC, with appointments on the Joint Planning Staff and as a Director of Operational Requirements at the Air Ministry, he was ideally suited to the role.

Unlike both the Army and the RAF, the Royal Navy had never placed a high value on staff work. For the other two services, postings to their staff colleges and the IDC, as student or instructor, were a vital part of the careers of those looking for appointment to the most senior ranks. For the Royal Navy, time spent at sea was much more important. Moreover, the Admiralty itself, unlike either the War Office or the Air Ministry, assumed some of the attributes of an operational headquarters, particularly during the war. This lack of rigorous training and experience in staff work, bringing with it the capacity to deploy arguments persuasively, was to prove a great handicap in the months ahead as the Royal Navy put forward the case for carriers and the RAF for the Island Strategy, each one at the same time seeking to demolish the arguments of the other. Healey was only too aware of the disparity in the quality of the two sides:

> The navy argued its case for the carrier badly; I had to keep sending its papers back to be more persuasive. The air force, on the other hand, was represented by two able lawyers – Sam Elworthy himself, the Chief of Air Staff, and Peter Fletcher, the Air Marshal concerned with policy. They made rings round the navy, carrying the army and the Chief of Defence Staff, Dick Hull, with them.[7]

Throughout the summer of 1965 and into the autumn, papers flew back and forth, the Navy Board presenting the case for carriers and setting out what the Royal Navy would look like without them, the RAF continuing to advance the Island Strategy and, at the same time, demolishing the Royal Navy's arguments with forensic thoroughness. As Healey indicated, the 'neutrals', in the shape of the CDS and the CGS, swung in favour of the RAF view. It was deeply unfortunate for the Navy that Mountbatten's term as CDS was not further extended beyond the additional two years; although he and Healey got on well together, the latter felt that he could never have full control of Defence whilst Mountbatten remained. He was succeeded by his old foe, Dick Hull, whilst General Sir James Cassels was appointed as CGS. This left David Luce, who was far better suited to the role of C-in-C than to that of CNS, somewhat isolated on the Chiefs of Staff Committee, on which he had been able previously to look for, and usually receive, Mountbatten's support. Luce was never inclined to mount the type of all-out attack adopted by the RAF, partly because he was too much of a gentleman and partly because the Royal Navy itself was not as united as the RAF, some of its senior officers believing that too much expenditure on carriers, in addition to that on the Polaris submarines, would prejudice the interests of the rest of the surface fleet.

As the Defence Review approached its conclusion in early 1966, the tempo rose. Over four days in the second half of January Sam attended no fewer than six meetings at No. 10 Downing Street to put forward the RAF's case.

There were numerous sessions with Healey and his staff and extra meetings of the whole Chiefs of Staff Committee, not only to discuss the carrier issue but also to consider all the other implications of the Defence Review. The Cabinet met to endorse it on 14 and 15 February and it was published on 22 February. By far the most newsworthy item was the cancellation of CVA-01. As a small sop to the Royal Navy, *Ark Royal* was to be given a major refit, which would allow a three-carrier force to be extended into the mid-1970s.

In the end, the argument had boiled down to cost, with the Government committed to a financial target for the Ministry of Defence in 1969/70 of £2,000m, against £2,400m set by the previous administration. The Treasury was the key player in the game and it had, from the earliest days of the debate, been a strong supporter of the RAF's position. Following the publication of the White Paper, the Government announced its intention to order fifty F-111s.

The Royal Navy was badly bruised by the contest, accusing the RAF of foul play, most memorably for having supposedly moved either Australia or one of the islands 500 miles to the west in support of its case![8] Luce and the Navy Minister, Christopher Mayhew, felt compelled to resign, the former to prevent the resignations of other senior admirals. Luce was replaced by Varyl Begg, whose background had been in the gunnery branch and who thus had no emotional links to naval aviation. He was determined not to allow the topic to re-surface, whilst rebuilding the morale of his service in other ways. He and Sam, both with experience as C-in-Cs of integrated commands, had always got on well together and were determined to do whatever was possible to reduce the bitterness between their two services. Sadly, this did not prove to be easy to achieve in the immediate future.

All the AOC-in-Cs of the home commands had been personally briefed by Sam on the day before the White Paper was published, and those in the overseas commands were sent letters in time for the announcement of its contents. This enabled the recipients to brief Group and Station Commanders and senior staff officers on the day itself. Sam, who deeply regretted the rift with the Royal Navy, was determined to prohibit any expressions of exultation by the RAF on what was nevertheless widely deemed by all to have been a victory. Relief at the outcome was expressed in the numerous letters he received after the White Paper's publication, from both serving and retired officers. Jack Slessor, one of his predecessors, expressed the view of many when he wrote, 'I have throughout never ceased to thank goodness that you were in that chair.'[9]

In spite of the congratulations of his colleagues, this had been a bruising experience for Sam. He had never been an opponent of carriers per se, but he believed that if the country could not afford enough of them to operate effectively, then their functions should be carried out by the RAF, which could perform them much more cheaply. The arguments in support of the RAF's case for the Defence Review and the representations to the Templer Committee had taken up a year of his time, during which he had been forced to cancel or scale back a number of engagements and devote much less of his time to his commands and units in the field than he would have wished. Some commitments had been sacrosanct, such as laying a wreath at the Cenotaph on each Remembrance Sunday and participating in the celebration of the 25th Anniversary of the Battle of Britain on 18 September 1965, when a service at Westminster Abbey was followed by a visit by the Queen and the Duke of Edinburgh to the Ministry of Defence Building, from the roof terrace of which they watched a fly-past of Lightnings. Another important event in early 1965 was Winston Churchill's funeral. The Chiefs of Staff, led by Mountbatten, stood in vigil around the coffin as it lay in state in Westminster Hall and then followed it in the funeral procession, Sam later remarking that the most difficult part of the march was trying to avoid horse droppings!

Sam had also managed to fit in his annual fishing trip to Eagle River, and he and Audrey snatched a week's holiday in Ireland which included a stay with Paddy Bandon, but otherwise opportunities for leisure were few and far between. Overseas trips on official business were also reduced to a minimum, although Sam and Audrey went on a long-planned visit to the Italian Air Force in September 1965 and another to Venezuela that December. On the latter, his hosts unexpectedly announced that Sam was to be presented with a medal. He had not received the permission of the Queen, so had to refuse the honour, much to the Venezuelans' dismay.

With the White Paper out of the way, however, Sam and Audrey were now able to embark on a round-the-world trip in March and April 1966, for him to visit both some of his overseas commands and a number of Commonwealth air forces and for the two of them to catch up with the family. Setting off on 11 March, their first stop was in Cyprus, where they were met by Tom Prickett, who was simultaneously C-in-C Near East Air Force, Commander British Forces Near East and Administrator, British Sovereign Bases in Cyprus. As there were no significant issues in his command, the meeting was a brief one, and Sam and Audrey flew on to Bahrain, whither Andrew Humphrey, recently appointed as AOC Air Forces Middle East, had flown up from Aden. One of the major commitments set out in the White Paper was the withdrawal of all British Forces from Aden before the Federation of South Arabia gained its independence in 1968, so there was much to talk about in the short time that the two men met.

Sam and Audrey then flew on to Ceylon. There was a formal visit to and events hosted by the Royal Ceylon Air Force, but this trip also enabled them to see Anthony, in whose flat in Colombo they stayed. After three days they left for Singapore, in Sam's case for meetings with John Grandy, now both an air chief marshal and C-in-C of the tri-service Far East Command and by this time identified as Sam's successor as CAS, as well as with Peter Wykeham, Commander of the Far East Air Force, and Christopher Foxley-Norris, the AOC of 224 Group. Confrontation with Indonesia would be brought to an end by a peace treaty five months later, but there was still some military activity in Borneo, and Sam flew there for two days and a night to visit units on the ground. For Audrey there were the usual visits to hospitals, SSAFA and service wives' clubs, and a lot of shopping.

After four days in Singapore, Sam and Audrey, accompanied by Foxley-Norris and his wife, took off for Perth. The stopped en route on the Cocos Islands, doubtless so that Sam could see a key component of the Island Strategy. They left with some additional passengers, a small boy with a fractured skull from a bicycle accident going to Australia for urgent hospital treatment, together with his mother, her baby and a hospital nurse. Having stayed the night in Perth, they left on the next day for Canberra, where they were given a very warm welcome by their hosts, their old friends from Aden, Charles Johnston, now the British High Commissioner, and his wife Natasha.

The main purpose of the visit was for Sam to attend the ANZAM (Australia, New Zealand and Malaya) Defence Committee Meeting. ANZAM had been set up in the early 1950s in response to the Malayan Emergency, to which both Australia and New Zealand had contributed armed forces, as they had to the Confrontation with Indonesia. Notwithstanding that the latter was coming to an end, there remained considerable concern about defence issues in the Far East, not least because of the Vietnam War, in which Australia was engaged alongside the USA. Denis Healey had been in Canberra at the beginning of the previous month, on a whirlwind round-the-world tour with Dick Hull to explain the contents of the Defence White Paper to the United Kingdom's allies prior to its publication, with a focus on the carrier and aircraft programmes and the decision to withdraw from Aden. As Healey had emphasised, it was the policy of the UK Government to remain East of Suez, but clearly some of the other implications of the White Paper were causing concern. One of the most important agenda items was thus a 'Review of British Defence Policy', on the implications of which Sam was able to elaborate and answer questions.

After four days in Canberra, including further meetings for Sam with the RAAF, the Elworthys departed for New Zealand on 23 March, Sam's fifty-fifth birthday. There was a guard of honour at the airport and champagne and a cake on the plane. They arrived in Ohakea that afternoon, to find waiting to meet them not only Bertha, with Tony and True, Di and Hamish Wilson and their son, James, but also Christopher. When his schooldays at Bradfield came to an end, Christopher had decided that he wanted to pursue a career in farming and had gone out to New Zealand, where he worked initially on a hill farm in Hawke's Bay. He was to go on to spend a short time at Gordons Valley before undertaking National Service and then attending Lincoln College, at the time part of the University of Canterbury[10] and one of the country's premier educational establishment specializing in agriculture and related subjects.

After a night at Ngaio-iti with more champagne and cake, Audrey and Sam flew down to Wellington, where Sam had business to discuss with the RNZAF, whilst the others were joined by John Elworthy, his wife Hester and other members of the family. Following a weekend back at Ngaio-iti, Sam and Audrey left for Auckland, flying out of there on 29 March. The first stop was Fiji, where they stayed the night before flying on to Honolulu, where they were entertained by the USAF and Audrey visited Pearl Harbor.

The next destination, after a quick stop for refuelling at San Francisco, was Ottawa, where they were met by Air Chief Marshal Frank Miller, the first officer to become Chief of the Defence Staff following the unification of Canada's armed forces. Miller had served in Bomber Command as a base commander in 6 (RCAF) Group in 1944/5, so he and Sam had much in common. After a day of meetings for Sam they flew on to Canadian Forces Base Chatham in New Brunswick, where Tim was serving on secondment. Two very enjoyable days were spent with Tim and Victoria and their two children, Kate and Lucy, the latter born in 1965. Sam and Audrey arrived back in England on 4 April.

Sam could now get on with the more routine aspects of running the RAF. Over the previous year he had been compelled to leave many of these to his colleagues on the air staff, particularly his VCAS, in which role Kyle, posted to Bomber Command as AOC-in-C, had been succeeded by Air Marshal Sir Brian Burnett. Although Sam's contact with Healey remained close, on a day-to-day basis his political opposite number was Lord Shackleton, the Minister of State for the RAF. Eddie Shackleton had been highly supportive during the aircraft carrier debate and was later to say that he never had a serious disagreement with Sam and valued his intellect very highly.[11] He was to remain a good friend.

As far as operations were concerned, the end of Confrontation had reduced the requirement for RAF aircraft in the Far East. In South Arabia, on the other hand, the statement on withdrawal from Aden had stimulated Egypt and Yemen, the supporters of rebellion against the government, into encouraging further unrest, and the RAF became much more active, with Hunters deployed to Beihan and air patrols instituted along the Yemen border, whilst the Radfan required constant policing. Acts of terrorism became commonplace closer to Aden itself and there were even mortar attacks on Khormaksar, although they did little damage. The RAF Regiment units there found themselves increasingly acting in conjunction with the Army.

One new international development was the Unilateral Declaration of Independence by the Government of Southern Rhodesia in November 1965, leading to the application of sanctions by the United Nations Security Council. As far as the British armed forces were concerned, the main burden of applying the sanctions fell on the Royal Navy's Beira Patrol, which policed the Mozambique Channel against blockade runners, but they were supported by a force of five Shackletons from 37 Squadron, based at Majunga on the north-west coast of Madagascar. A more significant military intervention against the regime in Southern Rhodesia was considered by the British Government and put to the COSC. It was considered to be impractical in any event, but there were also grave doubts expressed by the Chiefs on how such action would impact on the morale of the armed services, many of whose members remembered the Rhodesians' support for Great Britain during the war. Sam himself was later to say that this was the one issue on which he would have resigned.

A number of developments took place on the personnel front, notably the closure of the RAF Technical College at Henlow and its amalgamation with the RAF College at Cranwell, where all RAF officers would now train together. At the same time it was decided that advanced flying training would cease at Cranwell and be carried out at dedicated flying schools, enabling the course to be shortened by six months.

Over the course of Sam's tenure as CAS the strength of the RAF fell by approximately 25,000 to 124,000, due largely to budget cuts, but also to the disbandment of the Airfield Construction Branch, whose responsibilities devolved on to the Royal Engineers. However, even at this reduced level there were still difficulties in recruitment, largely because NCOs and other ranks became less inclined to extend their service when the time came to make a choice, but preferred instead to take better paid and less stressful civilian jobs, whilst many officers retired voluntarily. In spite of continuing reductions in the establishment, these factors would continue to be a problem.

Short overseas visits to Europe resumed, but there was only one other longer trip, in November 1965. This was primarily for Sam to make a formal visit to the Indian Air Force, but the journey took him and Audrey first to Teheran. They had been there once before, on a trip at the end of 1964 which also included Pakistan, and on both occasions Sam had an audience with the Shah. Arriving on the following day at Palam, the airport for New Delhi, they were met by the Chief of Staff of the Indian Air Force, Air Chief Marshal (later Marshal of the Indian Air Force) Arjan Singh, who had won the DFC commanding 1 Squadron of the Indian Air Force in Burma in 1944. After two days of talks for Sam and a combination of shopping and visits to various schools for Audrey, they moved on to Agra to see the Taj Mahal and then to Sam's old stamping ground at Bangalore, where their host was Air Marshal P. C. Lal, another holder of the DFC who was in due course to become Arjan Singh's successor.

The journey continued to Mysore, where they had an audience with the Maharajah, who left Audrey unimpressed, before they headed off for the Defence Forces Staff College at Wellington, in the Nilgiri Hills. This was later described by Audrey as 'A Day to Remember'. After very heavy rain the direct route was blocked by landslides, so the driver took them by an alternative road. Once again they met floods, accompanied by thunder and lightning, so a third route was tried. This road was blocked too, and there was no room to turn. A long queue of cars built up, with much shouting and gesticulation from the occupants. Eventually, they clambered on foot over the obstruction to be met by cars on the other side. They arrived at the college shortly before midnight, somewhat late for dinner!

The stay in India was rounded off by a visit to the National Defence Academy near Poona, after which they flew on to Aden. For Audrey this was an excellent opportunity to meet many old friends. For Sam, there was a much more important purpose, to hold preliminary talks with the Commander-in-Chief Middle East, Admiral Sir Michael Le Fanu, and with Andrew Humphrey and his Army and Navy opposite numbers, on both the withdrawal of all British Forces from the former colony, still expected to take place following the full independence of South Arabia on 1 January 1968, and the relocation of as many units as possible to Bahrain and Sharjah.

This visit was of particular interest to Sam, but not just because of the RAF's role in the evacuation. It was already known by then that he would be stepping down as CAS in the spring of 1967 and would subsequently succeed Hull as Chief of the Defence Staff. He would thus once again have a tri-service responsibility.

Chapter 16

Chief of the Defence Staff

J ust as had happened when Sam became CAS, there was a hiatus before he was able to take up his appointment as CDS. This time it was four months long and, as in 1963, the first month was spent 'down under', but it was entirely devoted to holiday. Accompanied by Clare, who celebrated her seventeenth birthday during the trip, Sam and Audrey flew by RAF, but the usual outbound and return stops were only fleeting ones, with no substantive meetings taking place. In New Zealand they stayed with Di and Hamish Wilson at Ngaio-iti, Tony and True at Heretaunga, near Wellington, Bertha at Ringstead, Audrey's cousin, Phyl Wilson, in Auckland and various Elworthys in the South Island. They also had a whole week at Gordons Valley, Sam's longest stay there since his summer vacation from Cambridge in 1932.

On their return to the UK there were still three months of relative idleness ahead, which were largely spent at Perseverance Cottage, interspersed with numerous visits to friends and fishing holidays in Scotland and, as in previous years, on the Eagle River. After all this leisure time, it was probably with a feeling of relief that Sam, now a Marshal of the RAF, took over as CDS from Dick Hull on 4 August 1967.

When David Craig was about to assume his own appointment as CDS in 1988 he met Sam for some guidance on the role and was told that he would find it 'a doddle'.[1] With the benefit of hindsight, Craig was unable to agree, but it is clear that Sam was making a comparison with his appointment as CAS, which he had found exceptionally trying. He was later to say that he enjoyed his term as CDS and found it much less traumatic than fighting his corner as a single service chief.[2] It was, nevertheless, far from undemanding.

At this time the role of CDS had only existed in its current form for the three years since the reorganization of the Ministry of Defence by Thorneycroft and Mountbatten. If anything, Hull had turned the clock back on the first of those years, during which Mountbatten had tended to push the boundaries of the collaborative model of the Chiefs of Staff Committee, on occasion behaving like the supreme commander he had once been and would have liked to be again. In contrast, Hull reverted to being simply the chairman of a committee, the single service chiefs becoming more powerful during his tenure as a result. Sam stood somewhere between the two: he was the voice of the chiefs, steering them into taking a common position on the issues with which they were presented, but he also provided a level of leadership which Hull had not. Nevertheless, although unquestionably *primus inter pares*, he was never the dominant service figure in the defence organization which his successors became a decade or so later and are still today.[3]

From his experience in Middle East Command, Sam was well equipped for his new role, recognizing that he had to be impartial when it came to disagreements between the three services, especially when the RAF was involved. He was fortunate in his colleagues. John Grandy, who was CAS for the whole of Sam's term as CDS, was an old friend in whom he reposed complete confidence. Arguably Grandy's greatest achievement was to oversee the merger of Bomber and Fighter Commands into Strike Command on 30 April 1968, joined by Signals Command on 1 January 1969 and Coastal Command on 28 November of the same year. Varyl Begg, who did much to calm the Royal Navy in the aftermath of the carrier decision, focusing instead on guided missile-equipped surface ships, was succeeded as First Sea Lord in 1968 by Michael Le Fanu. Like Begg, Grandy and Sam himself, Le Fanu was a former tri-service C-in-C and a most likeable individual, with a lively sense of humour, which included referring to himself on occasion as the Chinese admiral, Lee Fan Yew! For the Army, Jim Cassels was followed as CGS, also in 1968, by George Baker,[4] a sound and amiable gunner, who also did much to help heal the divisions between the services.

The colleague with whom Sam had to work most closely was his deputy, the Vice-Chief of the Defence Staff, Vice Admiral Sir Ian Hogg, who was followed in 1970 by Air Marshal Sir John Barraclough. Hogg had a relevant background from his previous job as Defence Services Secretary, responsible among other things for making recommendations in respect of the most senior tri-service appointments. The office of the VCDS was situated with

Sam's, and their personal staffs sat together. In addition, there were also the Deputy Chief of the Defence Staff (Operational Requirements), Air Marshal Sir Neil Wheeler, followed in 1968 by Lieutenant General Sir Noel Thomas, and two Assistant Chiefs of the Defence Staff, responsible respectively for Operations and Policy. From February 1968 to August 1970 the latter appointment was held by Air Vice-Marshal Neil Cameron, later to be one of Sam's successors as CAS and CDS.

The Chiefs were supported by the Chiefs of Staff Secretariat, under its Secretary, who in 1967 was Brigadier John Gibbon, succeeded in November 1968 by Commodore Peter Bayne. The Secretariat also consisted of an officer of the rank of colonel or its equivalent as Assistant Secretary and seven other officers of the rank of lieutenant colonel or its equivalent, each of whom was responsible for a specific part of the world, to which they were connected round the clock via a network of outposts. Between them they produced the papers for the COSC meetings, which were circulated to the Chiefs in advance, whilst one of them also took the minutes.[5] The meetings were always attended by the Permanent Under-Secretary, Sir James Dunnett, the Second Permanent Secretary, Sir Martin Flett, and the Chief Scientific Adviser, Sir William Cook, usually by a senior civil servant from the Foreign Office and sometimes by others, such as the Chief of the Secret Intelligence Service.

There were three officers at any one time on Sam's personal staff. The most senior was initially called the Military Assistant 1 or MA1, in which position David Craig, a wing commander before promotion to group captain, was followed initially by Commander Philip Cranfield. In early 1969 the position was renamed Personal Staff Officer and was held thereafter by a one-star officer, the first of whom was Commodore Peter White, who had been in the Paymaster's Branch of the Royal Navy and was regarded as a formidable Whitehall operator, but was not much liked by his colleagues. He was followed by Brigadier Patrick Howard-Dobson and then by Brigadier Robert Ford, both of whom were much more popular. The PSO handled the professional side of the office, dealing with policy and giving instructions to and receiving output from the CDS Briefing Staff, which was similar to the COS Secretariat in its composition and procedures. Next in seniority on the personal staff was the Military Assistant, initially called the MA2, who was responsible for the smooth running of Sam's office and for organizing his programme, including overseas travel. This was initially Major Alastair Tower, followed by Major Iain Ferguson and then by Squadron Leader K. F. Beck.

Finally, there was Sam's ADC, Flight Lieutenant Nick Adamson, succeeded by Captain Vyvyan Harmsworth. As well as accompanying him on most of his official visits, both at home and abroad, the ADC continued to be as concerned with Sam's household as with his office. Sam and Audrey were now accommodated in a spacious flat in Kingston House North, Knightsbridge, to which they had been accompanied by WO Ponsford, whilst 'Blackie' Blacklock remained Sam's driver.

Freed from the responsibility of leading his own service, Sam was now the professional face of Great Britain's defence establishment. Overseas trips continued at a considerable rate, but they were no longer to RAF commands and units, but rather to the United Kingdom's allies, who were grouped into a number of bodies, of which the most important and enduring was the North Atlantic Treaty Organisation. NATO had been founded in 1949 in response to the potential threat from the Soviet Union and subsequently the other countries of the Warsaw Pact. It consisted of the USA, Canada and the majority of the states of Western and Southern Europe other than France, which had withdrawn in 1959, and traditional neutrals such as Sweden and Switzerland. From 1952 it had also included Turkey. The UK had a permanent representative on the Military Committee, who during most of Sam's tenure as CDS was Air Chief Marshal Sir David Lee, an old friend. However, Sam always attended the Military Committee's formal meetings himself, as well as those of the Nuclear Planning Group, and was a frequent visitor to SHAPE (Supreme Headquarter Allied Powers in Europe), where the Deputy Supreme Commander was, by tradition at the time and more often than not thereafter, a British officer. For the majority of Sam's time as CDS this was Bobby Bray, by that time General Sir Robert, who, like David Lee, had served under him in Aden.

The second body to which the UK belonged was the Central Treaty Organisation. CENTO had begun life as the Baghdad Pact, an alliance formed in 1955 between Iran, Iraq, Turkey, Pakistan and the UK, with participation by the USA on its military committee. Iraq had pulled out in 1959 following the coup by General Qasim. Once again, this was an organization intended to defend against aggression by the USSR. It proved to be the least successful of the alliances, largely because of the difficulties posed by Arab/Israeli conflicts and by the unwillingness of the other members to side with Pakistan in its wars with India. During the late 1960s, however, it was still seen as an important buttress against the Soviet Union, and Sam made a point of attending its meetings at least once a year and frequently entertained its senior politicians and officers on their visits to London.

Finally, there was SEATO, the South East Asia Treaty Organisation, whose members were the USA, the UK, France, Australia, New Zealand, Pakistan, the Philippines and Thailand. Formed in 1955 to counter the threat of communist penetration in the region, it was again largely unsuccessful in its aims, notably after none of the countries other than Australia joined the United Sates in fighting the Vietnam War. It was eventually dissolved, as was CENTO, in the late 1970s.

Of rather greater longevity, to the extent that they still exist today, were the Five Power Defence Arrangements, a series of agreements binding together the UK, Australia, New Zealand, Malaysia and Singapore. The agreements do not commit the participants to mutual assistance, but to consultation in the event of an armed attack on Malaysia or Singapore. Although they were not formally concluded until 1971, they were the result of a Five Power Conference which took place in Kuala Lumpur in June 1968, to which the British delegates were Sam, Denis Healey, George Thompson, the Secretary of State for Commonwealth Affairs, and General Sir Michael Carver, the C-in-C Far East Command. The conference followed one of the most important post-war decisions on defence by the British Government, to withdraw substantially all the country's forces from East of Suez.

The first stage of this process, although at the time it was not part of any wider strategy, was the withdrawal from Aden, which had already been announced in the 1966 Defence White Paper. Sam had discussed the initial plans during his visit to Aden in the following November, at which time the decision had been taken to repatriate all service families between May and July 1967. This process was completed on schedule shortly before he took up his appointment as CDS. In the meantime, civil unrest had increased dramatically, not helped by the local police and armed forces being infiltrated by the nationalist movements. At the end of June the town of Crater on the Aden Peninsula had actually been occupied by the nationalists and was not retaken until nearly two weeks later, in a brilliant operation conducted by the Argyll and Sutherland Highlanders.

In a fast deteriorating situation, plans were made to accelerate the complete withdrawal of all British personnel, either to the Gulf or back to the UK, with the date for its completion brought back from early 1968 to the end of November 1967. To implement this, a massive airlift was mounted, supplemented by a seaborne evacuation by the Royal Navy which involved two carriers, HMS *Eagle* and HMS *Albion*, together with other ships. As the culmination of an exceptionally successful operation, the final departures took place on 29 November, on which date Middle East Command closed down and its remaining functions were assumed by Headquarters British Forces Gulf in Bahrain.

Eleven days earlier, an event had taken place which was to have significant consequences for the United Kingdom's armed forces. On 18 November, after a run on sterling which the Bank of England had attempted unsuccessfully to halt by the use of its gold and foreign currency reserves, Harold Wilson had announced the devaluation of the pound from $2.80 to $2.40. At the same time he announced considerable cuts in defence spending. With Confrontation at an end, the decision had already been taken earlier in the year that the UK should withdraw its forces from Singapore by the mid–1970s, but this was now brought forward to 1971. Moreover, with the UK's general economic situation deteriorating on top of the £/$ devaluation, it was announced in January 1968 that Britain would also be withdrawing from the Persian Gulf.

The practicalities associated with the closure of the bases East of Suez would now form a significant part of the remit of Sam and his fellow Chiefs over the remaining years of his appointment. The disengagement from both the Far East and the Middle East was, in due course, achieved smoothly. However, one of the consequences was to cause Sam particular distress.

Without bases in the Gulf and Singapore, the Indian Ocean would no longer be critical to Britain's defence policy, other than under its obligations as a member of CENTO and SEATO. This effectively put paid to the Island

Strategy, although it must be said that one seemingly intractable obstacle had already emerged, in the shape of the giant tortoises on the island of Aldabra. The fate of these rare reptiles had provoked the environmental lobby into waging a campaign, which proved to be highly successful, against any construction work there. Without Aldabra there would in any event have been a significant gap in the chain of island bases, with no obvious substitute.

The main victim of the defence cuts and the abandonment of the Island Strategy was the F-111, which the Government now cancelled. The first order, for a modest ten aircraft, had been placed in 1966, with an option for forty more. However, not only the lack of a need for such aircraft East of Suez, but also the devaluation of sterling, which increased the cost per aircraft commensurately, strengthened the Treasury's hand. Healey argued strongly in favour of its retention, but was overruled in Cabinet. In his words:

When the decision went against me I was on the point of resignation because I felt that my honour was at stake. I had been able to persuade the air force to cancel the TSR2 only by guaranteeing them the F111 in its place.

I had already formed the view that a minister should never resign unless either he felt he could improve the situation by resigning, or he knew the situation was irreparable. On the other hand, if I did not resign, there was a danger that Sam Elworthy would resign as CDS – he had got it into his head that I had done a deal with Wilson to scrap the F111 in return for becoming Foreign Secretary![6]

Whether or not Sam believed this cannot be confirmed, and in any event Healey decided, almost certainly correctly, that resignation would be a futile gesture. Nor is there any evidence that Sam ever considered resigning himself, but he was certainly deeply upset, and not just because the RAF's 'victory' over the Royal Navy in the Defence White Paper was now very clearly perceived to have been a Pyrrhic one. In his view the F-111 was a highly capable aircraft which could have added very considerably to the RAF's strike capability outside the East of Suez area. It was to be replaced by a combination of two aircraft, the first of which was the Buccaneer, which, whilst valued for its low-level flying characteristics, had always been considered unsuitable by the RAF, largely due to its subsonic top speed and a much shorter range than the F-111; in the event, those acquired were to include aircraft released by the Royal Navy as the carrier fleet was run down. The second aircraft was to be a tactical strike variant of the highly versatile F-4 Phantom, the interceptor variant of which was already on order and due to enter squadron service in 1969.

Although he was instrumental in putting together the new package, Sam, like many in the RAF, thought that it was inherently unsatisfactory and left a significant gap in capability until the introduction in 1982 of the Multi Role Combat Aircraft, by that time better known as the Panavia Tornado. It was only in 1967, two years after the cancellation of the Anglo-French Variable Geometry aircraft following the French withdrawal from the programme, that the United Kingdom had joined Germany, Italy and the Netherlands to develop the MRCA. Sam always believed that it would have made much better sense, for reasons of both cost and capability, to have gone ahead with the F-111 until the Tornado was available.

Neither of the other two services came out unscathed from the defence cuts. HMS *Victorious*, which had gone into a refit to extend her life, was instead decommissioned, and a decision was made to dispose of the other carriers in the early 1970s, ahead of the previously agreed schedule, although when the time came there was a stay of execution for HMS *Ark Royal* until the end of the decade. The Army lost a number of armoured regiments and infantry battalions and suffered cuts to the Brigade of Gurkhas.

All of this put some strain on the relationship between the services and the politicians, although it was generally recognized that Healey was fighting the former's corner as hard as he could, but held a weak hand relative to the Treasury. Sam's own relationship with Healey had necessarily become closer after his appointment as CDS. From being one of three single service chiefs he had become not only their spokesman but also, constitutionally, the senior adviser to the Government on defence, so they saw a great deal of each other. The relationship was built on mutual respect rather than friendship. There were a few who thought that Sam did not really like Healey, but it is more probable that he felt that he should not get too close to such a consummate political operator. He tended to decline opportunities to socialize with him alone, such as going off for lunch together, as this might have affected his ability to stand up to the Secretary of State, which he often had to do. On the other hand, he was very happy to meet Healey off-duty in other company, and it helped that Audrey and Edna Healey got on well together.

In their professional dealings Sam remained wary of Healey, who could on occasion act in a way which Sam felt bordered on the devious. This did not go as far as Mountbatten's habit of misrepresenting the Chiefs' positions, but it did on occasion involve Healey trying to pick off one or more of them from the rest. He would, in particular, take a newly appointed Chief aside, tell him how much he valued his opinion and suggest that he should deal directly with him in the future. Whilst Sam could not prevent any of his fellow Chiefs from meeting the Secretary of State alone – indeed, it was vital they should be able to do so on matters relating to their own service – he countered Healey's tactic by agreeing with them that on all significant issues they would establish a position to which they could all subscribe and, if they were not meeting Healey as a body, would trust him to convey it accurately. This he was well suited to do; as Neil Cameron was to write later of Healey, Sam 'was the only Chief whom he did not overshadow'.[7]

It did not help that Healey had decided in late 1966 to set up a unit under his direct control called the Programme Evaluation Group. In the words of Neil Cameron, who was selected to join it, the PEG 'was established to give him (Healey) independent advice on Services' proposals and to provide more valuable data on which to base his decisions'.[8] The Chiefs, however, regarded the PEG as having power without responsibility. Moreover, there were potential conflicts of interest for the members in recommending policies which might be in some way inimical to their own service. In the end, the opposition of the Chiefs proved irresistible and Healey was forced to abandon it, setting up instead a Defence Policy Staff which came under the CDS's direct control.

Communications between the Chiefs and ministers were helped in no small way by the civil servants. Other than Dunnett and Flett, the most significant of these was Frank Cooper, the Assistant Under-Secretary of State (Policy) from 1964, with promotion to Deputy Under-Secretary of State (Policy and Plans) in 1968. Cooper had served as a pilot in the RAF during the war, seeing action in Italy, and had spent most of his working life thereafter in the Air Ministry, so was well known to Sam and had, indeed, been instrumental in working with him on issues such as the cancellation of the TSR-2. That he was trusted implicitly by both Sam and Healey oiled the wheels between them, as did the relationship between Sam's staff and Healey's Private Secretaries, Patrick Nairne and then Ewen Broadbent, both of whom went on to more senior positions in the ministry, and later Alistair Jaffray.

Meeting his fellow Chiefs, inside or outside the COSC, Sam adopted much the same tactics which he had used so effectively in Aden. He would let the discussion on any subject take its course, before delivering a succinct summing-up which not only reflected his own views but also received the backing of all the others. There was one particular subject on which they were absolutely united, and that was service pay. In the aftermath of the financial crisis the Government attempted to cut this, which the Chiefs knew would be disastrous to morale and recruitment. They insisted on seeing the Prime Minister, Sam being called back from an overseas trip to lead them to Downing Street. Once there, Michael Le Fanu gave Wilson three or four minutes on the Invergordon Mutiny of 1931, which he had experienced in person. In the face of their united opposition, Wilson caved in.

It was now clear to all that the Government's defence policy was to be focused on NATO, and thus a significant proportion of Sam's time was to be devoted to the alliance. For the first time in his career, except briefly whilst serving in SHAEF in 1944, his job entailed frequent contact with his opposite numbers in the armed forces of foreign countries other than those of the Commonwealth. One of Sam's greatest attributes was his ability to form friendships, and this had by no means been limited to his private life or his RAF service. It was now extended to the leaders of the UK's allies, of which by far the most important were the Americans. Three US officers were particularly important: Lyman Lemnitzer, who had been the Chairman of the Joint Chiefs of Staff and, rather unusually, went on to become Supreme Allied Commander in Europe, his successor as SACEUR, Andrew Goodpaster, and the Chairman of the Joint Chiefs and thus Sam's American opposite number for the greater part of his appointment as CDS, Earle 'Bus' Wheeler. Sam visited Washington on a number of occasions and was a guest of President Nixon at the White House on two of them.

Perhaps the most important of the European officers was Ulrich de Maizière, Sam's opposite number as Inspector General of the Bundeswehr (German Armed Forces). After ten years of post-war disarmament, the Bundeswehr had only been established in 1955, but by the time of Sam's appointment as CDS, and in the absence of France from NATO, it had by the late 1960s become the largest conventional Continental European force committed to the alliance. Sam developed an excellent relationship with de Maizière, which was vital given the UK's own substantial presence on the ground in North-West Germany.

Relations with the Warsaw Pact countries remained tense throughout Sam's time as CDS, not helped by the Soviet invasion of Czechoslovakia in August 1968, conducted in order to overturn the reforms introduced by the Dubček Government in the 'Prague Spring'. With the combined forces of NATO invariably weaker than those of the Warsaw Pact, there was concern as to how any aggression against one or more of its members would be halted short of a full scale nuclear attack, which was likely to impact more severely on the Europeans than the Americans. The doctrine of 'flexible response', under which there would be a progression from conventional warfare to the deployment of tactical nuclear weapons and, only if this was unsuccessful, to strategic nuclear weapons, had been conceived by the Johnson Administration and had largely been accepted by its allies. It was the practical application of this doctrine which exercised the Nuclear Planning Group, whose meetings occupied much of Sam's time on NATO business.

Outside NATO there were, in the first two years of Sam's appointment, few major operational issues for the Chiefs other than the withdrawal from East of Suez; indeed, 1968 was the first and, until 2016, the only year since the Second World War in which no British servicemen lost their lives on active service. One small conflict became active again, the Dhofar Rebellion in the South of Oman. This had taken up a modest amount of Sam's time whilst he was C-in-C Middle East, before quietening down. After he had left Aden, however, the Dhofar Liberation Front had stepped up its activities once again, and Sultan Said's heavy-handed response, against the recommendation of his British advisers, served only to arouse deep resentment among the local population. Following the British withdrawal from Aden, the DLF, now renamed the Popular Front for the Liberation of the Occupied Arabian Gulf, was able to receive arms from across the border with the former Eastern Protectorate and during 1969, supported by the new government in Aden and equipped with Russian and Chinese weapons, it captured the greater part of the Jebel, the highland area of the province. The British Army had a small involvement by way of providing protection for the airfield at Salalah.

In July 1970 Sam's old friend, Sultan Said, was deposed by his Sandhurst-educated son, Qaboos. The Foreign Office was supportive of Qaboos from the outset, but the Chiefs were hesitant at first, before being persuaded that he offered the best chance of a satisfactory outcome. In addition to the units around the airfield and British officers who had been seconded to the Sultan's Armed Forces, detachments of the Special Air Service Regiment were flown in to direct attacks on the rebels in the Jebel itself. Although it was nearly six more years before the rebels were completely defeated, Qaboos gradually won back local support and territory with British help.

Another much more serious campaign also began during Sam's time as CDS, one which was to cause more British service fatalities than any since the Korean War. The civil rights movement in Northern Ireland, protesting about discrimination against Catholics and Nationalists, had been steadily gaining strength during the mid-1960s and, in August 1968, held its first march. Loyalists reacted violently, and with sectarian violence increasing, the civil authorities proved unable to cope on their own. In August 1969 the British Army was deployed on the streets of the province for the first time.

It was decided at an early stage in 'The Troubles' that this would be an exclusively Army commitment, with the GOC Northern Ireland reporting directly to the CGS, who in turn was responsible for advising the Secretaries of State for Defence and Northern Ireland. There were, however, some repercussions on the whole apparatus of defence, and the CGS also reported at regular intervals to the COSC. Sam went to see the situation on the ground for the first time in November 1969 and visited again during 1970, but the major escalations in the campaign, including the introduction of internment and 'Bloody Sunday', did not take place until after he had retired.

Other than the worsening situation in Northern Ireland, the major event of 1970 was the surprising victory of the Conservative Party in the General Election of 18 June. The new Secretary of State for Defence was

Lord Carrington. Peter Carrington had been Parliamentary Secretary to the Minister of Defence from 1954 to 1956 and First Lord of the Admiralty from 1959 to 1963, so was well informed on defence matters. He may have lacked the intellectual rigour of Healey, but he was full of common sense and easy to deal with. Moreover, he had taken over Healey's Private Secretary, Alistair Jaffray, so communications between the two offices remained smooth. As his political master, Sam found Carrington 'blissful',[9] whilst he and Audrey were able to establish a strong friendship with both him and his wife, Iona.

Sam's years as CDS were by no means all work and no play. The Elworthys entertained regularly at Kingston House North, where they were able to sit down twelve to dinner and liked to have a good mix of backgrounds amongst their guests. They managed to keep up with all their friends, often providing beds for the night to those visiting London, and from time to time they enjoyed an evening of bridge with a selected few. The Henley Royal Regatta was sacrosanct, not least because Sam was elected as a Steward in December 1968, which he regarded as one of the greatest honours of his life. He also used to enjoy playing golf, turning out regularly for the RAF side against the aircraft industry. One of his favourite partners was Gus Walker, a contemporary in Bomber Command during the war, who had lost an arm when he was blown up by an exploding bomb whilst rescuing the crew from a crashed Lancaster and played with his left arm only. Sam was particularly amused whenever their foursome also included the legless Douglas Bader!

There were other diversions from routine, such as the Investiture of the Prince of Wales in Caernarvon Castle on 1 July 1969. The Chiefs and their wives were invited as official guests, and there was an explicit instruction from the Earl Marshal that they were to travel on the special train laid on for the occasion. Sam was having none of it. Instead, he and Audrey, with John Grandy, George Baker and their wives, flew in a RAF Andover to RAF Valley on Anglesey, taking a helicopter from there to the house where they were staying for the night. On the following day they found themselves sitting in the front row close to the podium where the ceremony took place.

If anything, the pace of foreign travel picked up during Sam's last sixteen months as CDS, possibly because most of the big decisions for the future had been taken by then, so less time was needed to be spent in Whitehall and more in explaining their implications to allies. On 11 February 1970

Sam and Audrey, accompanied by Iain Ferguson and his wife and by Vyvyan Harmsworth, set out on a round-the-world tour, yet again in a Comet piloted by Basil D'Oliveira. They stopped off for three days in Ceylon, partly for Sam to attend meetings with the armed forces chiefs, but more importantly to catch up with Anthony and his wife, Penny (née Hendry), whom he had married in Harpsden, near Perseverance Cottage, three years earlier.

In Singapore their hosts were Admiral Sir Peter Hill-Norton, C-in-C Far Eastern Command, and his wife. They spent four days there, as Sam had much business to discuss with his service colleagues and with local politicians. The withdrawal from the Far East was already underway, and while Sam and Audrey were there they attended the disbandment parade for No. 20 and No. 45 Squadrons.[10] A day in Kuala Lumpur was followed by two in Hong Kong, the one outpost in the Far East which would continue to be garrisoned by British forces. They then went to Manila for Sam to hold meetings with the service chiefs in the Philippines, a member of SEATO, before flying on to Canberra, where they once again stayed with the Johnstons.

After a day in Canberra for Sam to meet the main figures of the defence establishment, the party flew on to New Zealand, this time directly to Christchurch, where the welcoming party included Christopher and his wife Annie (née Johnstone), whom he had married in 1968; Christopher and Annie's first child, Caroline, was born later that year and she was followed by Amanda in 1970. Sam always loved going to New Zealand, but was reluctant to spend too much time with the family whilst on duty, as he had no wish to attract criticism. The visit to the South Island was thus limited to 24 hours before they departed for Wellington, where Sam had official business to carry out, including attending a meeting of the New Zealand Defence Council. From New Zealand the flight back to London involved no great hardship, taking the party across the Pacific via Fiji to Honolulu and Las Vegas, where Harmsworth lost $80 on the slot machines, and then on to Jamaica.

One other overseas trip in 1970 was particularly memorable. Sam had been invited to attend the celebrations for the 50th Anniversary of the founding of the Ecuadorian Air Force on 26 October, which would allow him to fit in a meeting of the Nuclear Planning Group in Ottawa on the way home. Leaving London on the Comet, which by now Audrey considered 'a way of living, not just a means of transport',[11] they flew via Gander in Newfoundland to their initial destination, Guadeloupe, where the crew was required to have a mandatory rest. Quite why the island had been chosen in preference to one of the British overseas territories in the Caribbean is unclear, but the French authorities had been informed of what was very clearly an unofficial visit. Nothing was heard from them, and Sam assumed that, if he was met at all, it would at least be without fuss, so was wearing casual clothes on the flight. On landing at the airport, Harmsworth pointed out that not only was there a large reception committee waiting, but also a guard of honour. Luckily, the suitcase containing Sam's uniform was in the cabin, and the pilot was ordered to taxi extremely slowly to give him time to change into it. On disembarking he was greeted by the Governor, who presented the local army commander, the head of the chamber of commerce and various other dignitaries. Strangely, however, the guard of honour was not to be inspected! Cars had been provided, with police outriders, who escorted the party to its hotel at high speed and with sirens blaring.

After a very pleasant two nights the party left for Quito, the capital of Ecuador. The airport there, hemmed in by high mountains, had one of the most difficult approaches in the world. Aircraft were advised to land before 15.00, after which cloud tended to accumulate on the flight path, but the Comet arrived significantly later. Audrey described the landing:

> The approach to Quito, with high mountains looming out of thick cloud, roaring engines and not a glimpse of the ground had me praying aloud. When I could see something, there were hills higher than us and remarkably close on either side. Now descending into a deep valley, engines still roaring. We touched down and immediately into reverse pitch: we stopped in time.

They were met by a large delegation and, after the formalities were over, an album was produced containing photos of the numerous crashes around the airport!

On the following day Sam and Audrey attended the celebratory Te Deum in the cathedral and then Sam went off to inspect one of the Ecuadorian

Air Force's Canberras, whilst Audrey was taken on a sightseeing tour. On the following day there was to be a grand parade, but the news arrived early that morning that the Chief of the Ecuadorian Air Force, General Rohan Sandoval, had been kidnapped during the night. Apparently he had left a celebratory dinner, which they had all attended, to visit his mistress, but was attacked on leaving her and bundled into a car by men from a group demanding an end to the country's dictatorship. With rumours of a wider coup imminent, the parade was cancelled and a guard was placed on the British Ambassador's temporary residence, where Sam and Audrey were staying. Once Sam had managed to get the crew of the Comet released from detention, they left for Ottawa earlier than originally planned, with a stopover for a night at a particularly luxurious hotel in Acapulco.

That they went on this trip at all was unexpected, as Sam had been due to retire before it took place. That he did not do so was due to the news, which came just after the general election, that the ever-popular Le Fanu was very ill with chronic lymphatic leukaemia.[12] He had been the Royal Navy's choice to become the new CDS and was due to hand over as First Sea Lord to Peter Hill-Norton. Now it was clear that Hill-Norton himself would have to take on the more senior appointment, but he needed, and indeed wanted, to be 'played in' on the Chiefs of Staff Committee first. Sam therefore agreed that he would extend his term until the spring of 1971 in order to give Hill-Norton nine months at the head of his own service.

Hill-Norton was professionally well suited to the role of First Sea Lord and CDS, having served as Assistant Chief of the Naval Staff from 1962 to 1964 and Deputy Chief of the Defence Staff (Personnel and Logistics) in 1996–67, in which role he had been instrumental in the withdrawal from Aden, followed by appointments as Vice-Chief of the Naval Staff in 1967–68 and thereafter C-in-C Far East Command. He was, however, a very prickly character, to the extent, according to Hill-Norton himself,[13] that Sam had vetoed his appointment as VCNS in 1966. The reasons for this are not clear, but they may have had something to do with the bad blood between the RAF and the Royal Navy at the time. Be that as it may, it was actually Hill-Norton and Grandy who eventually put a stop to the damaging rivalry by issuing a 'concordat' to their senior officers promising to court-martial any officer who was heard to rubbish the other service.

There were those who thought that Hill-Norton went out of his way to make enemies, and he was certainly both short-tempered and a martinet, a man from whose office even relatively senior officers sometimes emerged in tears. Most disliked him, although his wife Eileen was very well regarded. There was one person who took a different view. Writing at the time of her and Sam's visit to Singapore in February 1970, Audrey wrote 'Peter is a super chap', a good example of her ability either to see the best in everybody or to charm the monkeys out of the trees, or perhaps both!

On 29 January 1971 Sam and Audrey set out on a grand valedictory tour, taking Sam's last PSO, Robert Ford, and his wife and Harmsworth with them. Their first major destination, after stops at Thule to refuel and Anchorage for the crew to rest, was Japan, where Sam was the first head of the British armed services to make an official visit since the war. They arrived escorted by two Japanese F-104 Starfighters to be met by Admiral Itaya Ryuichi, Sam's opposite number as Chairman of the Joint Staff Council of the Self Defence Force. They spent five days in Japan with an exceptionally full programme laid on for both of them, to the extent that Audrey, most unusually, wished that she could have a day off. The Japanese officers whom they met on the whole spoke good English, but their wives none at all, although they were full of smiles. Two full days in Tokyo were followed by a trip to Kyoto, stopping off on the way to visit a Japanese Air Force Base and an electrical factory. The hospitality was outstanding, but Audrey, at least, was pleased to be able to relax when they arrived in Singapore, where Air Chief Marshal Sir Brian Burnett, an old friend of Sam's who had been his VCAS in succession to Kyle, was now the C-in-C Far East Command, the last to hold the appointment before the withdrawal of British forces from the region.

On 9 February the Elworthys arrived in Canberra for Sam to attend for the last time a meeting of the Australian Chiefs of Staff. Once more they stayed with the Johnstons, but for only two nights, before leaving for Ohakea, where they were met by Clare, who was already in New Zealand. This time Sam had no compunction about spending time with his family, so having made arrangements for Harmsworth to be taken care of, they left for Lake Taupo, where a large family party was gathering for the wedding of Di and Hamish Wilson's youngest daughter, Victoria. Staying in their motel that night were eleven family members, nine of whom had the surname of Elworthy, whilst even more gathered over the next two days for the wedding itself.

On the day after the wedding Sam, Audrey and Clare drove back to Ohakea and flew down to Wellington, where they stayed at Government House. On the following day Sam attended a meeting of the Defence Council and he and Audrey were the guests of honour at a lunch given by the Defence Staff. They then flew down to Christchurch to stay with John and Hester Elworthy and on to Timaru to see Christopher, Annie and their two young daughters, Caroline and Amanda, before going to stay in Gordons Valley. Christopher was now working for the veterinary division of Merck, Sharp and Dohme, an American multi-national company, as its sales manager in South Canterbury and North Otago. After four nights Sam and Audrey drove back to Christchurch. Clare had decided to stay on in New Zealand, and they left her with Sam's first cousin, Betty Gould,[14] and her husband Derrick.

Sam and Audrey departed from Christchurch on 21 February and flew back to London across the Pacific to Tahiti and Easter Island and then on to Lima, Barbados and the Azores. On Easter Island they picked up Princess Alexandra, whom they had first met in Aden and who was returning to the UK after accompanying the Duke of Edinburgh and the Mountbattens on a visit to Panama and the Pacific Islands.

On the evening of 7 April 1971 Sam and Audrey were guests at a dinner at No. 10 Downing Street, and at 11.00 the next morning, followed by Hill-Norton and two very recent appointments to the COSC, Michael Carver as CGS and Denis Spotswood as CAS, Sam took the salute on the steps of the Ministry of Defence and inspected a farewell parade of all three services in his honour.

Chapter 17

Constable and Governor

It had been Sam and Audrey's longstanding intention to retire to Perseverance Cottage, which was well situated for him to be able to fulfil whatever appointments were to come his way. In the event, this was not to be. In May 1970, some four months before he was originally expecting to step down as CDS, he was approached to become Constable and Governor of Windsor Castle in succession to Field Marshal Viscount Slim.

Slim was then aged seventy-eight and had been in poor health for some time, having suffered a number of strokes and lost his sight to the extent that he was effectively blind. An informal tradition had long been established that the office of Constable and Governor was an appointment for life; indeed, this had invariably been the case since the first half of the eighteenth century. However, it was not a rule, and Slim, in the belief that he was no longer able to discharge his duties effectively, wrote to the Queen in early 1970 and asked to be permitted to retire. This was granted with effect from the middle of the year, and, in the meantime, the search began for his successor.

On 20 May 1970 Sam was invited to meet Lord Cobbold, the Lord Chamberlain and thereby the most senior officer of the Royal Household, who asked him a number of questions about his impending retirement before proposing that he should succeed Slim at Windsor. Sam was unenthusiastic, not least because he knew that this would not play well with Audrey, who was greatly looking forward to life at the cottage. She was also experiencing some trouble with her legs at the time, which Sam mentioned in the light of the numerous stairs in the Norman Tower, the Governor's residence at Windsor Castle. Cobbold countered with the news that a lift had now been installed and asked Sam not to make a final decision but to see Lord Tryon, the Keeper of the Privy Purse and responsible for the financial management of the Royal Household.

Sam was extremely busy at the time and it was not until 15 June that he was able to meet Tryon, who explained to him that the Queen wanted someone for the appointment with a background in both the armed services and the 'Old' Commonwealth; this had certainly applied to Slim, who had served as Governor-General of Australia. During their discussion it became apparent to Sam that there was only one name on the shortlist, his own. As a committed royalist and a great admirer of the Queen, her wish was his command, and he felt that he had no option but to accept the appointment. Three days later he met Slim at Windsor Castle.[1]

The meeting with Slim took place on the day of the General Election and, shortly afterwards, the news was received of Le Fanu's retirement due to ill health. Sam duly received permission to defer taking up his appointment until his extended term as CDS had been completed, but an announcement was nevertheless made to the press on 3 July. Sam and Audrey moved to Windsor a few days before his retirement as CDS and, to Audrey's sorrow, Perseverance Cottage was sold soon afterwards.

The building of Windsor Castle, which then commanded an important crossing of the River Thames, was begun by William the Conqueror shortly after the Norman Conquest, and it was first occupied as a royal palace by his son, Henry I. The first Constable was appointed in 1087. From the early nineteenth to the mid-twentieth century the office was usually held by a member or the husband of a member of the Royal Family, but from the early twentieth century it had also been the practice to appoint a Deputy Constable and Lieutenant-Governor. Slim himself had held and had later been elevated from that office, which was thenceforward devolved on to the Governor of the Military Knights of Windsor. The Military Knights were initially appointed in the fourteenth century as surrogates for the Knights of the Garter, their role being to pray daily for the monarch and the knights they represented. Originally called the Poor Knights, in 1833 their title was changed and they were thereafter recruited from the ranks of retired officers of the British Army holding any rank from major to brigadier, being of impeccable character and possessing no independent means other than their pensions. The eighteen knights and their wives – they are almost always married at the time of their appointment – occupy a row of houses against the wall of the castle opposite St George's Chapel.

The Governor of the Military Knights, and thus Sam's deputy for the duration of his own appointment, was Major General Sir Edmund Hakewill-Smith. Sam was in overall charge of the temporal activities of the castle, whilst the spiritual element, including all the services and other activities held in or associated with St George's Chapel, was in the hands of the second and equally important figure in the Castle hierarchy, the Dean of Windsor, who, because the Chapel is a 'Royal Peculiar', is chosen by and responsible directly to the monarch. When Sam arrived the position was held by the Right Reverend Lancelot Fleming, who was succeeded in 1976 by the Right Reverend Michael Mann.

In theory, Sam had responsibility for all the day-to-day management of the castle other than those matters under the control of the Dean, but in practice much of this, with the particular exception of security, was carried out by the Superintendent, who reported to the Master of the Household. Sam's duties as Constable and Governor included greeting the Queen at the Sovereign's Entrance whenever she arrived to take up official residence, but in practice she was there so frequently, as Windsor is said to be her favourite official residence, that this was rarely insisted upon. Greeting Heads of State on state visits, on the other hand, was very much an essential part of his job.

The Constable and Governor does not receive any remuneration, but he is provided with accommodation in the Norman Tower. This edifice, despite its name, dates from the fourteenth century and encompasses the Norman Gate, one of two entrances within the castle from the Lower Ward, which is largely occupied by St George's Chapel, and the Middle Ward, around the Round Tower, to the Upper Ward, where the Queen's apartments and the state rooms are situated. Sam's study was located directly above the gateway, reflecting its architecture – rectangular over the gate itself and round at one end[2] – with the portcullis forming one of its walls. There were carvings on another wall made by Royalist prisoners during the English Civil War. The most talented carver was Browne Bushell, who on the eve of his execution requested and was granted an additional twelve hours of life to finish his work. The other main feature of the study was a round desk which had belonged to the late King.

There were numerous rooms in the Norman Tower, including nine bedrooms, making it a fine place to entertain and to have guests to stay, of whom there were many during Sam's tenure. Whilst furniture was provided, the Elworthys had to buy curtains and carpets, which somewhat strained their financial resources. On the other hand, there were many pictures on loan from the Royal Collection, including a portrait by Anthony Van Dyck of King Christian IV of Denmark. One other attractive feature was the Moat Garden beneath the adjacent Round Tower, although this was overlooked from the Middle Ward, so tended to be used after public visiting hours were over.

Sam's job at Windsor actually required very little time, so he had to find other things to do. In this he succeeded triumphantly, indeed he took on so many roles that his own assessment, that he was 'overbusy, but not overworked',[3] was a major understatement. His appointment diary became significantly fuller than it had been at the height of his career and his time management must have been exceptional, as was most certainly his capacity for taking on appointments. The first of these occurred even before he retired as CDS, when, in February 1971 he was nominated by the Government to join the board of Rolls-Royce (1971) Limited.

Rolls-Royce had fallen into serious financial difficulty as a result of the excessive development costs of the RB211 aero engine for the Lockheed Tristar airliner. The company was placed in receivership and was then nationalized by the Government as Rolls-Royce (1971) to protect its strategic position. With two exceptions, an entirely new board was appointed. Lord Cole, the former chairman of Unilever, became Chairman, and a selection of the great and the good from finance, industry and the civil service were appointed as directors; they included Sir William Cook, who had been Chief Scientific Adviser at the Ministry of Defence whilst Sam was CAS and CDS.

Sam himself was very familiar with Rolls-Royce. He had flown in aircraft propelled by the company's engines from his earliest days in the RAuxAF in the Hawker Hart. Whilst DCAS he had been intimately involved in discussions with the company on the propulsion for the RAF's new aircraft, and this had extended into his time as CAS, when it was decided to fit Spey engines in the Phantom. Sam's appointment at Rolls-Royce (1971) was, however, to prove one of the shortest. He stepped down at the end of 1973, his position on the board being taken by Denis Spotswood, who had just retired as CAS. By that time the Lockheed Tristar had entered airline service and the RB211 was a proven technical success, largely responsible for transforming Rolls-Royce in due course into a global leader in aero engines.

Sam's other corporate directorships came thick and fast. Within weeks of his retirement from the RAF he was appointed to the boards of the National Bank of New Zealand (NBNZ) and the British Oxygen Company (BOC), followed in the ensuing months by Plessey and British Petroleum (BP), whilst he also sat on the board of BP's computer services subsidiary, Scicon. Subsequent corporate directorships were to include Lloyds Bank, the parent company of NBNZ, and the London Committee of AMP (Australian Mutual Provident Society), a leading insurance and financial services company in Australia and New Zealand with a substantial business in the UK.

In November 1971 BP provided Sam and Audrey with an overseas tour which must have been reminiscent of his last decade in the RAF, when she was invited to name the company's latest super-tanker, the *British Prospector*, which had just been completed in the Nagasaki yard of Mitsubishi Heavy Industries. They flew first to Anchorage, where their stay was organized by the local BP Manager, who had hosted a lunch for them there during their previous visit to Alaska at the beginning of the year. Whilst Sam went off to visit the company's North Slope oilfield, Audrey was well entertained by the BP wives. After three days in Alaska they flew to Tokyo, where they were joined by Clare, who had been travelling and working in New Zealand and Australia.

They then flew down to Nagasaki, accompanied by the British Ambassador and the Managing Director of the BP Tanker Company, and their wives. On 25 November, which Audrey described as a 'fabulous day',[4] with perfect weather, she carried out the naming ceremony in a loud and clear voice and then cut a cord with a presentation axe, which released balloons and doves into the air, whilst a band played the national anthems of the two countries! After a more detailed inspection of the ship, they returned to Tokyo via Fukuoka and then visited the Nikko National Park, before returning to London the way they had come.

Sam's appointments were by no means confined to the corporate sector. Shortly after stepping down as CDS he agreed to take on the Chairmanship of the Central Council of the Royal Overseas League for a five-year term. His predecessor was David Luce, and he may have been invited because of that connection or because the Grand President of the ROSL was Mountbatten. Sam in due course handed over the chairmanship to a fellow New Zealander, Lord Grey of Naunton.

Sam also became the Chairman of a number of charitable institutions, including King Edward VII's Hospital in Beaumont Street, London. One of the foremost private hospitals in the country, it had a very close royal connection from its foundation in 1899 on the initiative of the then Prince of Wales, later King Edward VII. The Queen was and is the Patron of the hospital, and she and many other members of the Royal Family have been patients there.

Another somewhat unusual organization chaired by Sam was the Royal Commission for the Exhibition of 1851. This also had a strong royal connection, set up as it was by Prince Albert, initially to administer the Great Exhibition itself and subsequently to invest the profits for charitable purposes connected with scientific and industrial education and later, more specifically, to fund postgraduate scholarships. It owns a great swathe of land between South Kensington and Hyde Park, its properties including the Royal Albert Hall, the Victoria and Albert, Natural History and Science Museums, the Royal Colleges of Art and Music and Imperial College, London. The other members of the Committee were largely scientists, with little enthusiasm for some of the trickier aspects of managing a large estate, such as evicting squatters. Sam, on the other hand, was ruthless in protecting the charity's properties. The Royal Commission had also initially funded and subsequently supported the British Schools in Rome and Athens, and Sam and Audrey were able to visit the former in June 1973.

One other charity of which Sam became a Trustee was the Richard Ormonde Shuttleworth Remembrance Trust, which played to two of his interests, flying and education. Richard Shuttleworth was a well-known racing driver and aviator who had joined the RAFVR at the beginning of the war, only to be killed on a training exercise in 1940. During the inter-war years he had put together a collection of vintage cars and aircraft and, when he died, his mother formed the trust to continue this work. The Shuttleworth Collection, at Old Warden Aerodrome in Bedfordshire, had been opened to the public in 1963.

The second objective of the Shuttleworth Trust was education, in the form of Shuttleworth College, established in the family home, Old Warden Park, as a centre for further education in farming and the environment, reflecting Richard Shuttleworth's strong interest in these subjects.

In addition to Shuttleworth College, Sam had a strong involvement with secondary education. Whilst still serving in the RAF he had become a Governor of both Wellington College and Bradfield College. He had also shown continuing interest in his own school, but this had been limited to inspecting the Combined Cadet Force in 1964 and occasional attendance at the Annual Dinner of the Marlburian Club. Following his retirement from the RAF, however, he became a more assiduous Old Marlburian, visiting the school on a number of occasions, including on an inspection of the CCF again in 1973, and attending its functions in London. He was elected President of the Marlburian Club for 1972/3 and became a Member of the Council in 1974.

Sam's involvement with schools was unexpectedly enlarged by an appointment of wider significance which occurred in 1973. Sometime before that he had been invited to become an Honorary Freeman of the Skinners' Company, one of 'The Great Twelve' City of London livery companies, those of the greatest antiquity. The Skinners were numbered either sixth or seventh in order of precedence, this having been a matter of dispute between the company and the Merchant Taylors, which on occasion escalated into physical conflict.[5] Exasperated by this behaviour, Sir Robert Billesdon, Lord Mayor of London in 1484, ordered that each company should have precedence over the other in alternate years, and that each should entertain the Masters and Wardens of the other annually.

The succession to the Mastership of the company is predetermined some years beforehand, those chosen progressing through various levels of Warden, with the First Warden in due course succeeding as Master. The First Warden for 1972/73 was unable to accept the nomination as Master in the following year due to unforeseen commitments, whilst the Second Warden was equally unable to arrange his affairs to be able to devote the time required a year earlier than planned. It was considered undesirable to have a Master serve two years running, and thus, following a precedent set in 1685, when an Honorary Freeman was chosen, Sam was approached and agreed to accept nomination as Master for 1973/4. Having become in quick succession a Liveryman, a member of the Court (the governing body) and First Warden for the remainder of 1972/3, he was elected Master on Corpus Christi Day, 21 June 1973.

Somehow Sam managed to fit being Master into his already crowded diary and he thoroughly enjoyed his year of office, made easier by the use of a flat in Skinners' Hall, a valuable facility for him and Audrey when attending functions in London, which included dinners at Lincoln's Inn, of which he had become an Honorary Bencher in 1970. His duties as Master involved, inter alia, chairing meetings of the Court and attending a large number of lunches and dinners, both at the Skinners' Hall and at a number of the other companies, which naturally included the Merchant Taylors, pleasingly in a year in which the Skinners ranked sixth in order of precedence! The company, like a number of others, had a strong interest in education, dating back to the sixteenth century. It supported four schools, Tonbridge School and The Judd School in Tonbridge, The Skinners' School in Tunbridge Wells and The Skinners' Company School for Girls in Stamford Hill. Sam attended meetings of each of the governing bodies and visited the schools for speech days and prize giving, continuing to do so for some time after his term as Master had expired.

Rather more than a year before his election as Master of the Skinners' Company, a quite unexpected honour had been bestowed on Sam. In March 1972 he received a letter from the Prime Minister, Edward Heath, who wrote that he had it in mind to submit his name to the Queen to be created a Baron of the United Kingdom. Having duly accepted, Sam's was one of eight new life peerages announced at the end of the month. He wrote shortly afterwards:

Some of the papers have implied that my peerage is connected with my appointment as Governor of the Castle. It is not so, it is connected solely with my military career and my chairmanship of the Chiefs of Staff. It is therefore a compliment to the three Services and I am just the lucky one who happens to get it. It has been represented that whilst the heads of the Foreign and Commonwealth Office and such like have collected the odd peerage over the past decades, no military man has had one since the spate of them at the end of the war, and therefore it was about time that the contribution of the armed forces to the country was publicly recognized. So once again in my life I have been boosted up as a result of the efficiency, helpfulness and unselfishness of my colleagues. I am glad and grateful if only because I think it may have done something for the morale of the three services at a time when they are hard pressed and in so called peacetime when it is fashionable to decry their value.[6]

Although every CDS since Sam, with three exceptions for good reasons,[7] has been made a peer on his retirement, he was being typically modest. At the time it was a remarkable achievement. Although no fewer than six RAF officers had received peerages in the past, the last of these had been Sholto Douglas in 1948, nearly two and a half decades earlier. Particularly since the decision was being made by the Prime Minister, the precedent would only have been established by a man of considerable stature, which is how Sam was clearly regarded in the early 1970s.

In his letter the Prime Minister suggested that Sam should consult Sir Anthony Wagner, Garter King of Arms, on the question of his title. In line with what was by then common practice, Sam decided that he should be known by his own surname, but Garter asked whether he would also like a territorial title. Sam said that he wished to be known as Lord Elworthy of Timaru. Garter responded that he was to become a Baron of the United Kingdom and it would not be permissible for him to associate the title solely with a New Zealand location. After a certain amount of debate, Sam suggested the possible place of origin of his family and they agreed on Baron Elworthy of Timaru in New Zealand and of Elworthy in the County of Somerset. Sam asked the Mayor of Timaru for permission, which the latter was delighted to grant, but felt that this was not necessary for Elworthy.

The discussion with Garter continued over his coat of arms and this became more complex. For a very long time the Elworthys had used a coat of arms consisting mainly of a shield with a blue background, on which were placed two horizontal bars of gold and silver, above the higher of which were three gold roundels – in the language of heraldry, 'Azure, two bars Or and Argent, in chief three bezants Or'. Garter suggested that this should be 'differenced', by way of reference to Sam's membership of the Royal Household, by the addition of a lion passant, as in the arms of England in the Royal Standard, placed between and in the same colours, albeit reversed, as the bars in the old Elworthy arms.

A difficulty arose over the crest. The Elworthys had always used one depicting a steel casque, an archaic type of helmet. Garter maintained that this would not be possible, as one exactly the same was already in use. Sam pressed the point, and after further research it was discovered that the family in question was long defunct, so Garter conceded the point. There was no argument about the 'supporters' on either side of the shield, Kotuku birds from New Zealand. Each of these was to have an 'astral' crown around its neck, denoting the RAF, from which hung double-warded golden keys, designed as back-to-back capital Es, for Elizabeth and Elworthy, representing his appointment at Windsor. The motto was the Latin one always used by the Elworthys, 'Fide et Sedulitate', roughly translated as 'By Faith and Conscientiousness' and highly appropriate to Sam.*

On 14 June 1972, watched by Audrey and other members of the family, Sam was formally introduced to the House of Lords by his two good friends, fittingly from opposing political parties, Peter Carrington and Eddie Shackleton. Sam himself had decided to sit as a cross-bencher, without any political affiliation. In the event, he never spoke in the Lords. He did, however, on at least one occasion carry the Great Sword of State at the State Opening of Parliament, which required not only walking in the procession in front of the Queen but also standing motionless on the dais with the sword raised for about an hour whilst the Queen read her speech from the throne setting out the Government's legislative agenda for the forthcoming session.

If membership of the House of Lords did not require any of Sam's time, his next major appointment certainly did. A little over a year after receiving the letter about his peerage from Ted Heath, another one dropped onto the mat at the Norman Tower. This time the Prime Minister wrote that he had been considering the choice of a successor to Sam's old friend

---

* See Appendix – Coat of Arms of Baron Elworthy of Timaru and Elworthy

Gerald Templer as Lord Lieutenant of Greater London.[8] Heath went on to say that he had consulted the Queen, who had assured him that Sam's duties at Windsor would not conflict with those of the Lieutenancy and had expressed a hope that Sam should find it possible to accept the appointment. Notwithstanding his numerous other commitments, Sam agreed to succeed Templer that September.

Lord Lieutenants no longer have the role for which they were originally created by Henry VIII, the defence of their counties by the raising of a local militia, although they still act as the liaison between the community and locally based military units. They do, most importantly, represent the monarch in their counties, escorting them and other senior members of the Royal Family on visits, and they advise on the award of honours. They are closely involved in major civic activities and are responsible for the local magistracy.

The Lord Lieutenancy would have represented an enormous burden for Sam if he had not had a large number of Deputy Lieutenants who could take on a number of his duties or engagements. Greater London is by far the largest county in terms of population, encompassing as it does all thirty-two boroughs. It is, moreover, somewhat unusual, in that the monarch actually lives in it for much of the time, as her most important residence and her private office are located in Buckingham Palace, right at its heart. It was thus not considered necessary for the Queen to be greeted by Sam or one of his Deputies every time she arrived. She was, however, accompanied by one of them on most of her formal visits and, moreover, was very often greeted or seen off, as were other senior members of the Royal Family, whenever she travelled through Heathrow, which lies within Greater London.

There was one type of occasion on which Sam's roles as Constable and Governor of Windsor Castle and of Lord Lieutenant of Greater London overlapped. This was the state visit, of which there were a number during his term. Usually on such occasions Sam would be at Heathrow to welcome the visiting Head of State, before leaping into a car and being driven the few miles from there to Windsor, if that was where he or she was staying, to perform the same function as Constable and Governor. At least one such dignitary was heard to remark that the Queen must be economizing on her household by having the same man for both occasions!

In the case of the state visit of the Queen of Denmark in April 1974, however, this was complicated by her arrival by ship at Greenwich. Greenwich is on the opposite side of London to Windsor and it was less certain that the traffic would enable Sam to get back to the castle first. The solution, or so it seemed, was for him to travel by helicopter, whilst the Duke of Edinburgh accompanied Queen Margrethe by car. The arrival at Greenwich went smoothly and the royal party set off, whilst Sam went to where the helicopter was parked, in the expectation that he would be at Windsor long before them. To his horror the engine refused to start. He tried to secure a car, but it was clear that he was at serious risk of failing in his duty. The pilot assured him that the problem could be fixed and, after a tense period of waiting, the engine coughed into life and Sam was able to get back before Queen Margrethe arrived. His reward was to be made a Knight Grand Cross of the Order of the Dannebrog, whose star and sash he wore at the state dinner that evening.

Sam was to succeed Gerald Templer in one other appointment, as President of the Council of the Order of St John for London in June 1976. Sam had been admitted as a Knight of the Order of St John in the previous month, following in the footsteps of his father. His new role proved to be one of the least demanding, with quarterly meetings of the Council and a small number of other functions through the year.

In the middle of all this activity, Sam managed to make time for his private life. Audrey was not as busy as he was, although she was a member of a number of committees, which included the Grants Committee of the RAF Benevolent Fund, of which she was deputy chairman, and the committee of the Homes for Officers' Widows and Daughters, a subsidiary charity of SSAFA, on whose council she had sat for many years. Friends and family frequently came to stay at the Norman Tower, with a number of important family events taking place there, the first, soon after they arrived, being a tea party following the christening of Anthony and Penny's eldest child, Tracy. There was usually a large gathering at Windsor for Christmas, often including old friends such as the Garrans and the Lords, whilst there was almost always a shoot at Blakeshall with the Kenricks in December.

Of the immediate family, Tim was rising through the ranks of the RAF. Having served in the Ministry of Defence and graduated from the Staff

College, he was posted in 1971 as a flight commander of a fighter squadron at Akrotiri in Cyprus. By that time he and Victoria had divorced and he had married Anabel Block (née Harding). In 1974, shortly before they returned to the UK, their son Edward was born. By 1977, after another MoD posting and a year at the National Defence College, the successor to the Joint Services Staff College, Tim was commanding a Phantom fighter squadron at Coningsby.

Anthony and Penny left Ceylon in early 1971 because of the civil war which had broken out there, and he worked in the London office of Harrisons & Crosfield for two years, living in Bracknell and seeing more of Sam and Audrey than during the rest of their married life. In the summer of 1973 they left to start a new life in South Africa, where Anthony worked as a tea buyer, blender and taster. Sam and Audrey visited them there for the first time two years later, staying in their house in Kloof, near Durban and, joined by Clare, enjoying a holiday in the Drakensberg.

Christopher was firmly settled in New Zealand, employed by Merck, Sharp & Dohme, before moving with Annie and the children to work at Gordons Valley. Their only visit to England, the first for Christopher since 1964, was for three months in the summer of 1977.

Clare returned from Australasia in 1972, living and working in London, with frequent visits to the Norman Tower. On 4 October 1975 she married Anthony Cary in St George's Chapel, the wedding being organized by Sam with military precision. From 1975 to 1978 they lived in Berlin, where Anthony, a member of the Diplomatic Service, was working for the British Military Government, and it was there that their first child, named Sam after his maternal grandfather, was born in May 1978. Sam and Audrey were able to visit them several times.

Other than an occasional game of golf and the invariable attendance at Henley, where he remained a Steward and was on occasion required to be a Timekeeper, Sam's sporting activities were largely limited to field sports. He was a good shot and often invited for days out during the season, and a keen fisherman. There were a number of visits to Scotland to pursue the latter sport, and on one occasion he found himself fishing alongside Prince Charles on the Spey.

European holidays became more frequent. There were several visits to Tim and Anabel whilst they were stationed in Cyprus, one of which was combined with a trip to see the sites of antiquity in the Levant, Tyre, Sidon, Byblos and Baalbek, whilst other destinations included Gibraltar, where John Grandy was now the Governor.

In January and February 1973 Sam and Audrey paid their first visit to New Zealand since his retirement.[9] They were transported once again by the RAF and, as a result, were taken on a somewhat circuitous route, initially via Akrotiri and Gan. The original intention was to go on from there to New Zealand via Singapore, but their plane was delayed by engine failure and instead they secured a lift on another which was being used by the Carringtons to fly to Hong Kong, from where Sam and Audrey flew to Fiji for the night and then on to Christchurch, where they were met by Christopher. They stayed in the country for three weeks, split as usual between the North and South Islands and mostly devoted to catching up with relatives and friends. In the South Island these included not only Christopher and Annie and their two children, Caroline and Amanda, but also Tony and True, who had relocated to Chalk Farm at Gordons Valley, where their second son, Mark, farmed Tuarangi, that part of the estate left to Tony by Percy. Sam and Audrey stayed at Gordons Valley, where Audrey described the house as 'still decrepitly gallant',[10] and also visited Sam's cousins at the other Elworthy property, Craigmore.[11] Whilst there, Sam received the Freedom of Timaru, Audrey finding the Mayor's eulogy so moving that she was almost reduced to tears.

In the North Island their first two days were spent by Sam on meetings with BP and NBNZ, before they moved on to spend time at Taupo with Di and Hame Wilson and with Bertha, who was now living in a flat next door, aged eighty-six but still in good heart. Their last few days were spent in Auckland, from where they took a commercial flight to Singapore, travelling back by RAF from there.

Sam and Audrey were back in New Zealand again for Christmas 1974 and most of January 1975, dividing their time much as before. This was in the aftermath of Bertha's death, which had come a few weeks earlier, on 4 December. She had reached the age of eighty–eight, outliving all the Elworthys of her generation. Bertha had not always been an easy person, having in particular had a difficult relationship with her daughter Anne, although they had become reconciled late in her life, but she was nevertheless much missed. Christopher was the only one of Sam's children to be able to attend the funeral.

Sam's next visit to New Zealand, in November 1976, was shorter and made for a specific purpose. Audrey did not accompany him but stayed with friends whilst he was away, the Barnetts, Luces, Garrans and also Leonard Cheshire and his wife, Sue Ryder. Sam went with one specific purpose, to organize the building of a new house at Gordons Valley. The old wooden building in which he had been born had become increasingly dilapidated and, on his instructions, was burnt down in August 1975, under the direction of Christopher and with the fire brigade in attendance. The new house was to be built on the same site but was considerably smaller and, unlike its predecessor, was of one storey. It had been designed by Sam himself, but was to be erected by the same builder who had been used by Christopher for his own house, some 200m away up the hill. During his stay Sam met not only the builder himself but also the individual tradesmen, the electrician, plumber, joiner, painter and others, to explain his plan. The resulting home, constructed during 1977 and early 1978, was solidly built of Oamaru stone and, whilst it may have lacked some of the character of its predecessor, it was much more functional as well as being warm and comfortable.

Sam and Audrey were able to inspect the site when they visited New Zealand for a very specific reason in October 1977. That July a new colour had been presented by the Queen to the Queen's Colour Squadron of the RAF Regiment during the Silver Jubilee Review at RAF Finningley. It was decided that the old colour should be laid up at St Paul's Cathedral in Wellington, and Sam, who had been at Finningley, was asked to accompany it and, with a detachment from the Regiment, to represent the RAF at the ceremony. They were in the country for only a week, the visit also including the unveiling by Sam of a portrait of Ralph Cochrane and a description of his role in establishing the RNZAF at the Museum of Transport and Technology in Auckland, to whose Hall of Fame Cochrane had been elected. Cochrane had been invited himself, but was seriously ill and his doctors refused to allow him to travel. He did, however, go to Brize Norton to see Sam and Audrey off and to give Sam a copy of the speech he would have made.

Cochrane, whom Sam probably admired more than any other RAF officer, died two months after the unveiling in Auckland, and Sam subsequently gave one of the addresses at his memorial service in St Clement Danes.

Some four months beforehand a momentous and totally unexpected event had taken place. It came during a particularly busy year for Sam as Lord Lieutenant, due to the Queen's Silver Jubilee, for which the organization began many months before the two most important occasions in London, the procession to St Paul's for a thanksgiving service on 7 June, followed by lunch at the Guildhall, and the Royal Progress up the Thames from Greenwich two days later. These were followed later by two further Royal Progresses, one for each of North and South London. Sam not only had to be in attendance on all of these and some other, more minor, occasions, but to ensure that, to the extent that they came within his own area of responsibility, they went off without a hitch. There had thus been a lot of communication with the Royal Household, notably the Earl Marshal, the Duke of Norfolk, who was responsible for all the ceremonial.

One day in April 1977, whilst this was all going on, Sam was at Windsor when he received a call from the Queen's Private Secretary, Sir Martin Charteris, asking if he could come to see him. Sam duly invited him for a drink in his study in the Norman Tower. Charteris then handed over a letter in which he had written that he had been commanded by Her Majesty to inform Sam that it was her pleasure that he be appointed a Knight Companion of the Order of the Garter.

This was the most astonishing news. The Most Noble Order of the Garter is the most senior British order of chivalry, founded by Edward III in 1348. Unlike most other honours, it is in the personal gift of the monarch and it is limited in number to twenty-four companion members, although there is also provision not only for royal knights and ladies, but also for extra knights and ladies who are usually members of other royal families. It had, until relatively recently, been confined to the most senior members of the hereditary peerage, to former prime ministers and other eminent politicians, and to outstanding wartime military leaders. The only RAF officer to have been so honoured was Charles Portal in 1946.

To Sam this came as a complete surprise. He had wondered if he might see his membership of the Royal Victorian Order upgraded from the LVO awarded to him at the time of the Coronation Review, to reflect his recent service to the Queen, but this was a much more exalted honour. The appointment was announced on 23 April and on 4 June he was invested by the Queen with the Insignia of the Order, wearing the robes, which he had to have made himself at great expense. On Garter Day, Monday 13 June, he was robed by the Queen in a private ceremony, with his supporter Knights, Mountbatten and Templer, standing on either side of him. He then walked alongside Lord Cromer, another new Knight, in the front rank of their fellows down the familiar path to St George's Chapel, where he was formally installed.[12] For the first time in many years, not only Audrey but every one of his children was present, together with his sister Anne, and their spouses.

Amidst all the celebration, however, there was a cloud on the horizon and it related to Audrey. For some time now, going back in small ways to even before Sam became CAS, she had become noticeably more forgetful and, on occasion, erratic. She remained on her committees, she still drove her car and she loved, as always, to entertain friends and relations, rising to the occasion when it mattered. She was, nevertheless, somehow diminished and no longer the sharp and insightful person she had once been. It did not help that she had, for the whole of her adult life, smoked too much and probably drunk too much as well, albeit never to the extent of intoxication, and she had never taken any exercise. As the years passed, Sam became more and more concerned.

Now in his seventh year at Windsor, he was also worried that, as he grew older, he himself would no longer be able to discharge his duties so capably, particularly where they related to the Queen's security. Although Slim had been allowed to retire as Constable and Governor, he was by then in very poor health, and Sam did not want to find himself in the same situation. He therefore requested a meeting with Lord Cobbold's successor as Lord Chamberlain, Lord Maclean, and argued that his post should not be considered a lifetime one, but that he should be allowed to retire when the time was appropriate. Maclean replied that he had been appointed for no particular term by the Queen and that he should stay on. He did say, however, that he would think about it further and asked that Sam should come and see him again three months later. When the meeting took place

Maclean once again said that he thought retirement was impossible. Sam asked if he might talk to Martin Charteris, to which Maclean agreed.

Charteris, on being approached, considered Sam's position to be entirely reasonable and volunteered to raise it with the Queen immediately. The Queen's reaction was totally sympathetic and she just asked that he should give her adequate notice when he felt that the time was right for him to go. By late 1977 it was clear that Audrey's mental health was only going to decline further, and he asked to be relieved, a request which was duly granted. Perseverance Cottage was long gone, but there was a good alternative in the shape of the new house at Gordons Valley, which Sam felt would suit her better than remaining in England. When they visited New Zealand in October 1977 he proposed moving there to Audrey and she agreed.

The last few months at Windsor were busier than ever, as Sam did not resign from most of his appointments until shortly before his departure. There were two particularly important occasions before they left. One was at the Norman Tower, where Sam and Audrey gave a dinner for the Queen and the Duke of Edinburgh, with Tim and Clare and their spouses and a few others attending as well. The second was a dinner given by the RAF at the Staff College at Bracknell. The host was the current CAS, Michael Beetham, and the dinner was attended by a large number of former colleagues with whom Sam had been particularly closely connected, together with their wives. Every single living Marshal of the RAF was present other than the Duke of Edinburgh and Jack Slessor, who was unwell, and, much to Sam's pleasure, they included Bert Harris. There were many others who had played a role in Sam's long career, including 'Connie' Constantine, Denis Barnett and Hugh Walmsley from the war years, Denis Crowley-Milling and Al Deere from the Staff College, David Lee and Fred Rosier from Aden, Peter Fletcher, Frank Cooper and Michael Quinlan from Whitehall, and Gus Walker, his favourite golf partner. It was a fitting send-off, demonstrating very clearly the respect and affection in which Sam and Audrey were held.

On Friday, 11 August 1978 a car provided by BP drove the Elworthys to Heathrow to catch a flight to their new life.

Chapter 18

Gordons Valley

Unlike his father, who had always considered himself to be an Englishman who happened to live the greater part of his life in New Zealand, Sam was unequivocally a New Zealander, albeit one who by 1978 had spent fifty-eight of his sixty-seven years living elsewhere, with only very occasional and invariably brief visits to his homeland. There were some who were surprised by his decision to live there after so many years away. Clearly, his concern for Audrey's welfare was paramount, and he was certain that she would be able to relax in Gordons Valley much more easily than in England, where, even without the tie to Windsor, the significant demands on Sam's time, not to mention her own, might well become increasingly confusing to her. In New Zealand he would be better placed to manage his diary to suit her, whilst his many relatives in the area were likely to be both supportive to him and understanding of her condition; from this perspective it was unquestionably the right decision. However, it seems likely that he was also drawn back on his own account, having a strong affinity for a country which was not only intrinsically beautiful but which also, after years of moving from one posting to another, represented continuity with the past and permanence in the future. Even Perseverance Cottage, whilst much loved, had always been a country retreat, whereas Gordons Valley was Home.

Ever since Edward Elworthy's death in 1899 and the consequential division of the original Holme Station among his three surviving sons, Gordons Valley had remained substantially within Percy's immediate family, apart from small blocks of land sold by him to finance his lifestyle. In 1937 the 900 acres of Tuarangi was split off for Tony, who later retired there after spending most of the post-war years in the North Island; his second son, Mark, assumed the management of the property in the early 1970s. The sense of continuity of occupation by the family had thus never been seriously interrupted. Even after Percy and Bertha moved to Havelock North they continued to return to Gordons Valley each summer, and the link was further strengthened when Christopher, who had worked there briefly in 1965, moved to the property permanently with his family in 1975, taking over its management from Robin Johnston in 1978 at much the same time that his parents took up residence there.

Sam and Audrey did not travel from the UK straight to New Zealand, but took the opportunity to spend three weeks in South Africa with Anthony, Penny and their children, Tracy and Alexander. On the journey onwards from there they parted in Sydney, with Audrey flying to Auckland to visit her cousin, Phyl Wilson, whilst Sam flew straight to Christchurch, staying with his cousin John overnight before going on to Gordons Valley. The new house had been completed since he was last there, and he and Audrey were able to move in to much more comfortable and convenient accommodation than the family had experienced in its rambling predecessor. That part of the property immediately surrounding the house still needed a lot of attention, and Sam was to enjoy creating a lovely garden there, carrying out much of the work himself and, on one occasion, falling out of a tree, chainsaw in hand. One of the new features was a croquet lawn. Croquet was a game which Sam had enjoyed for many years and which lent itself to the same level of competitiveness which he had once reserved for rowing and sailing. He and Peter Kenrick, who had a croquet lawn at Blakeshall, had long maintained a fierce but friendly rivalry, which they could now pursue on both sides of the world.

The close proximity of relatives was a great source of comfort to Sam. Christopher and Annie and their two daughters, Caroline and Amanda, lived just up the hill, and the two girls used to call in for soft drinks on their way home after being dropped off by the school bus. Tony and True were also relatively near at hand in Chalk Farm. There were two other couples of Sam and Audrey's own generation to whom they became very close. One of these, unsurprisingly, was John and Hester Elworthy. John, the younger of the two sons of Arthur Elworthy, had been more like a brother than a cousin to Sam and Tony, dating back to the years before the war when Percy and Bertha had offered him a home-from-home in England in whichever house they were occupying at the time He had also introduced Sam to Audrey. He and his wife Hester, who was very popular with them both, lived at Scarborough Hill on the outskirts of Christchurch, where they often provided a bed for the night, and they were frequent visitors to Gordons Valley.

The other couple with whom Sam, in particular, formed a great friendship, were Harold Elworthy and his wife June. Harold, the only son of Herbert Elworthy, was four years older than Sam and had been at Trinity Hall, Cambridge whilst Sam was at Marlborough, so they had not been particularly close hitherto. Harold had inherited Craigmore, but after farming it for many years he and June handed over the management to three of their sons and retired to a house on the outskirts of Timaru. They and Sam and Audrey were frequent guests in each other's houses, and Harold became one of Sam's regular golf partners.

Other popular visitors were Sam's sister Di and her husband Hame, whilst Sam and Audrey enjoyed going to Taupo to see them. Notwithstanding the eight years' difference in their ages, Sam and Di were very close, and he had appreciated her looking after Bertha in the last years of their mother's life. She had her own name for him, Hum, apparently because as a child she had been unable to pronounce Sam! Outgoing, upbeat and highly capable, Di provided just the tonic that Sam was to find he needed and, notwithstanding the geographical distance between them, she became a great support to him.

This was not, at least for the first few years, to be a retirement devoted largely to gardening, croquet and golf. Sam found himself immediately in demand and, within weeks rather than months, took on a number of appointments, three of which were with organizations with which he was already familiar from his positions as a non-executive director in the UK. He joined the main board of NBNZ, the local boards of both BP and AMP and the board of the latter's subsidiary, Perpetual Trustees. These appointments required travelling to board meetings, which were held mostly in Wellington but occasionally in other New Zealand cities. In all cases, however, there was a specified age limit for directors, and he retired from NBNZ and BP in 1982 and AMP in 1983 but retained close contact thereafter with all of them and was frequently invited to social events.

A number of other appointments involved no such age limits. Two of them, like the directorships, prolonged relationships which had been established in the UK, when Sam was invited on to the local committees of both the

Royal Overseas League and the Order of St John. The latter, established in New Zealand in 1885, had long been involved, as elsewhere, in ambulance and other medical services. Sam became a member of both its Appeals and Finance Committees, to which he devoted a lot of time. He also became the Chairman of the local committee of Operation Raleigh, a charity set up in the UK and elsewhere to enable young people to work in poor communities in developing countries, helping them, among other things, to establish sustainable agriculture and to provide fresh water and sanitation.

Sam continued to cultivate his Air Force connections, becoming a prominent member of the RNZAF Association, notwithstanding the fact that he had never served in the New Zealand Armed Forces, and developing a very keen interest in the Air Training Corps, regularly attending parade nights, visiting the cadets during their training and in camp and presenting trophies for achievement.

Living on the other side of the world, it might be thought that Sam would have lost touch with his connections in the United Kingdom. This was very far from the truth. Right from the start, visitors began appearing at Gordons Valley, and over the years they would amount to a very large number. Some, of course, were personal friends of long standing. Peter and Betty Kenrick came for the first time only five months after the Elworthys had themselves arrived, and were to return a number of times subsequently, usually in February when the weather in England was at its worst. There were multiple visits by former colleagues, such as Al Deere, himself a New Zealander, and Michael Quinlan, whilst other senior officers from all the services who had come to visit their colleagues in New Zealand often made time to see Sam; indeed, it seems that he became an important part of their itineraries, a visit to Gordons Valley almost amounting to a pilgrimage.[1]

The traffic was far from one-way. Notwithstanding his renewed attachment to New Zealand, the highlight of Sam's year was his visit to the UK in the summer, which he undertook with great enthusiasm every year for the rest of his life. Whilst the duration varied from year to year, the pattern remained the same. It was built around two events, Garter Day, which took place on a Monday in mid-June, and the Henley Royal Regatta, which was held over five days at the end of the same month and in early July. Sam had promised the Queen that he would faithfully attend the former, which he did in every year except 1984, when it was cancelled for no given reason. He was usually invited to stay at the Deanery, and there was often a meal and sometimes a bed for the night at the Norman Tower, where John Grandy had succeeded him as Constable and Governor. As far as the Regatta was concerned, Sam remained a Steward and the event provided an excellent opportunity to entertain others. In the early 1980s Tim was on a posting to Strike Command at High Wycombe and living nearby, which was geographically highly convenient.

The rest of the time was spent catching up with friends. The longest stay was always with the Kenricks at Blakeshall, but among others who were visited in most years were the Garrans, the Barnetts, the Beeslys, the Lords and Lancelot Fleming, the former Dean of Windsor, and his wife Jane. There was usually a week or more spent in London, crowded with meals with other friends, such as the Wrights, Johnstons and Besses, and often including the Corpus Christi Day Dinner at Skinners' Hall. Sam also usually received a briefing on the current defence position from the CDS or CAS. In some years there were visits further afield, notably to Scotland, to stay with Tim and Anabel whilst the former was Station Commander at RAF Leuchars, to see other friends and usually to fish, and to Ireland for Sam to see his sister Anne and her husband Shaun. The journey to the UK or back again was also occasionally extended to visit the immediate family, as Anthony was still living in South Africa, whilst Clare's husband, Anthony Cary, a member of the Diplomatic Service, was posted to Kuala Lumpur in 1986 and then to Brussels in 1989. There were reciprocal visits by all the family, with Anthony's at the end of 1980 being his first to New Zealand since leaving there in 1946.

Whilst both his new life at Gordons Valley and his annual visits to the UK provided Sam with a great deal of enjoyment, overhanging everything was Audrey's condition, which showed a gradual but unstoppable deterioration. The move itself had been tiring, but in its immediate aftermath she settled down and, at first, was able to accompany Sam on some of his trips to board meetings and other events. However, she showed a tendency to become overwhelmed, physically and mentally, not only by the real, but also by the imagined labours of life. As early as in March 1979, shortly after they had arrived in New Zealand, when Sam proposed a nine-day visit to the North

Island, both on business and to see Di and Hame, she declared that she could not face it. She was checked into a small private hospital for the duration, where at least she was able to relax.

Whilst she was in hospital she was examined and given tests by the doctors, who diagnosed primary dementia, which they believed would be progressive. A second opinion later confirmed that she had Alzheimer's disease. She was put on a drug regime to try to slow the deterioration and told that she must cut right down on her consumption of alcohol, to which her reaction was that if she couldn't drink she had no interest in prolonging her life. Sam wrote to Clare that he was 'filled with despair that her lovely and fertile mind should be threatened … I owe so much of whatever I have achieved to her and I am very distressed, but pleased to do my best to keep her as happy as I can.'[2]

Whilst the deterioration was steady, it was not so fast that Audrey was unable to cope; indeed, she continued to receive guests at Gordons Valley and to travel on occasion with Sam, notably to the UK in the years from 1979 to 1982. In 1983, however, they decided that she should not go. He cut his trip down to the shortest possible duration, arriving in England two days before the Garter Ceremony and leaving on the day after the end of the Regatta. Whilst he was away he arranged for a nurse to be with Audrey for a few days until Di arrived. Di then took her up to stay with her cousin Phyl Wilson in Auckland, where Sam picked her up on his way home.

In 1984 Audrey did accompany Sam to England and even up to Scotland for a week. On the whole she was on relatively good form and was particularly delighted by a family reunion just before they left, as Anthony and Penny had arrived in London. On the way back to New Zealand, however, she became completely disorientated on the plane and had to be given oxygen and later disembarked in a wheelchair. She settled back into life at Gordons Valley, but had no recollection of the journey to and from England. She never went there again.

That September, whilst Sam was in Australia as the guest of honour at two of the annual RAAF Europe reunion dinners in Melbourne and Brisbane, he arranged for a recently retired hospital matron, Alma Strang, to stay with Audrey, who had become much more dependent on him and whom he felt he could no longer leave alone. Alma was to carry out the same service on subsequent occasions, but by July 1985 it was clear that the strain on her and on Annie, who also looked after Audrey when Sam was away, was too great. Audrey was, moreover, experiencing pains in her chest and her legs, the former diagnosed as a heart condition, and she now needed full-time care. She was admitted to the Talbot Hospital in Timaru, where she was to remain for the rest of her life. Sam wrote to Clare that his misery was 'beyond belief',[3] but his morale was restored by a visit with Christopher to Di and Hame.

In the meantime, another family tragedy had occurred, when Tony died of a heart attack in Dunedin on 14 November 1984 at the relatively young age of seventy-two. Born only fifteen months apart, a shared childhood and then schooldays at Marlborough meant that Sam and Tony had once been very close, and it had been Tony's early enthusiasm for flying which had inspired Sam to follow him into the air, thereby in due course launching him on his career. After a spell in Australia in the mid-1930s, Tony had been summoned back by Percy to farm Tuarangi, so he and Sam saw relatively little of one another thereafter. Tony's war had been spent in the Middle East with the New Zealand Expeditionary Force, until injury had caused him to be invalided home. Never an enthusiastic farmer, he had Tuarangi managed professionally and, in 1946, moved to the North Island, establishing his own engineering business there and only retiring back to Chalk Farm many years later.

Sam and Tony were quite different characters, the former disciplined, the latter a free spirit. In their schooldays at Marlborough Sam was in many ways a model pupil, whereas Tony was invariably at the bottom of any class and frequently in serious trouble. Tony had been deeply disappointed to be refused by the RAF on medical grounds, but he retained his love of flying and went on to own a number of light aircraft and become an outstanding glider pilot. He was also a talented and inventive engineer and, in his spare time, a fearless mountaineer, but he lacked the sort of application to building a career which Sam had demonstrated. Like his sister Anne, he had had a difficult relationship with his mother. For Sam, Tony's passing was a very sad event, as over the previous six years they had grown closer again. On the other hand, his relationship with True, which had been somewhat fragile, now improved considerably.

Sam spent as much time as he could with Audrey, recognizing that her attention span was very limited and that she could seldom remember what she had been told. However, now that she was in full-time care, he was significantly more able to pursue other opportunities and interests. The first of these took place in November 1985, a few months after Audrey had entered the Talbot, when Sam was invited to join a VIP visit to Antarctica organized by the Antarctic Division of the New Zealand Department of Scientific and Industrial Research. Sam knew that Eddie Shackleton would be going, as he had invited him to stay before doing so, but it was not Shackleton himself, but a friend of Sam's in Timaru who engineered his invitation. The third VIP was Frank O'Flynn, Minister of Defence in the New Zealand Government, whose politics Sam deplored but who he found to be a congenial travelling companion.

The party left Christchurch for McMurdo Sound on a RNZAF Hercules on 25 November and proceeded from there by dog sledge for a night at the Scott Base, before flying on to the South Pole on the following day. On the day after that they visited both Ernest Shackleton's hut from his 1908–9 expedition and Captain Scott's hut from the fateful 1910–13 expedition. Over the next two days they took a helicopter further afield and looked at the work of the various defence and academic establishments in the area. They also tried some fishing through an ice hole, without success. In the words of the trip report:

> For old Antarcticans the toboggan ride back to Scott Base was nervewracking. Toboggans being driven by Lord Shackleton and Lord Elworthy were driven to their limit.[4]

Another memorable occasion was a 617 Squadron Reunion at Whenuapei on 19 March 1986. It was attended by thirty-five former aircrew, of whom only four were New Zealanders, whilst the others came from the UK, Canada, Australia and the USA. There were a number of speeches, of which the most important were those by Sam, who proposed a toast to the squadron, and Leonard Cheshire, who replied to it. Sam and Cheshire found much to talk about, and the former enjoyed the latter's company enormously.

Sam had by this time become a seasoned host at Gordons Valley, entertaining a large number of visitors; many were only there for meals, but some came to stay, and often for a few nights or even longer. One visitor was Ashe Windham, the son of Bill Windham, a fellow Steward of Sam's at Henley who had gained a double rowing Blue at Cambridge and been a member of the British VIII in the 1952 Olympics. The younger Windham, who was an officer in the Irish Guards on a secondment to the Australian Army, arrived after spending a month living rough and with clothes which badly needed laundering. Sam sent him off fishing, suggesting that he left them to be taken care of. On his return, Windham wrote:

I found three or four pairs of trousers, at least half a dozen shirts and sundry underclothes and socks beautifully washed and immaculately ironed, lying on my bed. As I had not spotted any helpers, and with Lady Elworthy in a nursing home, I asked Sam whom I could thank for doing such a splendid job on my dirty washing. He was surprisingly unforthcoming as to the identity of the excellent charlady but on being pressed he finally admitted that he had done it himself.[5]

Similar experiences were recorded by a number of others, evidence of both Sam's outstanding hospitality and his complete lack of pretension. Sam did have some help around the house and in the garden in the form of Dawn Drake, whose husband worked at Craigmore, but he did most of the cooking himself and much else besides. One thing which he never did was stand on his dignity. This would probably not have worked in the egalitarian Antipodean society, but it was in any event not in his nature. That he was a Lord, in particular, sometimes caused confusion amongst those he was meeting for the first time, who then asked how they should address him. 'Just call me Sam,' was the invariable reply.

There was at least one occasion on which Sam's innate friendliness did not work. Returning from a visit to Lake Tekapo one day, he picked up a Canadian hitch-hiker. It turned out that the young man was in New Zealand 'to get to know Jesus better'. Sam was intensely quizzed as to his own background and, on confessing that he had served in the armed forces, was informed that he could not therefore be a Christian. Having then suffered a long lecture on his sinful life, Sam stopped the Land Rover and invited the man to continue his journey on foot, with the suggestion that this would enable him to get to know Jesus better still. The hitch-hiker answered that God had told him to remain and to pray for Sam. At least the rest of the journey was passed in silence!

The two months following Sam's return from England in the late summer of 1986 were amongst the worst of his life. On 19 August one of his oldest friends, Pat Beesly, died; he had been a fellow rower at Trinity College and Sam's best man at his wedding. He was followed four days later by John Elworthy, who had been suffering from Parkinson's disease for some years. Sam gave the address at his funeral, and Christopher was one of the pallbearers.

It is said that bad news comes in threes, and in this case it was the third that was the worst of all. Audrey died peacefully at the Talbot Hospital on 13 September. Clare arrived from Kuala Lumpur and Di from Taupo to be with Sam on the next day. Audrey was cremated on 16 September and a thanksgiving service was held immediately afterwards at St Mary's, Timaru, the church where Sam himself had been baptized. The address was given by Archdeacon Sam Woods, who had first met Audrey on the ship in which she was returning from New Zealand with Tim, Anthony and Christopher in early 1946.

Sam and Audrey's marriage had been a partnership in every sense of the word, and an equal one at that. Right from the start she had supported him in his career, but without in any way losing her own identity. In the war years she had quickly realized that she must make her own contribution, which she achieved brilliantly through her work with 'Bundles for Britain' and then, more prosaically but no less enthusiastically, by making electric motors on a production line and repairing damaged Lancaster bombers. It was after the war, however, that the partnership really established itself, in the very different environments of places such as Karachi, Tangmere, Bracknell, Aden and, latterly, Windsor Castle. In each of these Audrey always made the very best of what she found, as she did when Sam was working in Whitehall and when she accompanied him on his many overseas tours.

Audrey had a fine brain, as her first-class honours degree proved. She had a deep knowledge of literature and an astonishing memory for poetry in particular. In a later age, her intellect would have undoubtedly led to a successful career of her own. As it was, she devoted herself to Sam's, easing his path in many ways. She was the opposite of a snob, treating lords or labourers the same and able without effort to engage the attention and approval of both. She was exceptionally well informed and could hold her own in any company. She handled the relatively mundane duties of the wife of a very senior officer, such as visiting hospitals or meeting the wives of Sam's more junior colleagues, with an enthusiasm which was entirely genuine; having met anyone once, on the second and subsequent occasions they would be old friends. She was much admired by Sam's staff, especially the junior members, whom she treated almost as family.

Audrey had a considerable sense of humour, which she used on occasion to defuse difficult situations. By way of example, she and Sam were at a cocktail party and dinner in Hong Kong as guests of the Governor and the event was not going at all well; indeed, there was a very awkward atmosphere until Audrey was offered a second Martini.

'You know what they say about Martinis', she announced to the large group around her. 'Oh how I love a Martini, but only one at the most, two I'm under the table and three I'm under my host'!

The Governor's wife, an American, dissolved in laughter, the ice was broken and the party went swimmingly thereafter. Sam told her off at the end of the evening, but, as she rightly said, someone had to do something.[6]

Audrey's notebooks, written over thirteen years, are a fascinating account not only of the places she visited, but also of the people she met. There were few whom she did not like; indeed, on the face of it she might have been thought an undiscerning judge of character. The truth was the opposite: she was a very good judge, but she would always focus on the best in people.

Sam always treated Audrey as an equal. They could, on occasion, be brusque with one another. David Craig felt that there was always a slight spark between them, but of the most endearing kind,[7] whilst Peter Carrington, who liked her very much, thought that she was actually tougher than Sam.[8]

The years of Audrey's decline had been exceptionally difficult for Sam, especially before she had gone into full-time care, and he later regretted that he had been somewhat impatient and unsympathetic during the early onset of her Alzheimer's. During her last few years, however, the aggression often associated with the disease had gone and she had been more like a child. In spite of all this, he missed her deeply. On the other hand, he was now considerably more free to lead his own life, and his morale improved considerably when he spent Christmas 1986 and the first week of January 1987 in Kuala Lumpur with Clare, Anthony and their four young children, Sam, Tom, Arthur and Harriet, and yet more when Peter Kenrick arrived for a three-week stay that February, much of it spent fishing.

During the last six and a half years of Sam's life he was far from idle. The visits to the UK were extended to two months or more, often incorporating stopovers with members of the family, wherever they happened to be, and in September 1990 there was an additional one, when he was invited to the celebrations for the 50th Anniversary of the Battle of Britain. On this occasion he was once more transported by the RAF, staying a night in Washington on the way and dining there with the British Ambassador. He was present at Buckingham Place for the fly-past on 15 September and for the Thanksgiving Service at Westminster Abbey on the following day.

In Gordons Valley, life continued at a gentler pace. There was much to do in the garden, where, among other things, Sam had developed a close relationship with a female magpie named Maggie, whom he used to feed by hand with cream crackers whilst her mate lingered in the background. Any human guests were invited to play croquet, a sport at which Sam now excelled. Visitors continued to come, there were frequent meals with family locally and games of golf, whilst the annual Gordons Valley duck shoot remained a highlight of the year. Always a keen fisherman, Sam now had plenty of time to indulge his enthusiasm, not only in South Canterbury but also further afield, notably in the rivers around Queenstown, further south on Lake Wakatipu. He developed a friendship with an American millionairess, Clara Spiegel, who had been introduced to him by Di and who rented a house there. She would hire a helicopter for the day, allowing her, her guide, Sam and sometimes Christopher to fish the more remote stretches of the mountain rivers.

Christopher took after his father and uncle in his love of flying and had his own aircraft, which enabled Sam to go further afield with him and his family, including to Stewart Island off the south coast of the South Island. Stewart Island was also the venue for a much larger family gathering towards the end of 1988. This had actually begun at Noosa on the Sunshine Coast of Queensland and Heron Island on the Great Barrier Reef in early November, when Tim, who was on leave before taking up a new job as Captain of the Queen's Flight, and Anabel were joined by Sam, Christopher and Annie for a week. A week before Christmas, Tim and Anabel's son Edward arrived for the duration of his school holiday, as did Anthony and his two children, Tracy and Alexander, three months after another family tragedy, when Anthony's wife, Penny, died of cancer, which she had been fighting for some time. It was the first time that Tim, Anthony and Christopher had been together since Sam's installation as a Knight of the Garter in 1977.

It was during this family reunion that Sam undertook a feat which was somewhat unusual for a man approaching his seventy-eighth birthday. He was persuaded, apparently without great difficulty and not just because it was free to one of his age, to undertake a bungee jump off the suspension bridge across the Kawarau River, not far from Queenstown. He executed a perfect swallow dive off the bridge, but said later that he found the experience of the 40-metre descent much less frightening than flying in a bomber over Germany!

Sam's health had been reasonably good up to this time, other than rheumatoid arthritis in his hands, which had been diagnosed whilst he was in London in 1987 and was treated with steroids. In November 1989, however, he collapsed at Gordons Valley. He managed to get to a telephone to ring Christopher, who immediately summoned an ambulance to take him to hospital, where he was placed in intensive care. It appeared that the scar tissue resulting from the operation to remove his gastric ulcer in 1956 had been perforated. He needed a blood transfusion and keyhole surgery to repair the damage and remained in hospital for a week before returning to Gordons Valley to convalesce. He had been planning a trip with Di, Hame and Hester to Golden Bay, but this was cancelled, and Di and Hame came to look after him instead, although the tour was later reinstated.

Many of his friends were not so lucky, and he was particularly distressed when Peter Kenrick suffered a stroke in 1988, leaving him partly paralysed, with some difficulty in speaking and loss of sight. He was to improve subsequently, but hopes of fishing and shooting in Scotland together had to be shelved indefinitely.

There were a number of highlights in the new decade, the first of which was the Queen's visit to New Zealand in February 1990. Sam was invited to a dinner for her at Government House in Wellington at which he was placed on her left, with the Prime Minister on her right. He found her full of conversation and good humour. He was to be horrified in November 1992, when a fire at Windsor Castle destroyed the Queen's Private Chapel, St George's Hall and many of the other State Apartments. He wrote to the Queen and received a handwritten letter in return.

Sam approved greatly of his nephew, John Jeffares, the only child of his sister Anne, and of John's wife Marjorie. He had been to stay with them on a number of occasions in Melbourne, where John was a consultant obstetrician and gynaecologist. John was very interested in photography and video recording and, together with Di, persuaded Sam to allow him to carry out a series of interviews with him about his life. The Jeffares and Di came to Gordons Valley for several days in December 1991, the result of which was seven and three quarters hours of footage covering the whole of Sam's life, an invaluable record for both his family and his biographer. Sam had been dreading it, but found the experience highly enjoyable.

The event, however, which Sam most valued and enjoyed was a party for his immediate family on 11 July 1992, during his annual visit to the UK. He had originally asked that it should be held in a pub near Henley, but Tim and Anabel insisted that it should be at their home, Coates House. Remarkably, every one of his children and grandchildren was there, together with Anabel's children by her first marriage.

Living alone at Gordons Valley, even with Christopher and Annie nearby, had by this time become too much for Sam and, whilst the house was to remain available for him and other members of the family, shortly before flying to England he moved into a small flat in a retirement development at Bishopscourt in Christchurch, on the same site as the house once occupied by his grandfather, Bishop Julius. Ten days earlier, he had undergone a colonoscopy in the hospital in Timaru, following problems with his bowels, and a polyp was discovered which was found to be malignant. Surgery to remove a section of bowel was deferred until after his return from the UK, but he then refused to have chemotherapy, writing to Clare that he was quite content and in no way despondent.

Sam was told that his life expectancy would be between one and five years and, full of optimism, he booked to fly to the UK in June 1993. It was not to be. As his health deteriorated, Clare flew out to stay for a fortnight at the end of February and into March, and she was followed to Bishopscourt by Di, but by mid-March Sam knew that the end was coming and wrote a touching letter to the Kenricks thanking them for the deep friendship between the two families. Chris and Annie were with him for much of the time, and Leonie Clent, the manager of Bishopscourt and a former nun, sat by his bed and read him poetry. He died in his own flat, in the care of Macmillan nurses, on 4 April 1993.

Chapter 19

Reflections

The day of the memorial service for Sam at St Mary's, Timaru, 8 April 1993, dawned still, clear and sunny, a fitting symbol for a life well lived. The address was given by a family friend, Adrian Kerr, an 'inspired choice' according to Hester Elworthy.[1] On Sam's last visit to Gordons Valley he had been heartbroken when his beloved magpie, Maggie, failed to appear, but as the guests gathered there after the service she carried out a fly-past and then mingled with them on the lawn.

Sam was cremated, and his ashes, combined with Audrey's, were later buried at Gordons Valley on a site with a view to both the mountains and the sea, marked by a stone cairn and bronze plaque. The banner which had hung above his stall as a Knight Grand Cross of the Order of the Bath in King Henry VII's Chapel in Westminster Abbey was gifted to the City of Timaru and still hangs at St Mary's, in a chapel whose doors are dedicated to Sam's grandmother, Sarah Elworthy.

On 3 June a service of thanksgiving was held at St Clement Danes, the Central Church of the RAF in London. The Queen was represented by John Grandy and the church was full, not only of the great and the good, but also of many friends, former colleagues and representatives of the organizations with which Sam had been associated. The lessons were read by Tim, Anthony and Christopher, whilst Clare read the poem 'Ebbtide at Sundown' by Michael Field.[2] The address was given by one of Sam and Audrey's oldest friends, Paul Wright. Two days earlier, Sam's banner in St George's Chapel at Windsor had been taken down in a ceremony attended by eight of his fellow Garter Knights and the Dean of Windsor and brought to St Clement Danes to hang alongside that of Lord Portal, at the time the only other RAF officer to have been admitted to the Order of the Garter.

The direction of Sam's life had, in retrospect, been hugely influenced by his father. Percy was the most pronounced anglophile of his family, and without his strong attachment to 'Home' and his decision to have his sons educated there it is difficult to see how Sam could have embarked on a career which would in due course see him become one of the United Kingdom's leading figures of his generation. Such a future would, in any event, have seemed highly unlikely in his early years. His performance at school, whilst satisfactory, was far from outstanding. At Cambridge he put rowing before his studies and graduated with little distinction, whilst he showed no enthusiasm for either the Law or stockbroking. It was only when he joined the Reserve of Air Force Officers, encouraged by the prospect of being paid to learn to fly, that he realized where his vocation lay, and thereafter he never looked back.

Sam's selection for one of a very small number of permanent commissions granted in 1936 to university graduates was the earliest indication that he might succeed in his chosen career. The enormous expansion of the RAF in the late 1930s meant that promotion came much more quickly to him than to the previous generation of officers, whilst his appointment as adjutant of XV Squadron and his subsequent selection to be personal assistant to the C-in-C of Bomber Command suggest that his quality was, by that time, already recognized by at least some of his superiors.

Luck, of course, played a part, as it always does in the life of any successful individual, but so did skill. Sam was lucky not to be included in the initial batch of aircrew to face the Germans during the Battle of France, but skilful in getting through a tour of over thirty operations in a woefully inadequate bomber, bringing his aircraft home safely on more than one occasion by exceptional flying ability and demonstrating at the same time two of his other qualities, courage and leadership. He was lucky to serve directly under Harris and Cochrane, two outstanding officers whom he counted amongst his most important mentors, but skilful in demonstrating to them that he knew his job as a staff officer as well as any and better than most.

By the end of the war Sam had risen to acting air commodore and, at this point, there were only a few contemporaries who had done as well, but the next few years were to see him mark time. The only occasion on which he took positive action to advance his career was his request to receive staff training, which the demands of his wartime postings had denied him. Luck then again played a role, when the rather dreary staff job to which he was subsequently posted brought him into contact with the fiery Basil Embry, who was big enough to react to explicit criticism of himself by giving Sam a job which was to propel him forward once again, command at Tangmere. His skill in organization then caused Paddy Bandon to select him to manage much of the Coronation Review, thus bringing him to the attention of Dermot Boyle, who as C-in-C Fighter Command and then CAS would have a hand in his next three major appointments, Commander of the Metropolitan Sector, Commandant at Bracknell and then DCAS. By that time he was on a fast track, and the patronage of Mountbatten, a highly successful tour as a tri-service C-in-C and the support of his superiors in the RAF would see him to the top of first his own service and then the armed forces as a whole.

It was Sam's misfortune to find himself as CAS at a time when Great Britain was coming to terms with the loss of its status as a world power. The reason for the most part lay with the country's finances. With the exception of a short period during the Korean War, defence spending after the Second World War began its gradual decline as a percentage of gross national product which has continued to this day. As far as conventional warfare was concerned, this was exacerbated by the cost of maintaining the country's position as a nuclear power.

Sam's time as CAS was the least happy of his career, the cancellation of major projects being followed by the conflict with the Royal Navy over its carriers. The latter could have been even more traumatic had it not been for his consistent integrity, which ensured the maintenance of good personal relationships at the top of both services, albeit sadly accompanied by bitterness amongst middle-ranking officers, which Sam deplored. As it was, the 'victory' proved to be short-lived when the British Government decided to pull out effectively all of its armed forces East of Suez, a process which Sam subsequently had to oversee as CDS and which went very smoothly. With the transfer of the nuclear deterrent to the Royal Navy's Polaris submarines, the role of the RAF, other than as a transport service, was effectively reduced for the time being[3] to the defence of the UK and participation in NATO, and it had to cut its cloth accordingly. Although he sometimes described himself as a 'military undertaker', Sam nevertheless provided exemplary leadership during a most difficult time and was a major contributor to the creation of a smaller but well-balanced force to fulfil the RAF's responsibilities, leaving it in as good shape as the circumstances permitted.

At the age of sixty Sam was disinclined to contemplate retirement into a life of ease. Instead, in addition to his role at Windsor Castle, he took on a large number of corporate and other appointments, but there is no evidence that the juggling of the time required to satisfy them all ever resulted in his dropping a ball. He remained much in demand, and it was only his decision to relocate to New Zealand which reduced the load. His years there were overshadowed by Audrey's condition but were by no means unhappy overall; indeed, there is more than ample evidence of contentment with his lot.

Audrey's outstanding contribution to Sam's life and career has already been described. They were dissimilar in some respects, he measured and softly spoken, she forthright and robust in her views. Where they were most alike, however, was in their huge capacity for friendship, which once given was never withdrawn. Many of their friends harked back to school, university and wartime, whilst others were developed during Sam's subsequent postings, particularly in Aden. Inevitably, a large number were from the RAF, but the most enduring friendships were not, and Sam must have relished these, where there was no need to 'talk shop' and his exalted position was of no consequence. In a number of these relationships Sam's children and those of his friends considered themselves to be part of each others' families. Sam's own family, of course, remained enormously important to him, especially after he and Audrey moved to New Zealand in 1978, when not only Christopher, Annie and Di, but also Tony and True and Sam's locally based cousins, provided much support. The fact that for much of their adult lives his and Audrey's children lived in countries other than the one in which their parents happened to be did not diminish their very close ties.

There was one particularly remarkable facet to Sam's character. As Sir Paul Wright said in his address at St Clement Danes, 'I can think of no one of similar stature who went through life without, so far as I know, making a single enemy.' It is difficult to rise to the top of any profession without treading on the toes of others, but Sam appears to have succeeded in doing so. That he was so universally liked and admired makes life difficult for a biographer, who therefore risks being accused of writing a hagiography, but it is nevertheless true. He somehow managed to remain the same person throughout, regardless of his rank, and to achieve his ends not by throwing his weight around but by deploying his considerable intellect. That he was determined was never in doubt, but determination was often accompanied by self-deprecation. His subordinates, especially those on his personal staff, found him a delight to work for, combining, as he did, high expectations with encouragement and a strong sense of humour.

It is his personal characteristics which resonate most with me, not least his humility, mentioned by many I spoke to and best illustrated by Bill Windham, who was deputed to show him the ropes as a recently appointed Timekeeeper at Henley. On being asked what he did and where he was based, Sam replied that he was an airman and worked in London. There was no mention at all of his being the Chief of the Defence Staff!

My own encounter with Sam over fifty years ago, referred to in the Introduction, must have lasted little more than half a minute and yet I remember it vividly to this day. Adrian Kerr, speaking at his memorial service in Timaru, put it best:

> People from all walks of life rejoiced in his company. He harboured no malice, looked down upon no one and had a unique ability of being able to make anyone with whom he came in contact feel good about themselves.[4]

It is, however, his thirty-eight years of service in the armed forces for which Sam will be remembered by posterity. It is difficult for a military man to make a great reputation for himself in a time of peace, and Sam would have been the first to admit that he could not stand comparison with the outstanding RAF leaders of the Second World War. On the other hand, his influence on the shape of the RAF for the last thirty years of the twentieth century was considerable and is, to some extent, still being felt today. Air Chief Marshal Sir Patrick Hine, who served under Sam at Tangmere and went on to become AOC-in-C Strike Command and Joint Commander British Forces in the First Gulf War, considered that he was the outstanding Chief of the Air Staff in his 40-year career,[5] whilst Sir Michael Quinlan summed up his contribution thus:

> He would have met with derision any portrayal of him as being, in the RAF's third generation, what Trenchard and Portal had been in earlier ones. But so indeed he was.[6]

The Arms of Baron Elworthy of Timaru in New Zealand and of Elworthy in the County of Somerset

The arms shown are those granted to Sam as a Peer. The shield, from which are suspended Sam's orders and decorations at that time, from left to right the DFC, DSO, GCB, CBE, LVO and AFC, is placed over the circlet of the Order of the Bath, outside which are laurel leaves denoting a member of the military division of the order. On his appointment to the Orders of the Garter and St John, the circlet would have been changed appropriately to that of the Garter, and the neck badge of a Knight of the Order of St John, another recent appointment, added below the shield.

Abbreviations

ACAS	Assistant Chief of the Air Staff
ACM	Air Chief Marshal
ADC	Aide-de-Camp
ADGB	Air Defence of Great Britain
AEAF	Allied Expeditionary Air Force
AFB	Air Force Base
AFC	Air Force Cross
AHQ	Air Headquarters
AM	Air Marshal
AMP	Air Member for Personnel
AMP	Australian Mutual Provident Society
AMSO	Air Member for Supply & Organization
ANZAM	Australia, New Zealand & Malaya
AOA	Air Officer Administration
AOC	Air Officer Commanding
AOC-in-C	Air Officer Commanding-in-Chief
ARDC	Air Research & Development Command
AVM	Air Vice-Marshal
BBC	British Broadcasting Corporation
BEF	British Expeditionary Force
BOAC	British Overseas Airways Corporation
BOC	British Oxygen Company
BP	British Petroleum
CAS	Chief of the Air Staff
CBE	Central Bomber Establishment
CBE	Commander of the Order of the British Empire
CBS	Columbia Broadcasting System

CCF	Combined Cadet Force
CDS	Chief of the Defence Staff
CENTO	Central Treaty Organisation
CFS	Central Flying School
CGS	Chief of the General Staff
CIGS	Chief of the Imperial General Staff
C-in-C	Commander-in-Chief
CNS	Chief of the Naval Staff
CO	Commanding Officer
COS	Chiefs of Staff
COSC	Chiefs of Staff Committee
CVO	Commander of the Royal Victorian Order
DCAS	Deputy Chief of the Air Staff
DFC	Distinguished Flying Cross
DFM	Distinguished Flying Medal
DLF	Dhofar Liberation Front
DS	Directing Staff
DSO	Distinguished Service Order
FAA	Fleet Air Arm
G/C	Group Captain
GCB	Knight Grand Cross of the Order of the Bath
GHQ	General Headquarters
GOC	General Officer Commanding
GPO	General Post Office
GS	General Staff
HM	His/Her Majesty
HMS	His Majesty's Ship/Her Majesty's Ship
HQ	Headquarters
HRH	His/Her Royal Highness
IDC	Imperial Defence College
JSSC	Joint Services Staff College
KCB	Knight Commander of the Order of the Bath
KCVO	Knight Commander of the Royal Victorian Order
KG	Knight Companion of the Order of the Garter
LCT	Landing Craft Tank

LRC	London Rowing Club
LST	Landing Ship Tank
LVO	Lieutenant of the Royal Victorian Order
MA	Military Assistant
MC	Military Cross
MC	Medium Capacity (Bombs)
MP	Member of Parliament
MRAF	Marshal of the Royal Air Force
MRCA	Multi Role Combat Aircraft
MTB	Motor Torpedo Boat
MV	Motor Vessel
MVO	Member of the Royal Victorian Order
NAAFI	Navy, Army and Air Force Institutes
NASA	National Aeronautics & Space Administration
NATO	North Atlantic Treaty Organisation
NBNZ	National Bank of New Zealand
NCO	Non-commissioned Officer
NORAD	North American Aerospace Defense Command
NZ	New Zealand
OTU	Operational Training Unit
PA	Personal Assistant
PFF	Pathfinder Force
POW	Prisoner of War
PSO	Personal Staff Officer
RAAF	Royal Australian Air Force
RAF	Royal Air Force
RAFO	Reserve of Air Force Officers
RAFVR	Royal Air Force Volunteer Reserve
RAuxAF	Royal Auxiliary Air Force
RCAF	Royal Canadian Air Force
RFA	Royal Fleet Auxiliary
RIAF	Royal Indian Air Force
RMS	Royal Mail Ship
RN	Royal Navy
RNZAF	Royal New Zealand Air Force

ROSL	Royal Overseas League
RPAF	Royal Pakistan Air Force
SACEUR	Supreme Allied Commander in Europe
SASO	Senior Air Staff Officer
SEATO	South East Asia Treaty Organisation
SHAEF	Supreme Headquarters Allied Expeditionary Force
SHAPE	Supreme Headquarters Allied Powers in Europe
SS	Steam Ship
SSAFA	Soldiers', Sailors' and Airmen's Families Association
STOL	Short Take-off & Landing
UK	United Kingdom
US	United States
USA	United States of America
USAAF	United States Army Air Force
USAF	United States Air Force
USSR	Union of Soviet Socialist Republics
VC	Victoria Cross
VCAS	Vice-Chief of the Air Staff
VCDS	Vice-Chief of the Defence Staff
VCNS	Vice-Chief of the Naval Staff
VE Day	Victory in Europe Day
VTOL	Vertical Take-off & Landing
WAAF	Women's Auxiliary Air Force
W/C	Wing Commander
WRAF	Women's Royal Air Force
WO	Warrant Officer

Acknowledgements

I must start by thanking Marshal of the Royal Air Force the Lord Craig of Radley for his excellent Foreword, which both encapsulates Sam's life and emphasizes his outstanding qualities. David Craig is uniquely qualified to give a view on Sam, having served on his personal staff at the Ministry of Defence and later become both CAS and CDS himself. As well as giving me a full interview, he commented most helpfully on the chapters on Sam's own time as CAS and CDS.

I could not have written this book without the wholehearted support of Sam's children. From our first meeting, both Tim Elworthy and Clare Cary have done everything in their power to help me, providing several suitcases packed with papers, diaries, log books, letters and Audrey's notebooks. They allowed me to record a long interview with them both, full of personal reminiscences of their parents, and always responded without delay to my many queries thereafter. The photos in the book are, almost without exception, taken from the family albums held by Tim. Although I have never met them, as they both live in New Zealand, and although they came into the process somewhat later, Anthony and Christopher Elworthy were no less helpful, with Christopher providing some particularly valuable information on the retirement years. All of them read and commented on drafts of the book.

I would also like to record my appreciation of the work of their cousin, David Elworthy, and his wife, Ros Henry, the authors of an outstanding family history, *Edward's Legacy – The Elworthys of South Canterbury*. This provided not only most of the material for my first chapter but also valuable information on the members of the family who were important to Sam. Without it by my side, I would have been completely lost in my attempts to understand the various relationships.

A large number of other people helped me in the writing of this book, to all of whom I extend my thanks. Their contributions are described below, for the most part in the chronological order of Sam's life.

Clare Russell and Gráinne Lenehan, the Archivists at Marlborough College, enabled me to plot Sam's school career and also provided some photos of the occasion on which I met him and which is referred to in the Introduction, albeit not of our encounter itself. Jonathan Smith, the Archivist at Trinity College, Cambridge, confirmed both Sam's academic achievements at the university and his college boat club appointments, whilst Frances Bellis, Assistant Librarian at Lincoln's Inn, confirmed the date and circumstances of his call to the Bar and his election much later as an Honorary Bencher. Frankie Maddox of the Henley Royal Regatta sent me details of Sam's participation in the Regatta whilst at Cambridge, his election as a Steward and his appointment as a Timekeeper.

As far as Sam's early RAF career was concerned, Martyn Ford-Jones, the Historian of XV Squadron, provided a package of material relating to Sam's service with the squadron and later read and commented on the draft of the relevant passage in the book.

Faith Clark, the daughter of Babs Wright (formerly Rathbone), lent me her mother's memoirs, which covered her friendship with Sam and Audrey during the war and the death of John Rathbone whilst serving with 82 Squadron.

I spent several days in Lincolnshire looking round a number of the former 5 Group stations, of which only Waddington and Coningsby remain in use by the RAF. My itinerary was helped considerably by advice from Phil Bonner, the Aviation Development Officer at Aviation Heritage Lincolnshire. He also introduced me to Mike Rogers, who took me on a guided tour of the former airfield at Bardney, which came under Sam's command whilst new runways were being built at Waddington. The main focus of my visit was on Waddington itself, where my host was Chris Dean of the Waddington Heritage Centre, whilst Craig Smith co-ordinated the arrangements. Chris also followed up a number of subsequent queries about Sam's posting there. I am also grateful to Flying Officer Andy Gosling, who arranged that I should see around the rest of the station.

My friend, Charles Nicholls, who served as a navigator in 106 Squadron at RAF Metheringham whilst Sam was SASO at 5 Group, provided a vivid personal account of the training and operational service of the aircrews in Bomber Command and lent me a number of books on the subject.

I had a great deal of help from Robert Owen, the Official Historian of the No. 617 Squadron Association and Chairman of the Barnes Wallis Foundation, not only on Sam's links to the squadron, but on Bomber Command as a whole; this included a valuable reading list. I was also able to meet John Cochrane, one of the sons of Air Chief Marshal Sir Ralph Cochrane, who very kindly gave me access to his father's papers.

Dudley Hooley and David Coxon, respectively Director and Curator of the Tangmere Military Aviation Museum, were most helpful during my visit there and introduced me to John Dyer, who had served as a pilot in 29 Squadron whilst Sam was Station Commander at Tangmere. His very positive view of Sam was corroborated by Air Chief Marshal Sir Patrick Hine, who also served there at that time, in his case in 1 Squadron. During my interview with him, Sir Patrick also told me of his admiration for Sam in the late 1960s, whilst he was serving in Whitehall as Personal Air Secretary to Lord Shackleton and sharing an office with Sam's ADC. An exceptionally well-informed observer of Sam's post-war career, he met him subsequently on a number of occasions, the last of which was at Gordons Valley in 1991.

For information on Sam's time as Commander-in-Chief Middle East I met both his ADCs of the period, George Norrie and Richard Novis, who told me a great deal about his day-to-day activities, including, in the case of the former, during Operation *Vantage*. I also met Lord Luce, the son of Sir William and Lady Luce and nephew of Admiral Sir David Luce, who was most helpful on Sam's relationships with them.

I met or spoke to a number of people who had encountered Sam in some capacity during his years in Whitehall, the most senior of whom was Lord Carrington, who was Sam's political master during his last year as CDS and became, with his wife, a close personal friend of Sam and Audrey. Lord Carrington not only described his own relationship with Sam but also commented on the preceding years and the inter-service struggle during Sam's appointment as CAS. Field Marshal Lord Bramall, who first met Sam when he was DCAS and who was subsequently to become the co-author of the definitive book on the Chiefs of Staff, provided some exceptionally valuable insights on the reorganization of the Ministry of Defence by Mountbatten, on whose staff he was serving at the time, and on the part played by Sam as CAS and thereafter. He was also one of Sam's successors as Lord Lieutenant of Greater London, whose duties he described to me.

I interviewed a number of members of Sam's personal staff whilst he was CAS and CDS, three of whom, Nick Adamson, David Hawkins-Leth and Vyvyan Harmsworth, had been his ADCs and one, Iain Ferguson, his Military Assistant. The ADCs in particular saw a lot of Sam outside office hours and knew Audrey well, so they provided a light-hearted counterpoint to Sam's professional life, whilst Iain Ferguson was excellent on the organization of Sam's office and the structure of the Ministry of Defence. I also interviewed Major General Julian Thompson, who served in the Chiefs of Staff Secretariat during the last sixteen months of Sam's tenure as CDS and gave me a glimpse of the workings of the COSC itself.

For Sam's time as Constable and Governor of Windsor Castle His Royal Highness the Duke of Edinburgh graciously agreed to answer a questionnaire, for which I am most grateful. In addition I met Air Marshal Sir Ian Macfadyen, who had been one of Sam's successors in the role and was most helpful on what it entailed. It turned out that, as an Old Marlburian himself, he had acted as a temporary ADC to Sam on the very day on which I met him during his inspection of the college's CCF detachment.

Bill Windham wrote to me with the story of his first meeting with Sam, who had just been appointed as a Timekeeper at Henley, whilst his son, Ashe Windham, set down his recollections of staying with Sam in Gordons Valley in 1985.

In addition to the numerous people who have helped me during the writing of this book, I need to thank those working at the various archives which I have accessed. I never fail to be astonished by the efficiency of the National Archives. A number of its files are being digitalized, and I was delighted to find that they included the Operations Record Book of 82 Squadron, which I was then able to read at home, obviating the need for yet another crack-of-dawn departure for Kew! I am also grateful to the Imperial War Museum, the Mountbatten Archives in the Hartley Library at the University of

Southampton and the RAF Museum, London for enabling me to access some key sources.

I am most grateful for the support of Pen & Sword, where Henry Wilson has been consistently encouraging, perhaps not least because he, too, was on parade at Marlborough on the day that I met Sam during his inspection of the CCF. My editor, George Chamier, has tidied up my drafting with a pleasingly light touch and Matt Jones, the Production Manager, has been as efficient as always.

Yet again I have had tremendous support from my wife, Sheelagh, and my sons, Timothy and Rupert. As always, Rupert has been invaluable as my first proof-reader.

Sources and Bibliography

Interviews
Mr Nicholas Adamson
Field Marshal Lord Bramall
Lord Carrington
Mrs Clare Cary
Marshal of the RAF Lord Craig of Radley
Air Commodore Sir Timothy Elworthy
Colonel Iain Ferguson
Mr Vyvyan Harmsworth
Air Vice-Marshal David Hawkins-Leth
Air Chief Marshal Sir Patrick Hine
Lord Luce
Air Marshal Sir Ian Macfadyen
Lord Norrie
Mr Richard Novis
Major General Julian Thompson

Primary Sources
National Archives

AIR 2/11652	RAF Staff College Establishment of Personnel
AIR 2/14019	RAF Staff College reports on courses 1948–58
AIR 2/15358	RAF Staff College reports on courses 1959–62
AIR 2/12193	Arrangements for RAF Coronation Review by HM the Queen
AIR 14/2491	RAF Waddington Raid Record Book July 1941–December 1943
AIR 14/2492	RAF Waddington Raid Record Book December 1943–June 1944
AIR 14/3880	Formation of Central Bomber Establishment
AIR 20/8662	RAF Coronation Review by HM the Queen at RAF Odiham
AIR 20/11425	Future Aircraft and the Island Strategy
AIR 20/11776	Defence Review – Carrier Studies 1965–66
AIR 24/204	Bomber Command Operations & Administration 1942
AIR 24/205	Bomber Command Operations & Administration 1943
AIR 24/206	Bomber Command Operations & Administration Jan 1944–May 1945

AIR 25/23	2 Group Operations Record Book 1941–43
AIR 25/33	2 Group Appendices July–December 1941
AIR 25/110	5 Group Operations Record Book January 1944–December 1945
AIR 25/50	2 (Indian) Group Operations Record Book October 1945–July 1947
AIR 27/202	XV Squadron Operations Record Book 1920–39
AIR 27/681	82 Squadron Operations Record Book 1940–41
AIR 27/851	108 Squadron Operations Record Book 1937–45
AIR 27/2058	600 (City of London) Squadron Operations Record Book 1925–39
AIR 28/8	RAF Abingdon Operations Record Book 1932–40
AIR 28/63	RAF Bicester Operations Record Book 1936–40
AIR 28/903	RAF Watton Operations Record Book 1941–43
AIR 28/905	RAF Watton Operations Record Book 1940–41
AIR 29/648	13 OTU Operations Records Book 1940–43
AIR 29/650	13 OTU Nominal List of Personnel 1940–45
AIR 29/2484	HQ Metropolitan Sector Operations Centre 1951–55
AIR 29/2767	RAF Staff College Appendices for 1957
AIR 29/2962	RAF Staff College 1956–1960
AIR 32/146	Review of RAF by the HM the Queen – Air Ministry papers
AIR 38/399	Transport Command Plan for Operation Vantage
AIR 63/21	CBE Liaison Mission to New Zealand April 1947
AIR 63/63	CBE Monthly Progress Report June 1946
AIR 63/64	CBE Monthly Progress Report September 1946
CAB 148/26	Secretary of State for Defence on Fixed Wing Aircraft and Carriers
DEFE 4/128	Command Organization Aden
DEFE 4/129	Command Organization Aden
DEFE 5/105	Review of HQ & Administrative units Aden
DEFE 5/116	Report of working party on Operation Vantage
DEFE 6/77	Summaries of positions on Operation Vantage June–October 1961
DEFE 13/505	Defence Review 1966 Statement to the House of Commons
DEFE 13/506	Defence Review 1966 Press Conference Statement
DEFE 13/507	Defence Review 1966 Defence Estimates
DEFE 13/589	Secretary of State for Defence on the case for abandoning the carrier force
DEFE 13/590	Defence Review 1966 – Carrier Plan
DEFE 25/219	Templer Committee on the Rationalisation of Air Power

Imperial War Museum
The Papers of Air Chief Marshal Sir Denis Barnett
Recorded interviews with Sam and with MRAF Lord Hill-Norton

RAF Museum London
The Papers of MRAF Sir Arthur Harris

Marlborough College Archives
College Alphabetical Lists and Summerfield House Lists and photographs

Hartley Library, University of Southampton
Mountbatten Papers

Private Elworthy Records
Diary 1924
Appointment Diaries 1952–1993
Pilots Flying Log Books 1933–58
RAF Staff Interviews conducted on 7 & 21 March 1975
Letters from Sam in Pakistan to Audrey September 1948–February 1949
Letters from Sam to Clare 1979–1993
Audrey's journey notebooks 1960–1973
Video interview of Sam by John Jeffares
Photograph albums, including Rowing Album
RAF Service Record

Other Sources
Air Force List
Dictionary of National Biography
London Gazette
The Times Digital Archive
Who's Who
Journal of the RAF Historical Society
5 Group News September 1944–November 1945
5 Group Tactical Notes
Wikipedia and other web sites

Books
Allen, H. R., *Fighter Station Supreme – RAF Tangmere*, London 1985
Baker, Richard, *Dry Ginger – The Biography of Admiral of the Fleet Sir Michael Le Fanu*, London 1977
Bishop, Patrick, *Target Tirpitz*, London 2012
Bowyer, Chaz, *Royal Air Force – The aircraft in service since 1918*, Feltham 1981
Bowyer, Michael, *2 Group RAF – A Complete History, 1936–1945*, London 1974
Boyle, Dermot, *My Life*, Privately Printed 1990
Bramall, Dwin & Jackson, Bill, *The Chiefs – The Story of the United Kingdom Chiefs of Staff*, London 1992

Cameron, Neil, *In the Midst of Things – The autobiography of Lord Cameron of Dalhousie*, London 1986

Carrington, Charles, *Soldier at Bomber Command*, London 1987

Churchill, Winston S, *The Second World War, Volumes I–VI*, London 1949–1954

Daly, M. W., *The Last of the Great Proconsuls – The biography of Sir William Luce*, San Diego USA 2014

Delve, Ken, *Fighter Command 1936–1968 – An Operational & Historical Record*, Barnsley 2007

Dyndal, Gjert Lage, *Land Based Air Power or Aircraft Carriers?*, Farnham 2012

Elworthy, David & Henry, Ros, *Edward's Legacy – The Elworthys of South Canterbury*, Christchurch NZ 2011

Elworthy, Gertrude & Anthony, *A Power in the Land – Churchill Julius 1847–1938*, Christchurch NZ 1971

Falconer, Jonathan, *Bomber Command Handbook 1939–1945*, Stroud 1998

Grounds, Eric, *The Quiet Australian – The Story of Teddy Hudleston*, Cirencester 2015

Grove, Eric J., *Vanguard to Trident – British Naval Policy since World War Two*, Annapolis USA 1987

Helmore, W., *Air Commentary*, London 1942

Hamlin, John, *'For Faith and Freedom' – Royal Air Force Waddington – The first eighty years*, Peterborough 1996

Harris, Arthur, *Bomber Offensive*, London 1947

Hastings, Max, *Bomber Command*, London 1979

Healey, Denis, *The Time of My Life*, London 1989

Holland, James, *Dam Busters – The Race to Smash the Dams, 1943*, London 2012

Horsley, Peter, *Sounds from another Room – Memories of Planes, Princes and the Paranormal*, Barnsley 1997

Johnson, Franklyn A., *Defence by Ministry – The British Ministry of Defence 1944–1974*, New York USA 1980

Johnston, Charles, *The View from Steamer Point – Three Crucial Years in South Arabia*, London 1964

Leach, Raymond, *An Illustrated History of RAF Waddington*, Bognor Regis 2003

Lee, David, *Flight from the Middle East*, London 1980

Luce, Margaret, *From Aden to the Gulf – Personal Diaries 1956–1966*, London 1987

Melinsky, Hugh, *Forming the Pathfinders – The Career of Air Vice-Marshal Sydney Bufton*, Stroud 2010

Messenger, Charles, *'Bomber' Harris and the Strategic Bombing Offensive, 1939–1945*, London 1984

Middlebrook, Martin & Everitt, Chris, *The Bomber Command War Diaries – An Operational Reference Book 1939–1945*, Harmondsworth 1985

Mondey, David, *The Hamlyn Concise Guide to British Aircraft of World War II*, London 1994

Mondey, David, *The Hamlyn Concise Guide to American Aircraft of World War II*, London 1996

Mondey, David, *The Hamlyn Concise Guide to Axis Aircraft of World War II*, London 1996

Norrie, George, *Portals of Discovery*, Kibworth 2016

Onderwater, Hans, *Gentlemen in Blue – 600 Squadron*, Barnsley 1987

Probert, Henry, *High Commanders of the Royal Air Force*, London 1991

Probert, Henry, *Bomber Harris – His Life and Times*, London 2001

Rosier, Frederick with Rosier, David, *Be Bold*, London 2011

Tedder, Arthur, *With Prejudice – War Memoirs*, London 1966

Thorburn, Gordon, *The Squadron That Died Twice – The Story of No. 82 Squadron RAF*, London 2015

Trevenen James, A. G., *The Royal Air Force – The Past 30 Years*, London 1976

Ward, Chris, *5 Group Bomber Command – An Operational Record*, Barnsley 2007

Ziegler, Philip, *Mountbatten – The Official Biography*, London 1985

Notes

Chapter 1

1. After two other changes of name it became Taunton School in 1899.
2. It is now a hotel and conference centre.
3. Percy Elworthy, 'Memoir'
4. Ibid.
5. Arnold Wallis was both the grandson of William Elworthy, Thomas the Younger's elder brother, and the younger brother of the Right Revd Frederic Wallis, Bishop of Wellington.
6. The name was subsequently changed to Brent Knoll to avoid confusion with a village of the same name in Devon.
7. When Percy tired of a car, or they broke down and were difficult to repair, he would drop them into potholes around Gordons Valley!

Chapter 2

1. The *Prinz Eitel Friedrich* had a short but successful career between December 1914 and March 1915, sinking eleven ships totalling over 33,000 tons. She was later interned in the United States and then used as an American troopship.
2. From 1918 to 1933 Grove Lodge was the home of John Galsworthy, who wrote *The Forsyte Saga* there.
3. He was to become one of Churchill Julius's successors as Bishop of Christchurch.
4. When the author was in the same house in the 1960s, the number of baths had increased to three, but the system remained the same, as did the mud in suspension!
5. The reason for this was simply lack of space. It was only in 1953, when Summerfield took over part of the school sanatorium for additional dormitories and studies, that it became a fully fledged senior house in its own right.
6. 'You are old, Father William', the young man said, 'and your hair has become very white; and yet you incessantly stand on your head – do you think, at your age, it is right?'

Chapter 3

1. The two merged in 1946 to become the First and Third Trinity Boat Club.
2. Sam's oar no longer exists. There is a story, possibly apocryphal, that it was put on a bonfire by a cleaner at Trinity, furious at the state of his room.

3. Armstrong Whitworth, Bristol, Blackburn and De Havilland.

4. Jimmy Wells remained with 600 Squadron after Sam left, going on to become its CO and a squadron leader. He was killed when his Blenheim was shot down on 10 May 1940, the first day of the German invasion of France and Belgium.

Chapter 4

1. The General Duties Branch at this time was composed entirely of commissioned officers who were qualified pilots. With the expansion of the RAF and the introduction of aircraft which required large crews, it was in due course expanded to include air gunners, navigators, bomb aimers, wireless operators and flight engineers, many of whom were non-commissioned officers with the rank of flight sergeant or sergeant.

2. XV Squadron was one of only ten RAF squadrons which used Roman rather than Arabic numerals in their titles.

3. This was in spite of his having displayed the squadron badge in the lavatories, where he thought that the motto – 'Aim Sure' – would be appropriate. The CO was not amused!

4. Selway was always known as 'Mark' by his friends and colleagues.

5. Elizabeth Elworthy, later Borthwick, always known as 'Spud', was the fourth of five daughters of Herbert Elworthy.

6. This was possibly the same plane which Sam had flown up to Queen Mary's School, Duncombe Park in Yorkshire on the previous day in order to bring the headmistress, Margaret Bowen, a cousin by marriage, down to the wedding.. He passed low overhead for the children to get a good view. His daughter Clare was a boarder at the school from 1959 to 1962.

7. IWM interview.

8. Interview by John Jeffares.

9. There were five effective schemes in total between 1934 and 1939, respectively A, C, F, L and M.

Chapter 5

1. Letter from Foster to Sam, 16.1.41.

2. The armour plate behind the seat was popularly known as 'The Tombstone'.

3. Not so! It was repaired and taken on by Squadron Leader, later Wing Commander Ken Burt, who had served under Sam and was later to be CO of 82 Squadron. Sadly, he was to die over Heligoland in that very aircraft some months later.

4. Letter from Sam to his family, 18.4.41.

Chapter 6

1. Churchill, *The Grand Alliance*, p.729.

2. Letter from Mrs Paul White to Audrey, 24.4.41.

3. Sir Paul Wright had a long and successful post-war career in the Diplomatic Service and was to give the address at Sam's London memorial service in 1993.
4. The *Gneisenau* was so badly damaged that she never left port again. The *Scharnhorst* was repaired in due course, but sunk in the Battle of the North Cape in December 1943.
5. RAF Staff Interview, 21.3.75.
6. Later renowned for holding the Rhine Bridge at Arnhem for four days against constant German attack during Operation *Market Garden*.
7. Interview by John Jeffares.
8. RAF staff interview 7.3.75.
9. It was not considered necessary to bomb Lübeck in strength for the rest of the war, although this was in part due to Britain later agreeing with the International Red Cross not to bomb the city after it became the entry port for that organization's humanitarian supplies.
10. He would go on to become an outstanding AOC at 2 Group, which in 1943 left Bomber Command to join the Second Tactical Air Force.
11. Maschinenfabrik Augsburg-Nürnberg

Chapter 7

1. There was a second 'guest' on this trip, Major John Mullock MC of the Royal Artillery, who was the 5 Group Flak Liaison Officer. He took the place of the mid-upper gunner.
2. RAF Staff Interview, 21.3.75.
3. IWM interview.
4. Sharp was not as keen on the Thunderbolt as Sam and in due course persuaded the USAAF to exchange it for a P-38 Lightning!
5. Shortly afterwards, Doubleday was appointed to command 61 Squadron at Skellingthorpe. Sam kept in touch with him and stayed with him in Sydney in 1987.

Chapter 8

1. RAF Staff Interview, 21.3.75.
2. Harris had attended the Army Staff College at Camberley in 1928/9 when Montgomery was an instructor there, and the two men later served together in Palestine in 1938.
3. Carrington, *A Soldier at Bomber Command*, p.151.
4. In his book *The Quiet Australian* Eric Grounds identifies two other air commodores at the time who were younger than Sam: they were both good friends of his, later to become ACM Sir Augustus Walker and ACM Sir Kenneth Cross.
5. RAF Staff Interview, 21.3.75. Although Sam gave his total support to Cochrane he believed that Bennett had not been adequately recognized for his

achievements and added his weight to a campaign for him to receive a belated knighthood, writing to the Prime Minister on the subject in July 1978. No knighthood was conferred.

6. Guy Gibson, the first commander of 617 Squadron, had returned to duty as a staff officer at 54 Base at Coningsby. For reasons which have never been adequately explained, he was appointed to act as Master Bomber on a raid to Mönchengladbach and Rheydt on the night of 19/20 September. Flying an unfamiliar Mosquito borrowed from 627 Squadron, he and his navigator crashed in the Netherlands and both were killed.

7. RAF Staff Interview, 21.3.75.

8. Letter from Tedder to Sam, 23.2.45.

9. So called because of his personal architecture, standing 5ft 5ins tall and with a huge chest!

Chapter 9

1. AIR 14/3880.

2. Ibid.

3. Now Sydney Kingsford Smith Airport.

4. Tony had joined the New Zealand Army during the war and was wounded at El Alamein. He later became a tank instructor, but was invalided home after injuring his back.

5. Now Indira Gandhi International Airport.

6. Liaquat Ali Khan was assassinated in 1951.

7. Later the first President of the Republic of Pakistan.

8. The C-in-C of the Pakistan Army, General Sir Frank Messervy, followed in 1948 by Lieutenant General Sir Douglas Gracey, had his headquarters in Rawalpindi. Therefore, like Perry-Keene, he nominated a substitute for the Defence Council. Akbar Khan, the most senior Pakistani in the Army, was the Commander of Sind Area, with his HQ in Karachi.

9. Letter to Audrey, 6.10.47.

Chapter 10

1. RAF Staff Interview, 21.3.75.

2. Now the Goodwood Racing Circuit.

3. Horsley, *Sounds From Another Room*, p.158. In April 1953 Horsley became a full-time equerry to the Duke of Edinburgh, not returning to the RAF until 1957.

4. So called because he had been educated in South Africa.

5. Following his time in command of 82 Squadron, Bandon had commanded two stations in 2 Group, West Raynham and Horsham St Faith, whilst Sam was on the group operations staff.

6. Interview with Sir Patrick Hine, 8.8.2016.

7. In 1984 the MVO (4th Class) was re-designated LVO (Lieutenant of the Royal Victorian Order), with the MVO (5th Class) becoming simply the MVO.
8. Letter from Dermot Boyle to Sam, 16.7.53.
9. Kelvedon Hatch is open to the public as a museum.
10. Letter from Hubert Patch to Sam, 15.9.54.
11. Letter from Dermot Boyle to Sam, 31.10.55.

Chapter 11
1. Rosier, *Be Bold*, p.209.
2. Richmond was succeeded in October 1956 by Vice Admiral Sir Robin Durnford-Slater.
3. Interview by John Jeffares.
4. Ibid.
5. Mills was preceded by Embry and followed by Broadhurst, Bandon and Hudleston.
6. Commander, later Rear Admiral, Peter Howes, Naval Assistant to the First Sea Lord.
7. Letter from Mountbatten to Sam, 19.11.57.
8. The RAuxAF was, indeed, disbanded in 1957, only to be re-formed on a much reduced basis in 1959. It was expanded subsequently, but currently has no flying units.
9. Probert, *High Commanders of the Royal Air Force*, p.59.

Chapter 12
1. RAF Staff Interview, 21.3.75.
2. The circumstances are set out in *The Quiet Australian: The story of Teddy Hudleston, the RAF's troubleshooter for 20 years* by Eric Grounds, Hudleston's nephew by marriage.
3. RAF Staff Interview, 21.3.75.
4. Letter from Sam to Mountbatten, 5.7.61.
5. Norrie, who had accompanied Sam to Kuwait, obtained permission to rejoin his regiment temporarily.
6. Interview by John Jeffares.
7. Letter from Mountbatten to Sam 5.7.61.
8. Ibid.

Chapter 13
1. Johnston, *The View from Steamer Point*, p.209
2. Rosier, *Be Bold*, p.219
3. Yaur Adu was a Ghanian civil servant who subsequently became Deputy Director-General of the Commonwealth Secretariat.

4. Adu was brought back to England after Sam's tour and died at the age of fourteen.
5. RAF Staff Interview, 21.3.75.
6. Following the nationalization of his business in 1969, Besse became the Chairman of the International Board of United World Colleges, of which Mountbatten was the President.
7. Norrie, *Portals of Discovery*, p.104–5.
8. Johnston, *The View from Steamer Point*, p.209–10.
9. Norrie, *Portals of Discovery*, p.105.
10. Audrey Notebook 1.
11. Ibid.
12. Audrey Notebook 7.
13. Audrey Notebook 3.
14. Ibid.
15. Response to aide-memoire by Richard Novis.
16. Brunei later elected not to join Malaysia.

Chapter 14
1. Interview with Lord Bramall.
2. RAF Staff Interview 21.3.75.
3. Ibid.

Chapter 15
1. RAF Staff Interview 21.3.75.
2. Remarkably the last sortie by a RAF photo-reconnaissance Canberra took place in 2006.
3. *Flight International*, 17.6.65
4. DEFE 215/19.
5. RAF Staff Interview, 21.3.75.
6. HMS *Intrepid* was to play a major role in the Falklands War in 1982.
7. Healey, *The Time of My Life*, p.276.
8. A mistake had, in fact, been made by a RAF officer on the distance from Aldabra to the Kenyan coast, but this was relatively trifling and made no difference to the argument.
9. Letter from MRAF Sir John Slessor to Sam, 19.2.66.
10. It is now independent of the University of Canterbury as Lincoln University.
11. British Oral Archive of Political and Administrative History 1920–1980.

Chapter 16
1. Interview with Lord Craig, 12.10 2016.
2. Interview by John Jeffares.
3. It was Admiral of the Fleet Lord Lewin, exasperated by the failure of the Chiefs to produce a joint position for the Defence White Paper of 1981, who

began the process of strengthening the powers of the CDS into a position of pre-eminence.

4. Baker's real first name was Geoffrey, but his height and fair hair had led to the nickname of 'Swedish George' early in his career and this had stuck. Nevertheless, in circumstances similar to Sam's, he had been compelled to retain his proper name when he was knighted as Sir Geoffrey.

5. Following a dictum by Mountbatten that no one below the rank of lieutenant colonel could attend, one of them also served the tea!

6. Healey, *The Time of my Life*, p.273.

7. Cameron, *In the Midst of Things*, p.149.

8. Ibid. p.147.

9. Interview by John Jeffares.

10. Both squadrons were later re-formed, No. 20 as a Harrier squadron in Germany, No. 45 as a Hunter ground attack training squadron in the UK.

11. Audrey, Notebook 23.

12. He died on 28 November 1970.

13. Hill-Norton, IWM interview.

14. Betty Gould was one of the daughters of Arthur Elworthy and the sister of John Elworthy.

Chapter 17

1. Slim died on 14 December 1971 and Sam attended his funeral in St George's Chapel, Windsor, eight days later. Aileen, Lady Slim, was Sam and Audrey's guest at Windsor on a number of occasions thereafter.

2. The other end is incorporated into the Elizabethan Long Gallery.

3. Interview by John Jeffares.

4. Audrey, Notebook 26.

5. This was the origin of the expression 'At sixes and sevens'.

6. Undated note by Sam.

7. The exceptions were MRAF Sir Andrew Humphrey, who died in office, Admiral of the Fleet Sir Edward Ashmore, who was a 'caretaker' CDS after Humphrey's untimely death, and MRAF Sir Peter Harding, who resigned his commission as the result of an affair being made public.

8. The Lieutenancy excludes the City of London, in which the Lord Mayor has his own Commission of Lieutenancy.

9. This was the last journey recorded in Audrey's notebooks.

10. Audrey, Notebook 27.

11. Holme Station had been sold by Arthur Elworthy shortly after the end of the war.

12. Sam's stall had been occupied at one time by Sir Winston Churchill.

Chapter 18

1. Field Marshal Lord Bramall, who came in 1983 when he was CDS, described it thus in an interview on 6 July 2016. His predecessor, Admiral of the Fleet Lord Lewin, had been to Gordons Valley a year earlier. Air Chief Marshal Sir Peter Harding, then CAS but subsequently CDS, came in 1990. Sam maintained regular contact with his former Military Assistant, David Craig, who became CAS in 1985 and CDS in 1988.
2. Letter from Sam to Clare, 28.3.79.
3. Letter from Sam to Clare, 31.7.85.
4. Itinerary of VIP visit to Antarctica by the Department of Scientific and Industrial Research.
5. Ashe Windham, 'My Recollections of Lord Elworthy', written for the author.
6. Interview with Iain Ferguson, 12.12.16.
7. Interview with Lord Craig, 12.10.16.
8. Interview with Lord Carrington, 29.6.16

Chapter 19

1. Letter from Hester Elworthy to Clare, 11.4.93. Sam had not wanted any eulogy. When Christopher suggested Adrian Kerr, Sam just smiled, which Christopher took as a sign of tacit approval.
2. Michael Field was the pen name of Katharine Bradley and Emma Cooper, who published a number of works of verse in the thirty years leading up to the Great War.
3. In the Falklands, to a limited extent, and in the Gulf Wars, Afghanistan and Syria, the RAF once again deployed its strike aircraft outside Europe.
4. Adrian Kerr, Tribute to Sam, 8.4.93.
5. Interview with Sir Patrick Hine, 8.8.16.
6. Michael Quinlan, obituary written for the Royal Aeronautical Society.

Index I

Individuals, Military Formations and Units, Organizations and Institutions

Index II

Place Names